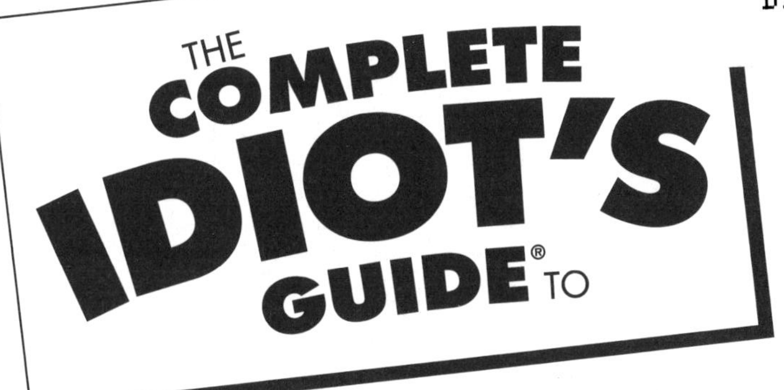

The Cold War

by Robert T. Mann

ALPHA
A Pearson Education Company

To Senator John Breaux who encouraged me to pursue my dream.

International Standard Book Number: 0-02-864246-5

Library of Congress Catalog Card Number: Available upon request.

04 03 02 8 7 6 5 4 3 2 1

Interpretation of the printing code: The rightmost number of the first series of numbers is the year of the book's printing; the rightmost number of the second series of numbers is the number of the book's printing. For example, a printing code of 02-1 shows that the first printing occurred in 2002.

Printed in the United States of America

For marketing and publicity, please call: 317-581-3722

The publisher offers discounts on this book when ordered in quantity for bulk purchases and special sales.

For sales within the United States, please contact: Corporate and Government Sales, 1-800-382-3419 or corpsales@pearsontechgroup.com

Outside the United States, please contact: International Sales, 317-581-3793 or international@pearsontechgroup.com

Publisher: *Marie Butler-Knight*
Product Manager: *Phil Kitchel*
Managing Editor: *Jennifer Chisholm*
Acquisitions Editor: *Randy Ladenheim-Gil*
Development Editor: *Tom Stevens*
Production Editor: *Billy Fields*
Copy Editor: *Susan Aufheimer*
Illustrator: *Chris Eliopoulos*
Cover/Book Designer: *Trina Wurst*
Indexer: *Julie Bess*
Layout/Proofreading: *Mary Hunt, Brad Lenser*

Contents at a Glance

Appendixes

Contents

Foreword

As Rudolph Anderson, a U.S. Air Force major on loan to the Central Intelligence Agency, took off from Florida's McCoy Air Base early in the morning of October 15, 1962, he saw the first orange streak of the Atlantic sunrise off to his left and far to the east. His aircraft was a U-2, a light-weight, high-flying spy plane, specially equipped for aerial photography. As he reached the northern shoreline of Cuba, at 70,000 feet, he banked toward the southwest. It was just 7:00 A.M., a time the CIA had chosen with care. At that hour in the middle of October, the sun would have risen just enough that shadows on the ground would be long and sharp: For agency photoanalysts, objects captured by U-2 cameras would stand out in clear silhouettes.

As he started to cross the western tip of Cuba, Anderson activated his cameras. Moments later, having passed over the island, he returned to Florida. By mid-morning, the pictures he had taken were developed and aboard another airplane, heading for CIA headquarters in northern Virginia, just across the Potomac River from the White House. By noon the photos were on the desk of President John F. Kennedy. They showed unmistakably that the Soviet Union had put missiles in Cuba—missiles aimed right at the United States.

The Cuban Missile Crisis was the most dangerous point of the Cold War. The United States and the Soviet Union were at the brink of a nuclear conflict. Secretary of State Dean Rusk later said that we and they had stood eyeball to eyeball, and they had blinked first. After the crisis was over, both Washington and Moscow realized that they had to look anew at their long-standing hostility. With all the perils of the nuclear age, they had to bring about some relaxation of tensions. Both knew that they had to rein in the dangers of the Cold War.

What was the Cold War? However exactly you date it, the Cold War was an ideological, economic, and political struggle between the United States and the Soviet Union. Sometimes the struggle was actually military: During the Korean War (1950–1953), American pilots on occasion engaged in combat with Russian ones. But, more broadly, the United States and the Soviet Union competed with each other for influence in Latin America, Europe, Africa, and the Middle East. The Cold War thus divided most of the world into mutually hostile organized alliances. As John Foster Dulles, President Eisenhower's secretary of state in the 1950s, put it, "If you're not for us, you're against us."

What caused the Cold War? What made it so important? What, in the late 1980s, finally brought it to an end? You are holding in your hands the best single answer to those questions you will find anywhere, *The Complete Idiot's Guide to the Cold War*, by Robert Mann. It gives you an expert and all-encompassing picture of the Cold War in its beginning, middle, and end. The author has already written *A Grand Delusion*, an excellent view of America's war in Vietnam. Here he has repeated his bravura performance. You will enjoy it.

Robert Smith Thompson

Robert Smith Thompson, author of *Empires on the Pacific: World War II and the Struggle for the Mastery of Asia.*

Introduction

The Cold War between the United States and the Soviet Union was really the twentieth century's Third World War. Although it wasn't a war in the conventional sense of the century's other major conflicts, the Cold War influenced and shaped the world in profound and lasting ways. It spawned the nuclear arms race, the space race, the Korean War, the Vietnam War, and the Soviets' war in Afghanistan—just to name a few.

Our world was shaped by the Cold War. Such influence is understandable, considering that the two superpowers were on opposite sides, openly hostile to each other for the much of the century. Indeed, from the 1917 Bolshevik Revolution to the late 1980s, the Soviet Union and the United States were almost always adversaries. Even their alliance of necessity during World War II was an uneasy one.

What was the Cold War fought over? The answer is not simple. It was about military power, political, cultural, and economic power. To many, it was about world dominance. At its core, however, the Cold War was a Herculean struggle between two competing ideologies—democracy and communism.

Those of us in the post-Cold War era know how the story ends. But if you lived in the United States, the Soviet Union, or in Europe during the 1940s and 1950s, the outcome was not clear at all. Communism was on the march around the world. Capitalism, still recovering from the body blows of the Great Depression, was not universally recognized as the supreme economic system. Which would prevail? No one knew for sure.

Ultimately, that is the story of this book: the titanic clash of two diametrically opposing views of the world.

How This Book Is Organized

The Complete Idiot's Guide to the Cold War is broken into five parts:

Part 1, "The Origins of Warring in the Cold," recounts the troubled history of U.S.-Soviet relations leading up to World War II. We look at the Bolshevik Revolution, World War I, the first U.S. "Red Scare," and the period of isolationism that gripped America in the years after the First World War.

Part 2, "Global Responsibility," examines the alliance between the United States and the Soviets during World War II and looks at how the Cold War erupted in the months after the war's end. We see how President Harry Truman dealt with this new threat from a former ally, and we also examine the impact of the first proxy war of the Cold War era—the Korean War.

Part 3, "Living in the Cold War," is devoted largely to examining how Americans lived under the constant threat of nuclear war during the 1950s and 1960s. We look at how Presidents Eisenhower, Kennedy, and Johnson dealt with the Russians and also examine early American involvement in Vietnam.

Part 4, "Doubting the Commitment," analyzes the tragedy of the Vietnam War and how U.S. humiliation over Southeast Asia caused Americans to question their place and role in world affairs. We look at the Nixon years and discuss how Vietnam and Watergate undermined American confidence in government. We also discuss how U.S.-Soviet relations, which warmed under Presidents Nixon and Ford, turned sour during the presidencies of Jimmy Carter and Ronald Reagan.

Part 5, "Coming Out of the Cold," documents the latter days of the Cold War, when Soviet leader Mikhail Gorbachev enacted a series of ambitious political, social, and economic reforms that ultimately led to the collapse of the Soviet Union. We examine President George Bush's passive role during the Cold War's decline and also look at how his successors, Bill Clinton and George W. Bush, grappled with the world's problems in the post-Cold War era.

Extras

Through *The Complete Idiot's Guide to the Cold War* you find three types of sidebars:

Quotes from the Cold

This features cogent and sometimes-eloquent quotations about the Cold War, drawn from speeches, memoirs, and books by world leaders, journalists, and historians.

Cold Facts

This feature presents little-known facts and figures, and interesting anecdotes about the Cold War and related events, as well as biographical sketches of key world figures.

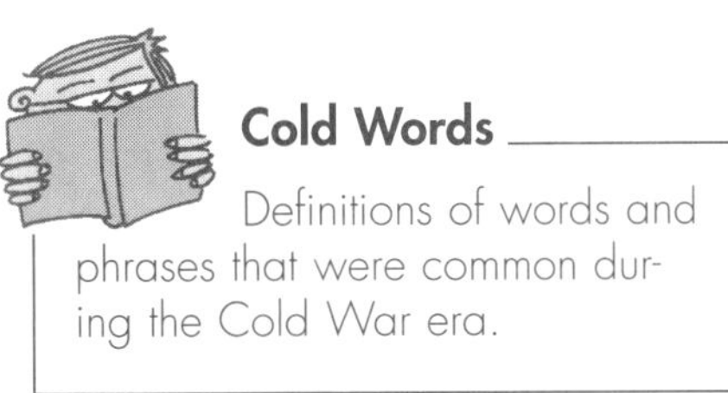

Cold Words

Definitions of words and phrases that were common during the Cold War era.

Acknowledgments

While researching and writing this book, I stood on the shoulders of several distinguished historians. More so than the other books I have written, this project is a work of synthesis. As in all my books, I benefited greatly from the scholarship of others. I am particularly indebted to the authors of several outstanding works for their contribution to my understanding of the Cold War. They are: Ronald E. Powaski, author of *The Cold War: The United States and the Soviet Union, 1917–1991;* H.W. Brands, author of *The Devil We Knew: Americans and the Cold War;* and James T. Patterson, author of *Grand Expectations: The United States, 1945–1974.* I also benefited from the research of other historians whose works are listed in Appendix C, " Further Reading."

I am deeply indebted to Tim Maga, author of *The Complete Idiot's Guide of the Vietnam War* and other fine works, for encouraging me to write this book. Tim began this project and then turned it over to me. I am deeply in debt to him for the research and creative thought that he put into the project during its early stages.

I wish to thank the delightful editors—especially Randy Ladenheim-Gil and Tom Stevens—at Alpha Books who guided me with good humor and patience through this process. Literary agents Gene Brissie and Bert Holtje at James Peter and Associates are consummate professionals and aggressive author advocates.

My colleagues in Senator John Breaux's office were, as always, understanding and supportive of my writing. Senator John Breaux of Louisiana, my employer and friend, has always supported and encouraged my extracurricular literary pursuits. I have dedicated this book to him with profound gratitude for the way that he has enabled and encouraged my passion for writing about history.

My family also gave me enormous support and encouragement. I thank my parents, Robert and Charlene Mann, and my wife's parents, Al and Gerry Horaist. No one gives me more support, encouragement, understanding, and love than my wife, Cindy. She is my partner, my best friend, the world's best mother and wife, and the person with whom I look forward to spending the rest of my life. I cannot thank her enough for the ways that her unconditional love and support have made this and other books possible.

Finally, I am deeply in debt to the late Clyde Taylor, my literary agent for more than a dozen years. Were it not for Clyde's enthusiasm for my writing, my first book—and certainly the subsequent ones—would never have been published. His untimely death in December 2000 left an enormous hole in my personal and professional life. Hardly a day passes that I do not think of him and how his faith in me changed my life.

Special Thanks to the Technical Reviewer

The Complete Idiot's Guide to the Cold War was reviewed by an expert who double-checked the accuracy of what you'll learn here, to help us ensure that this book gives you everything you need to know about the Cold War. Special thanks are extended to Mark McGuire.

Trademarks

All terms mentioned in this book that are known to be or are suspected of being trademarks or service marks have been appropriately capitalized. Alpha Books and Pearson Education, Inc., cannot attest to the accuracy of this information. Use of a term in this book should not be regarded as affecting the validity of any trademark or service mark.

Part 1

The Origins of Warring in the Cold

Many believe that the animosity between the United States and the Soviet Union began after World War II. But the two countries have never enjoyed the greatest of relations. Even when they were allies, they never completely trusted each other.

This is the story of the prelude to the Cold War—a period spanning the Bolshevik Revolution, World War I, and the years of post-war U.S. isolationism leading up to World War II. It is a story of America's deeply ingrained distrust of the Russians—a state of mind that did not begin in 1945, but in 1917.

Chapter 1

Do Commies Have Mommies, Too?

In This Chapter

- The Cold War is defined
- The titanic struggle between capitalism and communism
- The roots of Soviet communism
- The Bolshevik Revolution
- Woodrow Wilson and the First World War

In a way, it was actually World War III. The Cold War between the United States and the Soviet Union involved much of the world during the latter half of the last century. It was an epic struggle in which the future of the planet sometimes hung in the balance. Its outcome was no less important than that of the first two world wars.

Which form of government would prove superior? Which economic system would succeed? What kind of society would prevail? These and other important questions—matters of life and death for hundreds of millions—were determined by the outcome of a war that isn't considered a real war. In this chapter, the earliest beginnings of this historic conflict are explained.

What Was the Cold War?

Cold War. The phrase seems an oxymoron. How could a war be anything other than a hot, violent conflict between two or more belligerents? Well, the odd-sounding term is actually a most apt description of the open, yet limited conflict that erupted after World War II when the relationship between the United States and the Soviet Union chilled considerably.

It was certainly a conflict (one in which both sides aggressively competed for global influence); but it wasn't war in the conventional sense. Unlike a "hot" war, in which two or more nations send their military forces into battle, this was a different kind of contest. Despite all the mutual hostility, a direct military encounter between the United States and the Soviet Union never occurred during this period of icy relations.

Nonetheless, it was a chilling and potentially dangerous period of open belligerence, mistrust, propaganda, spying, and deception that spread to almost every continent. Armed to the teeth with staggering numbers of nuclear weapons, both sides seemed poised to destroy the world in a matter of minutes.

Cold Words

It's not entirely clear who coined the term **Cold War.** Some historians contend that it was American journalist Walter Lippmann. A renowned newspaper commentator and author, Lippmann's 1947 book, *The Cold War: A Study in U.S. Foreign Policy* (Harper, 1947), helped to popularize the term. However, Lippmann doesn't have clear title. Some historians credit American financier and diplomat Bernard Baruch, who used the term during congressional testimony in 1947.

Cold Facts

A war with no direct military fighting between the nations involved is a cold war. Usually cold wars are waged between countries with differing political, economic, or social ideologies. Most often, the term is used to describe the intense, 45-year struggle between the United States and the Soviet Union and their respective allies.

Hot Rhetoric, Hot Attitudes

The conflict between the United States and the Soviets may not have been hot in the traditional sense, but the rhetoric and attitudes that characterized it were. During most of the latter half of the twentieth century, the two sides circled each other like angry polar bears sparring over prime hunting ground. For the better part of 45 years their thundering growls reverberated around the world.

Yet, it would be wrong to conclude that while neither party battled directly, real armed combat—and millions of deaths—did not occur. Indeed, during the post–World War II period, numerous *proxy wars* and conflicts were fought on both sides, mostly in developing, or Third World, countries: Vietnam, Korea, Iran, Guatemala, Lebanon, Czechoslovakia, the Dominican Republic, and Grenada.

Millions died on all sides in those wars and conflicts. And both sides expended enormous sums of money to wage war and bolster their military forces. In all, the United States spent about $4 trillion for national defense and foreign assistance during the period. While this is a fantastic sum, the Soviets spent even more, if calculations are based on which side's spending accounted for a larger portion of its gross domestic product.

Cold Words

A proxy war is a conflict in which the major combatants remain on the sidelines and allow the military forces of other countries to fight on their behalf.

Considered by some a fierce struggle between communism and democracy, the Cold War touched virtually every part of the world. This poster from the early 1950s, depicts the threat that communism posed to the Philippines.

(Courtesy of the Library of Congress)

Lasting Changes

The Cold War struggle also had an enormous and lasting impact on American politics, science, industry, and culture. Political careers were made and ruined during this period, the causes of science and industry were advanced, and popular culture influenced and changed by the rivalry between the two nations.

The Cold War accelerated the modern-day space programs of both sides and sparked the United States' herculean effort during the 1960s to reach the moon. The resulting technological discoveries and advances have been applied to virtually every industry and walk of life in the world, including aerospace, medicine, computers, and telecommunications.

The Cold War dominated virtually every aspect of American and Soviet existence during the latter half of the twentieth century. And even now, more than a decade after its end, the Cold War's legacy is still powerful. While the United States and Russia are now allies, many Americans still don't trust Russia's leaders. And the attitude of the Russian people and their leaders is not always one of total trust and acceptance of the United States.

The U.S.–Russian relationship can best be described as an uneasy and evolving alliance. How it will evolve, no one knows. But it will certainly be an easier and safer evolution if more Americans understand the history of the conflict that dominated the world's stage for a great portion of the last century.

The Great Fear

The Cold War was basically a 45-year titanic struggle between the United States and the Soviet Union for economic, political, and military superiority. Yet, for many Americans, the fight over superiority was much simpler. It was about whose economic and governmental system would prevail—the capitalistic democracy of the West, or the Soviets' brand of communist *totalitarianism*.

Cold Words

Totalitarianism is a system of government under which every aspect of a society—political, social, economic, and religious—is completely subject to policies established by a nation's leader. Totalitarian governments usually try to impose their ideologies on the entire population, often resorting to violent or repressive measures.

It is difficult for younger generations to believe, but many Americans in the 1950s and 1960s were not so sure that their way of life would prevail. They seriously feared that the Cold War might end with a Soviet victory. Many believed that *communism* was so pervasive and its proponents so determined and ruthless, it might emerge victorious and become the world's dominant governmental system. These fears bolstered public support for our country's vast military expenditures, and they were the basis for the public's initial strong support for the American military roles in Korea and Vietnam.

Cold Words

Communism, in theory, is a system in which all goods and property are owned in common and available to all. In practice, it has largely failed. Soviet-style communism is a totalitarian system of government in which an authoritarian party directs every aspect of a nation's life.

The nation's fear of communism also launched, enhanced, or sustained numerous political careers during the Cold War years, including those of Dwight D. Eisenhower, John F. Kennedy, and Richard Nixon. Conversely, many political leaders who were judged to be insufficiently vigilant in the war against domestic and international communism saw their careers come to abrupt ends. In one of the ugliest and most destructive periods of the Cold War, during the early 1950s, Republican Senator Joseph McCarthy of Wisconsin (see Chapter 11, "The Senator from Wisconsin") exploited the public's fears of communism by asserting that the U.S. government was crawling with subversives.

What was it about communism that caused such fear and loathing among Americans in the years after World War II? Actually, Americans had disdained and feared communism since 1917, when the Russian communists came to power following the Bolshevik Revolution. By 1919, a full-fledged Red Scare was underway in the United States, as the federal government rounded up and deported hundreds of aliens who were suspected of communist activities. For much of the next 70 years, Americans would live in mortal fear of communism and the ways they believed it threatened their way of life.

What Is Communism?

At its core, communism is an economic, and social system in which most property and industry is owned by the larger community. Theoretically, a communist society would be characterized by the equal sharing of all labor according to ability, and of all benefits according to need.

A pure communist society would be utopia, marked by the virtual absence of injustice and class distinctions. This concept of an ideal society, free of poverty and oppression, is thousands of years old and is based upon examples in the Bible (the first Christian communities were classic communist societies) and Plato's *Republic.*

Modern communism, however, was articulated in 1848 by the German social philosophers Karl Marx and Friedrich Engels in the *Communist Manifesto.* Marx and Engels believed that capitalist societies of the mid-nineteenth century had fallen miserably short of their promise. The Industrial Revolution, despite the improvements in efficiency and productivity, had not abolished poverty. To the contrary, Marx and Engels saw privation at every turn. Furthermore, they concluded, democratic forms of government had failed to banish injustice and corruption.

Cold Facts

One reason so many Americans despised communism was its atheistic nature. Karl Marx was notoriously hostile to organized religion. He called it "the opium of the masses." When the Bolsheviks came into power in 1917, they seized the property of the Russian Orthodox Church, persecuted priests, and outlawed all religious teaching. During the 1930s, the communist rulers of the Soviet Union shut down and destroyed thousands of churches. The term "Godless communist" became a common, derisive refrain in the United States.

Marx and Engels also believed that all social systems in history had been organized so that the powerful would profit from the labor and misery of the powerless. Eventually, all of these systems had collapsed of their own weight, and they believed that a similar fate awaited capitalism.

This time, however, the two philosophers believed that capitalism would be destroyed by political revolution. The poor masses, the *proletariat*, would rise up and depose their oppressors. Private ownership of property would be banished. Ultimately, this new communist system would be driven, not by profits, but by the needs of the people. Goods would be available in abundance. Justice and freedom would prevail.

Cold Words

Proletariat was how Marx and Engels characterized the lowest social or economic class in a society. Engels defined it as "the class of modern wage laborers who, having no means of production of their own, are reduced to selling their labor power in order to live."

Cold Words

Bourgeoisie was the term used by Marx and Engels to designate the class of modern capitalists and employers of wage labor.

In their *Communist Manifesto*, German philosophers Karl Marx and Friedrich Engels boldly predicted the downfall of *bourgeois* society. The means by which this would be accomplished, included …

- An end to property ownership and application of all rents of land to public purposes.
- A heavy progressive or graduated income tax.
- Abolition of all rights of inheritance.
- Confiscation of the property of all emigrants and rebels.
- Centralization of credit in the banks of the state by means of a national bank with state capital and an exclusive monopoly.
- Centralization of the means of communication and transportation in the hands of the state.
- Equal obligation of all to work and establishment of industrial armies, especially for agriculture.
- Combination of agriculture with manufacturing industries; gradual abolition of all the distinction between town and country by a more equable distribution of the populace over the country.
- Free education for all children in public schools and abolition of children's factory labor.

"In short," Marx and Engels wrote in the *Communist Manifesto*, "the Communists everywhere support every revolutionary movement against the existing social and political order of things. … Let the ruling classes tremble at a communist revolution. The proletarians have nothing to lose but their chains. They have a world to win."

Of course, we know that the grand vision of Marx and Engels never materialized. It was communism, not capitalism, that ultimately collapsed. But in the latter part of the nineteenth century, and in the early years of the next, no one could be quite sure. Many people thought that maybe these two brilliant philosophers were on to something. Perhaps capitalist society would soon be threatened, even overthrown, by revolution.

In only a matter of years, certainly by the 1919, many Americans no longer viewed communism as just another abstract philosophy of government and society. It was a burgeoning worldwide revolutionary movement that appeared to pose a direct threat to the American and Western European way of life.

The Bolsheviks Are Coming!

In some ways, communism was already in practice in Russia when the 1917 Russian Revolution transformed it into an ideology more closely associated with totalitarianism. Russia of the late nineteenth century was an agricultural nation. Under the absolute rule of the tsar—the Russian monarch—85 percent of the country's people were peasants, a class of people who worked the soil as laborers. Most of these Russian peasants lived in communes until the early years of the twentieth century. In many ways, they were classic communist communities. Workers communally cultivated land for the greater good. Private property ownership was virtually unknown.

That changed after the 1905 "revolution" ended the autocratic and corrupt rule of the tsar. Forced to yield some of his power to the people, Emperor Nicholas II oversaw the formation of a representative assembly, the State Duma, and creation of a constitution that granted fundamental civil liberties to Russian citizens. The governmental reforms also weakened the commune system of agriculture by allowing peasants to own their land. These and other reforms held off a full-scale revolution—but not for long.

World War I changed everything. Humiliated by Germany on the battlefield, Russia's suffering was exacerbated by a transportation breakdown that resulted in soaring consumer prices and urban food and fuel shortages. Misery was widespread. After riots broke out in Petrograd (formerly St. Petersburg) in February 1917, the tsar abdicated, ending more than 300 years of the Romanov dynasty.

Initially, the Duma appointed a provisional government to run the country, an enterprise that was doomed by the vigorous opposition of the rival Petrograd Soviet of Workers' and Soldiers' Deputies. Leaders of the *soviet* quickly demonstrated their power by directing the nation's military to obey only their orders.

Cold Words

Soviet is the Russian word for council. A soviet is an elected governmental council in a communist society.

This rivalry drastically worsened Russia's political and economic woes. The country bordered on anarchy. Peasants seized land, nationalist independence movements sprung up, and the military's morale disintegrated at the German front.

Cold Facts

Also known as The Great War, World War I was an international conflict that began in 1914 and was the deadliest war in history up to that point. Europe had been a bonfire awaiting a spark, which came on June 28, 1914, in the Bosnian capital of Sarajevo, when a Bosnian Serb nationalist murdered Archduke Francis Ferdinand, the presumptive heir to the Austrian and Hungarian thrones. Believing the assassination the work of the Greater Serbian movement, Austria declared war on Serbia. Fueled by nationalistic, political, and economic rivalries between European nations that had simmered for decades, the war quickly spread throughout Europe. In all, 32 nations were involved, including the United States and Russia.

Lenin

At this point, Vladimir Lenin, leader of the *Bolsheviks*, the most radical of Russia's several major revolutionary parties strode onto the world's stage. For years, Lenin had lived in exile, first in Siberia and, by 1917, in Switzerland. Lenin had long believed that Russia was ripe for a peasant-led revolution that would depose the tsar and establish a socialist economy and state. Virtually alone among Russian revolutionary leaders, he was a "defeatist" who contended that Russia's defeat in the war would hasten the desired new order.

Cold Words

The Russian word **Bolshevik** is derived from the Russian word *bolshii,* which means "greater" or "majority."

Aware of Lenin's sentiments, the German government—hoping that victory could be secured if Russia negotiated a separate peace—arranged for Lenin's homecoming. Amply funded by the Germans, Lenin returned to his homeland in April 1917. His stay was short-lived. After an aborted Bolshevik coup in July, Lenin's collaboration with the Germans was exposed and the Bolshevik leader fled the country for Finland.

In a matter of months, however, the tides of fate shifted. Feuding and intrigue among leaders of the provisional government drastically weakened its grip on the country and undermined the crucial support its leadership enjoyed among military leaders. Bolshevik political strength, meanwhile, grew among local soviets. When Leon Trotsky, the brilliant Marxist leader, became chairman of the Petrograd Soviet, the stage was set for a successful coup.

Cold Facts

A Russian lawyer, union organizer, and Marxist revolutionary and theorist, Vladimir Lenin (1870–1924) was the Russian leader who, along with Leon Trotsky, led the Bolshevik revolution that toppled the Russian government in October 1917. Prior to the revolution, Lenin spent much of his time abroad—in Switzerland, France, and Germany—championing the cause of Marxism as a writer and newspaper publisher. After the revolution and once in power, Lenin ruled the new Russian government, as well as the Union of Soviet Socialist Republics, established in 1922. He became a brutal leader, responsible for killing as many as 140,000 political opponents. His rule was cut short in 1924, when the last of four strokes took his life. After his death, Lenin's body was embalmed, where it remains on display in an elaborate mausoleum near the Kremlin in Moscow.

As the inspirational revolutionary leader of the Russian Bolshevik Party, Vladimir Ilich Lenin brought communism to power in 1917.

(Courtesy of the Library of Congress)

The Coup

Before calling a national congress of local soviets in late October 1917, the Bolsheviks secretly assembled an armed force. On the evening of October 24, Trotsky placed

Bolshevik Red Guards at strategic points throughout Petrograd, including telegraph stations and government buildings. The next morning, he boldly declared the end of the provisional government. Incredibly, except for some scattered fighting, the Bolsheviks assumed power after very little bloodshed. Russia's government had fallen effortlessly into the hands of the communists.

Cold Facts

Leon Trotsky (1879–1940) was one of the most dynamic and inspiring Russian leaders during the early years of the Soviet Union. It was Trotsky who masterminded the 1917 Russian Revolution and led the Bolshevik coup that deposed the Russian Provisional Government. A passionate and eloquent proponent of Marxism, Trotsky was also an excellent administrator and military strategist. Under Bolshevik rule, he held the posts of commissar of foreign affairs and, later, commissar of war. Driven into exile after Joseph Stalin took power, Trotsky settled in Mexico City, where one of Stalin's agents murdered him in 1940.

Once in control, the Bolsheviks gave themselves a new name: The Russian Communist Party. Now that they had the government in their grip, Lenin and Trotsky were determined not to lose it. They dismantled the Duma, closed all opposition newspapers, and assaulted their political opponents with a new, powerful secret police force, the Cheka.

Russians celebrate May Day, also known as International Workers' Day, in Znamenski Square in Petrograd in 1917.

(Courtesy of the Library of Congress)

True to his defeatist ideology, Lenin moved quickly to end Russia's involvement in the war. In exchange for German financial assistance, he agreed to an extremely harsh peace deal in December 1917: Russia forfeited a sizeable portion of the territories it had captured—the Baltic states, Finland, Poland, and Ukraine.

Although German leaders had believed that ending the fighting on the Eastern Front would guarantee their victory, Allied leaders eventually prevailed. By November of the following year, Germany was forced to surrender and, under terms of the Treaty of Versailles, renounced the territories it had gained from Russia the previous year.

Cold Facts

Before the 1917 Russian Revolution, Lenin's rallying cry was "All power to the soviets!" It proved a meaningless slogan. After he took office, the new Russian leader failed to deliver on his promised changes, including land reform and workers' control of factories.

War Communism and Red Terror

Russian communism swept away virtually every remnant of private property and free enterprise. "The right to private property in the land is annulled forever," the Bolsheviks decreed, although they did exempt land and property already owned by peasants.

The harsh policy became known as "War Communism," primarily for how it eventually sparked a civil war. It also included the nationalization of all industrial production and transportation; abolition of money, which was replaced by barter tokens and goods and services; introduction of a centralized, planned economy; and the establishment of a system of compulsory labor.

War Communism proved enormously unpopular. Unwilling to accept barter tokens, the peasants revolted and refused to send their goods and produce to the cities and to the newly organized Red Army. Lenin quickly "solved" that problem with brutal measures that included dispatching armed soldiers throughout the countryside to seize grain supplies.

Public support for the communists plummeted, prompting Lenin to even more extreme measures. In July 1918, he ordered the murder of the ex-tsar and his family. After an attempted assassination in which Lenin was seriously wounded, the Soviet leader reacted with even greater brutality, ordering the Cheka to carry out mass executions of his political opponents. And he murdered thousands of political prisoners. In all, Lenin ordered the deaths of about 140,000 Russian citizens.

In his ruthless attempts to preserve his regime, however, Lenin jeopardized it. His unbridled brutality, combined with the actions of Britain, the United States, and their allies, sparked a bloody and destructive rebellion.

Wilson Takes Sides

President Woodrow Wilson had no desire to choose sides in the civil war that broke out in Russia in the winter of 1917–18. But British leaders were very persuasive. After Russia and Germany had agreed to peace terms, there was no longer any *Eastern Front* that could sap German fighting strength on the bloody *Western Front.* And Britain and France desperately wanted to force the Germans into another two-front conflict.

Cold Words

The **Eastern Front** was the battle line in eastern Europe between Russian troops and the forces of Germany and Austria-Hungary. It stretched from the Baltic Sea in the north to the Black Sea in the south. The **Western Front** was the battle line between French and British troops and the German forces in western Europe. It extended from Belgium to the Swiss border.

In July 1918, after the Germans launched a renewed offensive on the Western Front, Wilson reluctantly agreed to dispatch a joint Japanese-American expeditionary force of 19,000 troops to Vladivostok (in southeastern Siberia). Ostensibly, the American troops' mission was to help Czechoslovakian troops on a westward advancement to rescue members of their army trapped at Irkutsk. The president also approved sending a contingent of American forces to join other Allied troops at the White Sea port city of Archangel, in northern Russia, and at Murmansk, another port city north of the Arctic Circle.

Cold Facts

For much of the war, the U.S. public wanted no role in the fighting. In fact, President Woodrow Wilson was reelected in 1916 using the slogan "He Kept Us Out of War." But U.S. public opinion began to shift in 1917, when German submarine attacks on U.S. and British shipping escalated. Disclosure of an attempt by Germany to involve Mexico in a plot against the United States also influenced public attitudes, as did the March 1917 revolution in Russia that briefly installed a democratic regime.

The United States declared war on Germany in April 1917. American involvement soon proved decisive, shifting the balance of power toward the Allies, who accepted the Central Powers' surrender on November 11, 1918.

Wilson insisted that the troops, which landed in August and September, should not intervene in internal Russian affairs and he forbade them to do little more than guard military stores and protect supply lines. But it was an unavoidable fact that American forces were taking sides in the Russian civil war. Russia and the United States—recent allies in the World War—were now engaged in a de facto war.

President Woodrow Wilson led the United States into the First World War.

(Courtesy of the Library of Congress)

Russian leaders were outraged by the foreign intervention. The Soviet Central Executive Committee declared that "the socialist fatherland [is] in danger." They called the "toiling masses" in the Allied countries to force their leaders to end the expedition. But the fighting continued and U.S. soldiers were sometimes more than innocent bystanders. They engaged in several clashes with Bolshevik forces during the fall and early winter of 1918.

The armistice signed on November 11, 1918, ended the war with Germany and eliminated the ostensible reason for the presence of the U.S. troops. But the fighting continued. Sometimes, it was savage.

Despite the armistice, Wilson was reluctant to withdraw U.S. forces so long as the battered Czechoslovakian troops remained in danger. And he was not ready to allow the Japanese—eager to establish a territorial foothold in Manchuria and Siberia—a free hand to wage war with a force that had grown to 62,000. Wilson resolved to wait until the upcoming Paris peace talks before he withdrew the American troops.

In Great Britain, some leaders, primarily Minister of War Winston Churchill, argued for an increased Allied presence in Russia to combat spread of Bolshevism. Wilson rejected this strategy, agreeing with Secretary of State Robert Lansing that more war was futile and that "empty stomachs mean Bolsheviks. Full stomachs mean no Bolsheviks."

Cold Facts

Woodrow Wilson (1856–1924) was the twenty-eighth president of the United States and led his country into World War I in 1917. An attorney and academic, Wilson was president of Princeton University from 1902 to 1910.

In 1910, Wilson ran successfully for governor of New Jersey as a Democrat. Two years later, he was elected President of the United States and championed numerous governmental reforms, including lowering tariffs on imports and the creation of the Federal Reserve System and the Federal Trade Commission.

After the war, Wilson relentlessly, but unsuccessfully, campaigned for U.S. membership in the League of Nations, the forerunner to the United Nations. For his efforts, he was awarded the Nobel Peace Prize in 1919. That same year, Wilson suffered a crippling stroke and did not seek a third term. He died in 1924.

In February 1919, after the Bolsheviks rejected an American offer of food aid, Wilson finally ordered the withdrawal of the troops from northern Russia. But the U.S. troops stationed in Siberia did not depart until April 1920, primarily because their removal would have undermined the Czech troops, who were gaining ground against Bolshevik forces in Siberia.

The United States was finally out of Russia after almost two years. Although the civil war continued, the White armies were doomed. The Bolsheviks enjoyed numerous advantages, primarily greater numbers, the industrial capacity to produce military hardware, and a near-complete control over much of the Soviet interior.

The civil war over, the Bolsheviks, led by Lenin, consolidated their power and proclaimed creation of the Union of Soviet Socialist Republics, a confederation that included Russia, Belorussia, Ukraine, and the Transcaucasian Federation. Russia, however, dominated this new union of republics. And its leader, Lenin, would not be content with the dictatorial powers that gave him complete authority in the USSR.

Lenin saw a world upturned by revolution and ruled by communism. Europe would fall first, but he fully expected that the communist fires that blazed in Russia would soon engulf the United States.

The Least You Need to Know

- The Cold War was an intense, 45-year ideological struggle between the United States and the Soviet Union that began, in earnest, after World War II.
- While there was no direct fighting between the two nations, each side participated in or supported various "proxy wars," most prominent of which were the Korean and Vietnam wars.

- The Cold War impacted virtually every aspect of American and Soviet life, as each country diverted trillions of dollars into their national defense programs.
- Much of the domestic U.S. fervor for the Cold War was founded on the American dread of communism, a form of government that abolishes all private property and has usually resulted in totalitarianism.
- Hostility between the United States and the Soviet Union actually predated World War II, beginning in the years following the 1917 Russian Revolution when U.S. forces in Russia took sides in that country's civil war.

Chapter 2

Better Dead Than Red

In This Chapter

- Woodrow Wilson's Fourteen Points
- After the war: The Treaty of Versailles
- Wilson promotes the League of Nations
- The impact of communism in the United States

World War I transformed the world, but especially Europe. The war had laid waste to the continent's landscape, caused the deaths of millions and wreaked economic and social chaos. In short, the war's wreckage was immense and its long-term consequences enormous. The smoldering anger and resentment among nations after the conflict would lead directly to the outbreak of the Second World War in the 1940s.

For millions of Americans, who could never have imagined their nation waging war in Europe, the globe now seemed smaller. America had fought in Europe and its intervention not only made the difference, it turned the United States from a reluctant partner of the Allies into the world's leading military and economic power.

This chapter examines the war's aftermath, the new role the United States played in world affairs, and the American reaction to the threats Soviet communism posed to the United States.

Wilson's Idealism

President Woodrow Wilson was an idealistic man who believed that "the world must be made safe for democracy." Although he had hoped to keep the United States out of the war, remaining out had become impossible after Germany's intensified attacks against American shipping and its attempts to turn Mexico against the United States.

When Wilson finally asked Congress to declare war in April 1917, his speech was filled with idealism, but also indignation over the way Germany had undermined democracy in Europe. He summoned the country to support American involvement in the war, "for democracy, for the right of those who submit to authority to have a voice in their own governments, for the rights and liberties of small nations."

Quotes from the Cold

We seek no indemnities … no material compensation; we desire no conquest, no dominion …We have no selfish ends to serve …We would fight for the principles that gave this country birth … for the things which we have always carried nearest to our hearts … for a universal dominion of right by such a concert of free peoples as shall bring peace and safety to all nations and make the world itself free ….

—President Woodrow Wilson urging Congress to declare war against Germany on April 3, 1917

The Bolshevik Revolution in Russia, however, had been a severe blow to Wilson's spirited defense of democracy in Europe. Under the country's new communist leader, Vladimir Lenin, Russia was now eager to remove itself from the war, and expressed hostility for all sides in the conflict, not just the Germans. Lenin took great delight in publishing copies of the secret, self-serving treaties the European allies had negotiated with the Russian tsar. Those who read the treaties now knew that the Allies in Europe were for fighting for *imperialistic* goals, not unlike the Germans.

The secret treaties may have been a surprise to Wilson, but the true war aims of the Allies were not. Most of the Allied nations—particularly Germany, France, Great Britain, Russia, and Austria-Hungary—had been motivated by imperialistic interests.

Cold Words

Imperialism is the means by which a powerful nation exerts and maintains formal or informal control over less powerful nations.

In 1908, Austria had annexed Bosnia and Herzegovina. Later, Germany's designs on Morocco brought it into direct conflict with France. Ultimately, the long-simmering ethnic and economic rivalries had only exacerbated the territorial and imperialistic disputes among European nations.

Fourteen Points

Although he understood the reasons for the secret treaties, Wilson was disgusted by the self-interest that seemed to dictate so much of the world's affairs. And he was idealistic enough to believe that world unity and cooperation could be achieved, or at least enforced, by a League of Nations—an international alliance of countries whose aim would be to maintain peace.

Announcing his plan for a just and lasting peace in Europe to Congress in January 1918, Wilson spelled out what he called his "Fourteen Points." They included an end to secret diplomacy between nations; freedom of the seas; freer trade between nations; arms reduction; solutions to colonial disputes; and, most important, the creation of a League of Nations.

The speech and the lofty vision that Wilson had articulated made him a savior in the eyes of millions throughout Europe, even among the Germans who later sued for peace, prompted by their trust in his vision for postwar Europe. More than 60 million pamphlets containing Wilson's points were distributed across the war-torn continent, where he was roundly hailed as a heroic figure. It is this image of a selfless, idealistic leader that Wilson hoped would carry the day when the war ended and the victors divided up their spoils and extracted revenge from the Germans.

Cold Facts

While most everyone credits President Woodrow Wilson with the idea for the League of Nations, the organization's outline was actually formulated by British diplomats. Wilson loved the idea and eventually claimed it as his own. By the end of the negotiations at Versailles, the concept was thoroughly and permanently associated with the American president.

Alas, Wilson's Fourteen Points did not capture the imagination of at least one European leader, French Premier Georges Clemenceau, who remarked scornfully, "Even God Almighty gave us only 10—and we broke those."

Wilson's considerable worldwide prominence did not translate into greater popularity at home. After characterizing the November 1918 elections as a referendum on his foreign policies, the Republicans captured both houses in Congress—an outcome that would have a profound impact on Wilson's vision for world peace. His political opponents would now control the Senate and its Foreign Relations Committee—a situation that did not bode well for his postwar dreams of the League of Nations.

The Treaty of Versailles

When the war ended in 1919, Wilson shocked the American public and most of Washington by traveling to Paris to personally represent the United States in the peace talks. Until that time, an incumbent president had never left the United States. The notion of a president spending several months in a foreign country was most unusual and controversial.

Cold Facts

The treaty that formally ended World War I got its name from the Palace of Versailles, the massive, extravagant rural palace, about 10 miles southwest of Paris, built by King Louis XIV in the seventeenth century.

Wilson arrived in Europe to a tumultuous, enthusiastic welcome and believed that his popularity would help him to sell his European counterparts on the League of Nations. And he had high hopes for the league at home, believing he could persuade the Senate to ratify U.S. membership in the new world body. But, as Wilson would soon discover, the first goal would prove difficult, and the second, impossible.

To begin with, Wilson had blundered by not including a prominent Republican in the American delegation to the peace talks. He had not even bothered to consult the Senate and its new Republican leadership on the makeup of the delegation and, in fact, did not invite one member of the Senate to accompany him to Paris.

Cold Words

Reparation is a form of restitution—money or other assets—that a defeated nation pays to its victorious foe to compensate for damages or expenditures incurred by the victorious nation in a war or conflict.

However, by force of his personality and as a result of his dogged persistence, Wilson finally persuaded the European leaders to include the League of Nations in the final Treaty of Versailles.

The treaty itself was a harsh document that forced Germany to take major responsibility for the war and, as such, to make substantial *reparations*—$65.5 billion—for the damage it had caused to the various Allied nations. Forced to sign the document, the Germans also agreed to reduce their army to 100,000 men, give up a substantial portion of the country's naval fleet and other armaments, and relinquish control of all their colonial possessions. Historians would later conclude that the treaty's harsh, unrelenting, and punitive terms helped set the stage for the German aggression that led to World War II.

Cold Facts

Stalking the halls of the Palace of Versailles during the treaty negotiations was a skinny, young Vietnamese man who worked in Paris as a photo finisher. Inspired by Wilson's Fourteen Points, Nguyen That Thanh wanted negotiators to consider equality for the Vietnamese in French-occupied Indochina. When no representative of the Allied nations would meet with him, the man who would later be known as Ho Chi Minh, the inspirational wartime leader of North Vietnam, turned to the French Socialists for help. It was a fateful turn of events and it led the 28-year-old Vietnamese nationalist to embrace communism as his life-long guiding philosophy.

Versailles Under Siege

In theory, the League of Nations, as envisioned in the Treaty of Versailles, would insure that the world's nations behaved peacefully. Each member nation (Germany would be excluded) would agree to respect and preserve other members' political independence and territorial integrity. They agreed to use military and economic sanctions against nations that resorted to aggression. All conflicts that threatened to erupt into war would be brought before the league for resolution. Each nation would reduce its military armaments. The nations would create a world court to settle disputes between nations.

After seven months in Paris, an ailing Wilson returned home in July 1919 to begin selling U.S. membership in the league to the Senate and to the American public. In the months since he had left the United States, however, Wilson's political opponents had been busy. For months, they had disparaged the league as an "international quilting society" and "the most impudently un-American proposal ever submitted to the American people by an American president." Now, they were determined to ensure the country would never be counted among its members.

Lodge Attacks the Treaty

It did not help that Wilson's chief antagonist in the Senate, Republican Henry Cabot Lodge of Massachusetts, was now chairman of the influential Foreign Relations Committee—the very committee charged with responsibility for conducting hearings into the treaty.

As chairman of the Senate Foreign Relations Committee, Republican Henry Cabot Lodge of Massachusetts became the most determined opponent of U.S. participation in the League of Nations.

(Courtesy of the Library of Congress)

Particularly hostile to U.S. membership in the league, Lodge vehemently objected to the treaty's provision requiring member nations to preserve each others' territorial integrity. The United States, he complained, was being asked "to give up in part our sovereignty and independence and subject our own will to the will of other nations."

Cold Facts

Henry Cabot Lodge (1850–1924), a Republican from Massachusetts, was first elected to the Senate in 1893 and was among the strongest of President Woodrow Wilson's Senate opponents after World War I. A prominent lawyer and historian, Lodge was a distinguished scholar who, prior to his political involvement, authored biographies of Alexander Hamilton, Daniel Webster, and George Washington. Serving as chairman of the Senate Foreign Relations Committee from 1919 until his death, Lodge opposed Wilson's postwar proposal for U.S. membership in the League of Nations.

Lodge's grandson Henry Cabot Lodge Jr. (1902–1985) served as U.S. senator from Massachusetts from 1937 to 1944 and from 1947 to 1953. He later figured prominently in the history of the Cold War when he served, under presidents Kennedy and Johnson, as ambassador to South Vietnam.

Cold Facts

When Wilson arrived home from Paris after negotiating the Treaty of Versailles, those in the crowd meeting him at the dock were handed leaflets that read: "Everybody's business: To stand by our government. To help the soldier get a job. To help crush Bolshevism."

Even before Wilson returned home to seek the treaty's ratification, Lodge had secured signatures of 37 senators—more than enough to block the treaty's passage—who said they would never vote for U.S. membership in the league.

Adamant that the treaty was wise and sound, and determined to change the Senate's mind—"Dare we reject it and break the heart of the world?"—Wilson went about the task of selling his treaty to the American people. In September, Wilson embarked on an arduous cross-country speaking tour that would take him to all but four states west of the Mississippi River.

Fear of Bolshevism

Much of Wilson's fervor for ratification of the treaty was fueled by his fear of Bolshevism and his belief that a united world community could halt the spread of communism. During the Paris negotiations, Wilson's doctors had begged him to rest. He refused, explaining, "We are running a race with Bolshevism and the world is on fire."

Wilson also firmly believed that ratification of the treaty and active U.S. participation in the League of Nations was the only way to avoid another world war. "I can predict with absolute certainty," Wilson told a crowd in Omaha, Nebraska, "that within another generation there will be another world war if the nations of the world do not concert the method by which to prevent it."

After a month of cross-country travel, during which he delivered 40 major speeches, Wilson was exhausted, having never recovered from the strain of the Paris negotiations. His trip cut short, he returned to Washington, where he suffered a massive stroke near the end of October.

The Treaty Fails

Despite Wilson's failure to generate an emotional outpouring of public support for the treaty, Republican leaders knew that it was popular with a significant portion of the American public. Indeed, anything that promised to keep the United States out of another war was appealing. For that reason, Lodge and his allies sought to compromise, attaching to the treaty a series of amendments (called "reservations"). Debilitated by his stroke and his judgment possibly impaired, Wilson stubbornly rejected any compromise. "Better a thousand times to go down fighting," he told his wife, "than to dip your colors in dishonorable compromise." It was a decision that doomed the treaty.

Quotes from the Cold

We are in the midst of all of the affairs of Europe. We have entangled ourselves with all European concerns. We have joined in alliance with all the European nations which have thus far joined the League and all nations which may be admitted to the League. We are sitting there dabbling in their affairs and intermeddling in their concerns.

—Republican William Borah of Idaho, an opponent of the Treaty of Versailles, addressing his colleagues in November 1919

On November 19, 1919, the Senate rejected both versions of the treaty—one with Wilson's language and the other containing Lodge's reservations. Several months later, senators voted once more on the treaty, again with the reservations the president so adamantly opposed. This time, it fell seven votes short of the two-thirds majority required for passage. It would have passed had only seven of the 23 Democrats defied Wilson and supported the amended treaty.

While the League of Nations came into formal being in 1920—with 42 member nations—the absence of U.S. membership, and the accompanying prestige, would cripple it from the beginning.

The First Red Scare

America's long antipathy toward Russian communism began, in 1917, with feelings of profound betrayal. Many Americans believed their country had entered the war to fight for democracy in Russia, as well as in the rest of Europe. But the events of October 1917—when the Bolsheviks took power in Russia—were greeted with dismay and fear in the United States.

Even after German submarines began their relentless attacks on American and British shipping, many Americans were still somewhat reluctant to see their country take sides in the European war. But the March 1917 Russian revolution that toppled the tsarist regime, installing the ill-fated democratic Provisional Government, finally gave President Wilson reason to assert that American troops would be fighting, as he often said, to make the world "safe for democracy." The United States declared war the following month.

To many Americans, the Bolshevik Revolution and Russia's resulting peace agreement with Germany posed not only a threat to the war aims of the Allies, but also to American democracy. Lenin's "Letter to American Workers," published in August 1918, was hailed as proof of the threat Russian communism posed to the United States. In his message, Lenin summoned "American revolutionary workers" to overthrow the "American multi-millionaires" whose dollars were "stained with blood" from World War I.

Speak No Evil

Already, fears of revolution and sedition ran high in the United States, especially in Washington. During the war, Wilson and members of Congress had reacted harshly to those who dared to question American involvement in Europe, enacting laws that severely curtailed the civil liberties of all Americans. In essence, free speech was outlawed; the First Amendment, suspended.

Quotes from the Cold

Congress shall make no law respecting an establishment of religion, or prohibiting the free exercise thereof; or abridging the freedom of speech, or of the press, or the right of the people peaceably to assemble, and to petition the Government for a redress of grievances.

—From the First Amendment to the U.S. Constitution

The Espionage Act of 1917 made it a crime to interfere with the draft or to encourage behavior deemed disloyal to the United States. The post office was authorized to prohibit the mailing of materials determined to be seditious. The Sedition Act of 1918 criminalized, among other things, incitement of insubordination and discouragement of military recruiting. The law also provided for prison sentences of up to 20 years for anyone who spoke or published "any disloyal, profane, scurrilous or abusive language about the form of government of the United States, or the Constitution, or the flag."

Cold Facts

In 1919, five Russian immigrants were convicted on charges of violating the Espionage Act for publishing two leaflets that denounced the efforts of capitalist nations to interfere with the Russian Revolution. The men also attacked Woodrow Wilson and the "plutocratic gang in Washington" for sending American troops to Russia. Although the Supreme Court upheld the convictions, Justice Oliver Wendell Holmes, in his passionate dissent in *Abrams* v. *United States,* wrote: "[T]he best test of truth is the power of the thought to get itself accepted in the competition of the market."

That year, Congress also passed legislation, the Trading-with-the-Enemy Act, giving the government broad authority to censor all international communications, as well as the foreign-language press in the United States. The Wilson administration used the law to establish a widespread program of press censorship. In all, the government prosecuted 1,500 people for violating the Espionage and Sedition laws.

Cold Facts

Employing provisions of the Trading-with-the-Enemy Act, the U.S. government sent a film producer to jail for 10 years after he produced a movie about the American Revolution. Prosecutors feared the film might incite anti-British sentiment. In Vermont, a minister was sentenced to 15 years in prison for citing Jesus Christ as an example of pacifism. The Sedition Act was used to jail a Wisconsin congressman Victor Berger for editorials in his newspaper that condemned the war as a capitalist conspiracy. Although his constituents elected him twice after his conviction, the U.S. House refused to seat him.

Lenin's Call to Arms

After the war, in the early days of the new communist regime in Russia, the American fear of disloyalty turned into panic. With Lenin virtually begging American workers to join the worldwide communist revolution, the U.S. government and many citizens were persuaded that a bloody American revolution was imminent and must be suppressed at all costs.

In January 1919, Lenin again called on American workers to revolt. In March, as communists from around the world gathered in Russia to found the Third Communist International (the "Comintern"), Lenin would confidently express his belief that communism would sweep Europe within a year.

The workers' strikes that occurred in January in Seattle were cited as proof that communist revolutionaries were poised to stage the revolt Lenin had predicted. The Industrial Workers of the World (IWW) only helped to solidify that perception when it declared: "Every strike is a small revolution and a dress rehearsal for the big one."

The year 1919 was a year ripe for turmoil, marked as it was by political and social upheaval: Congressional approval of Prohibition and voting rights for women, labor unrest in several cities (in all, four million workers went on strike that year), and race riots in Chicago, Washington, D.C., and two dozen other cities and towns. Into this volatile mix, on May 1, 1919, came word of a plot to assassinate a number of prominent American political and business leaders, including Cabinet members and Supreme Court justices.

Bombs Across America

Thirty-six bombs were mailed from New York, timed to arrive on May Day and armed to explode when opened. While only one actually exploded (blowing off the hands of a domestic employee of Georgia Senator Thomas Hardwick), the conspiracy was promptly identified as the work of an IWW-Bolshevik alliance.

Veritable riots broke out across the country in response to the failed plot, as mobs attacked those attending mass meetings and rallies of groups identified as radical. Then, a month later, on June 2, an explosion severely damaged the house of U.S. Attorney General A. Mitchell Palmer.

While Palmer was not injured in the bombing, he was deeply affected by his close brush with death. And he was soon persuaded, despite little or no evidence, that the bombings of May and June were the work of radicals—including Bolsheviks—who were dedicated to overthrowing the government. Communism, he concluded, was "eating its way into the homes of the American workman."

Authorities inspect the Washington, D.C., home of U.S. Attorney General A. Mitchell Palmer after it was bombed in May of 1919. Palmer suspected the bombing was the work of communist radicals.

(Courtesy of the Library of Congress)

The Palmer Raids

Palmer promptly persuaded Congress to appropriate money to investigate and suppress the nation's growing radical movement. Appointed to head the Justice Department's new "Radical Division" was a 24-year-old official, J. Edgar Hoover. With Palmer's permission and under Hoover's direction, federal agents stormed union offices and the headquarters of the American Communist and Socialist parties, arresting about 10,000 aliens.

In all, about 500 aliens were deported for their political beliefs and activities. In December 1919, for example, Palmer's agents arrested 249 resident aliens—Palmer later called them "alien filth"—and placed them on a ship bound for the Soviet Union. Hoover and others called the ship a "Soviet ark."

These drastic actions reflected a popular opinion, expressed by Palmer in 1920, that the radicals …

> have stirred discontent in our midst, while they have caused irritating strikes, and while they have infected our social idea with the disease of their own minds and their unclean morals. We can get rid of them! And not until we have done so shall we have removed the menace of Bolshevism for good.

Ultimately, Palmer and Hoover went too far. Instead of simply investigating and arresting those responsible for the May and June bombings, the Justice Department declared open war on much of the nation's radical movement. Furthermore, Hoover rashly attacked as disloyal civil libertarians and religious leaders who questioned or criticized the government's tactics.

Hoover Fumbles

In the spring of 1920, Hoover committed a drastic misstep. He persuaded the House Rules Committee to consider impeachment proceedings against Louis Post, the assistant secretary of labor who had courageously tried to prevent deportation of aliens for their alleged membership in the Communist Party. During his testimony, Post turned the tables on Hoover and Palmer and managed to transform the proceedings into an inquiry of Justice Department misdeeds.

The ridiculous and dangerous nature of the Red Scare finally became evident in May. In April 1920, Hoover had issued dire warnings of a rash

Cold Facts

A devoted Quaker who had served in the U.S. House, A. Mitchell Palmer (1872–1936) justified his actions in 1919 as the only way to combat what he believed was a Bolshevik plot to overthrow the U.S. government. Critics believed the raids were politically motivated and designed to further Palmer's political aspirations. Palmer was discredited by his actions and failed in his bid for the Democratic presidential nomination in 1920.

Cold Facts

As Attorney General Palmer's point man for the persecution of domestic radicals during World War I, J. Edgar Hoover helped investigate 60,000 suspected subversives in preparation for the Palmer raids in 1919. Five years later, Hoover became Director of the Bureau of Investigation (later known as the Federal Bureau of Investigation). He held that position until 1972.

of assassinations, strikes, and bombings that he believed would occur that summer in response to Lenin's call for a worldwide communist revolution. Police departments were placed on alert. And many Americans braced for another round of violence and terrorism.

It was all for naught. None of the predicted violence or unrest came to pass. The finale to the Red Scare came in June, when a federal judge in Boston ruled that membership in the Communist Party and the Communist Labor Party were not deportable offenses. Those aliens not yet deported by Palmer and Hoover were freed.

By the summer of 1920, the nation's yearlong Red Scare was exhausted—but not until Palmer and Hoover had cynically fed a public frenzy resulting in the systematic denial of basic civil liberties for thousands of Americans. It was a dark, ugly chapter in American history and a vivid demonstration of just how fearful Americans were, and would continue to be, of Soviet communism.

The Least You Need to Know

- Before the end of World War I, President Woodrow Wilson, envisioning a peaceful world rising from the ashes of war, proposed creation of the League of Nations, the last of his Fourteen Points.
- Wilson's idealistic Fourteen Points captured Europe's imagination but, at home, the League of Nations was decidedly unpopular among his Republican opponents in the U.S. Senate.
- After negotiating the Treaty of Versailles, Wilson embarked on a cross-country tour to build public support for the postwar agreement, but could not finish the trip. Shortly thereafter, he suffered a debilitating stroke.
- The U.S. Senate rejected the treaty of Versailles in 1919, and again in 1920, ensuring that the United States would not participate in the postwar effort to maintain world peace.
- In 1919, the country was gripped by fears of a Soviet-inspired communist revolution, prompting deportation of hundreds of aliens and the arrests of many citizens for criticizing U.S. involvement in the war.

Chapter 3

Stalin and the Great Depression

In This Chapter

- Stalin comes to power in the USSR
- Postwar isolationism in the United States
- America disarms after World War I
- The impact of the Great Depression
- The rise of American communism

Americans were largely repulsed by the carnage wrought by the First World War. To many, the conflict would be remembered as "the war to end all wars." Despite the United States' role in the defeat of Germany, as well as its president's role in creating the League of Nations, the country began to shrink from world leadership and quickly returned to its isolationist norm.

This chapter explores the postwar political changes in the Soviet Union and in the United States. We also examine the Great Depression and how it gave life to domestic U.S. radical movements, particularly the Communist Party.

The New Face of Soviet Communism

Lenin was a brilliant revolutionary leader and theorist whose intense passion for communism transformed his nation. Yet, when faced with the daily administrative and political tasks of presiding over the new nation he had created, the dynamic revolutionary had met his match.

Stalin

Lenin was a charismatic revolutionary, not a bureaucrat. In April 1922, he named Joseph Stalin, a skilled administrator who was then commissar of state control, to serve as the Communist Party's general secretary. In his new position, the 42-year-old Stalin had authority to make appointments to official party positions and immediately began using that power to install his allies in important posts.

A committed Bolshevik and disciple of Lenin, Stalin was of Georgian birth, not Russian. He had been named Ioseb Dzhugashvili, born into a poor family in the town of Gori in 1879. As a young adult, while studying Orthodox Christian theology at a nearby seminary, Stalin first learned about the writings of Karl Marx. He was captivated and soon adopted the philosophy as the guiding principle of his life.

His mother hoped he would enter the priesthood, but Stalin was destined for politics. In 1900, he became a labor activist, sowing discontent among railway workers and organizing a workers' demonstration that was so successful it resulted in his exile to Siberia in 1902.

> **Cold Facts**
>
> Dzhugashvili is a mouthful, but that's not why the young Georgian changed his name. The name Stalin was derived from the Russian word *stal*, meaning steel. The name was also Russian, not Georgian. It conjured an image of power and strength.

By 1904, he had escaped, returned to Georgia and resumed his underground labor organizing. This time, however, he affiliated with Lenin's Bolshevik party. A talented organizer, Stalin stood out among Lenin's devoted followers.

What really distinguished him, however, was his complete devotion to the revolutionary aims of the Bolsheviks. Between 1902 and 1913, Russian authorities imprisoned or exiled Stalin seven times. But he repeatedly escaped and resumed his revolutionary activities.

In 1912, Lenin appointed Stalin to the ruling Bolshevik Party organization, the Central Committee. When the 1917 Bolshevik coup unfolded, Stalin was there, but played a subordinate role to the coup's masterminds, Lenin and Leon Trotsky.

Lenin's decision to elevate Stalin to general secretary in 1922 was a fateful one. Unlike Lenin, Stalin thrived in the bureaucratic environment. As the Soviet Union consolidated its power, taking over most, if not all, of the functions of private enterprise, Stalin's power and influence grew exponentially.

Stalin Versus Trotsky

To many, Trotsky—the revolution's co-leader—should have been Lenin's heir. But Stalin was far more skilled at politics and government administration. Unlike Trotsky, the Georgian had long been associated with the Bolshevik movement; Trotsky had affiliated with Lenin only in August 1917. Moreover, Trotsky was a Jew, among the most unpopular minorities in Russia.

In May 1922, Stalin's opportunities grew even more. Lenin suffered a stroke. He recovered, briefly, but was stricken again in December. He would suffer two more strokes. The last one, in January 1924, would take his life.

Cold Facts

In the early 1920s, Stalin and Lenin disagreed about the future of Soviet communism. Believing the Russian Communist Party was a model for communist parties worldwide, Lenin repeatedly called on foreign revolutionaries to rise up in the manner of the Russian Revolution. Stalin, meanwhile, favored intensive efforts to first revolutionize the Soviet Union's economy and its political system, adhering to what he called "Socialism in one country."

Lenin's death in 1924 meant victory for Stalin's philosophy. During Stalin's reign, the Soviet Union would not attempt to export its revolutionary communist philosophy as much as it would try to control other governments, particularly those in Eastern Europe.

Before he died, Lenin turned on Stalin. In a political "testament," the father of the Soviet Union condemned his former devotee for having undermined his authority and demanded his dismissal as secretary general. Lenin's decree would have ended the career of a less skillful politician. As it was, Stalin adroitly suppressed the testament and emerged strong as ever.

When Lenin died, Stalin moved quickly to fill the resulting leadership vacuum, outmaneuvering Trotsky and other leaders for the top Soviet position. By 1929, after Trotsky's expulsion, Stalin was the undisputed leader of the Soviet Union.

Five-Year Plans

Stalin's brutal, iron-fisted rule made Lenin's style look mild by comparison. Even before his dominance was undisputed, he had begun to dismantle Lenin's New Economic Policy, a postwar, semicapitalist program for Russia's economic recovery. In its place were a series of severe, centralized agriculture reforms and industrialization programs that aimed to increase the nation's productivity by brute force.

To accomplish his ends, Stalin drove more than 25 million peasants off their land, herding them into state-run farms, called "collectives." Meanwhile, he inaugurated his first Five Year Plan for the country's rapid industrialization—a deadly program that was financed by exporting the nation's precious agriculture resources. What followed was an apocalyptic famine in the Ukraine and the deaths of about 10 million peasants who died from starvation as Stalin cruelly continued exporting grain that could have saved countless lives.

Cold Facts

In enacting his first Five-Year Plan to rapidly industrialize the Soviet Union, Soviet leader Joseph Stalin relied heavily on American know-how. Stalin contracted with numerous American companies for their technical assistance. Furthermore, during the same period, as many as 1,000 American engineers were employed in the Soviet Union under individual technical aid contracts. Prominent American business providing the assistance included the Ford Motor Company and General Electric. While the leaders of some of these companies hoped to expose Stalin to capitalism, it was soon apparent that the Soviet leader had used them only to solidify and consolidate his iron grip on the country.

By the 1930s, Stalin would prove himself capable of even greater brutality, ordering a program—from 1934 to 1938—that resulted in the systematic murder of as many as seven million of his political opponents. Millions more were shipped to forced labor camps.

Stalin's industrialization program succeeded, as did his program to secure his leadership by killing or imprisoning virtually every political opponent. But his success came at an awful cost—in lives and lost human potential for the Soviet Union. By 1938, as the clouds of World War II gathered on the horizon, Stalin's nation—its military leadership decimated by years of deadly purging—found itself ill-prepared to meet the threat of the mighty German military machine commanded by Adolf Hitler.

Cold Facts

When the Bolsheviks came to power in Russia in 1917, some in the United States wanted the Wilson administration to extend formal diplomatic recognition to the new government. Wilson refused, arguing that "Bolshevism is a mistake and it must be resisted as all mistakes must be resisted." The three Republican presidents who succeeded Wilson—Harding, Coolidge, and Hoover—maintained Wilson's policy of nonrecognition. The United States would not formally recognize communist Russia until the administration of Franklin Roosevelt.

Isolationism Breeds Contempt

In early 1921, after eight years out of office, the Republican Party was back in the White House. President Warren G. Harding promised a return to "normalcy" and promptly led the country on a retreat from active involvement in world affairs.

Normalcy

No one would have ever called Warren Harding a statesman. In retrospect, it appears that he presided over the most corrupt administration in American history. But at the time of his election in 1920, the country was weary of war and ready for a president who promised to return the nation to the pre-war status quo of economic and political isolation.

President Warren G. Harding led the United States back into isolationism—he called it "normalcy"—in the years following World War I.

(Courtesy of the Library of Congress)

A handsome, amiable former newspaper publisher, Harding and his running mate, Calvin Coolidge, played to the nation's weariness with war. Their campaign slogan "return to normalcy" seemed to capture a sentiment expressed by many Americans who wanted less government intervention in business affairs, abolition of the income tax (first imposed under Wilson), and a more protectionist international trade policy. To many Americans, normalcy also meant suppressing the urge to meddle in other countries' affairs. In Harding-speak that meant: "Not submergence in internationality but sustainment in triumphant nationality."

Retreat

To win votes, however, Harding sometimes played both sides of the fence. To voters more inclined to support an activist foreign policy, he promised to support an "association of nations," but for isolationist voters, he pledged to put "America first!"

As one might imagine, the Democrats disagreed with Harding's promise to lead a U.S. retreat from world affairs. Wilson's secretary of the treasury, William Gibbs McAdoo, attacked the Republican's platform as "an army of pompous phrases moving over the landscape in search of an idea." The voters, however, disagreed, electing Harding and Coolidge with 61 percent of the vote over the Democratic nominees, Ohio Governor James M. Cox and running mate Franklin D. Roosevelt, the assistant secretary of the Navy under Wilson.

Many in Congress, especially Senate Republicans, greeted Harding's election with glee. To Senator William Borah of Idaho, the election was nothing short of "the judgment of the American people against … any political alliance or combination with European powers." The voters, he said, had pulled the country back from internationalism and had restored "the foreign policy of George Washington and James Monroe, undiluted and unemasculated."

Quotes from the Cold

George Washington warned the nation against alliances with foreign powers, especially those in Europe. The United States mostly took Washington's advice to heart until World War II.

> Europe has a set of primary interests, which to us have none, or a very remote relation. Hence she must be engaged in frequent controversies, the causes of which are essentially foreign to our concerns. Hence therefore, it must be unwise in us to implicate ourselves, by artificial ties, in the ordinary vicissitudes of her politics, or the ordinary combinations and collisions of her friendships or enmities.

—George Washington in his 1796 farewell address

Uncle Sam Lets Down His Guard

The war had put Congress in a mood to disarm the nation. In the months after Harding's election, Congress approved a resolution offered by Senator Borah, urging the president to negotiate with Great Britain, France, Italy, Japan, and other nations to reduce naval armaments and prevent a postwar arms race. Borah's proposal led to the International Conference on Naval Limitation, convened in Washington, D.C., in late 1921. Out of that conference emerged moratoriums on naval construction, as well as several other agreements on mutual security in the Pacific.

Cold Facts

William E. Borah (1865–1940) served six terms in the United States Senate from Idaho, from 1907 until his death in 1940. In domestic affairs, the Republican Borah sometimes took progressive stances. He opposed monopolies and fought for a national income tax and the popular election of senators. On foreign affairs, however, he was an isolationist and vigorously opposed U.S. membership in the League of Nations and the World Court. As chairman of the Senate Foreign Relations Committee, Borah played an instrumental role in Senate ratification of the Kellogg-Briand Pact, which renounced war. Later, in the 1930s, he opposed U.S. steps toward American involvement in what would become World War II.

When representatives of the respective nations (the United States, Great Britain, Japan, France, Italy, The Netherlands, Portugal, Belgium, and China) gathered in Washington, they were greeted with an astonishing U.S. proposal. In a speech to the delegates, Secretary of State Charles Evans Hughes offered to end virtually all U.S. Navy construction, if Britain and Japan would agree to do the same.

Isolationist Senator William E. Borah of Idaho (left) played an instrumental role in Senate ratification of the Kellogg-Briand Pact. The treaty, which renounced war, was negotiated by U.S. Secretary of State Frank B. Kellogg (right).

(Courtesy of the Library of Congress)

The treaty the nations signed in February 1922 established a 5:5:3 ratio in naval tonnage among the United States, Britain, and Japan (France and Italy also agreed to reduce their navies). In other words, Japan's total tonnage of battleships and aircraft carriers would be only 30 percent of the combined tonnage of the United States and Britain. Under terms of the Five-Power Naval Limitation Treaty, the nations agreed to scrap about 1.9 million tons of warships and to halt construction of capital ships (vessels weighing more than 10,000 tons).

Seeds of War

While the treaty was hailed as a great instrument that would ensure world peace, it actually planted seeds of a second world war. To win Japan's consent, the United States promised not to reinforce its military bases in the Pacific west of Pearl Harbor, and Britain agreed to the same terms regarding its bases east of Singapore and north of Australia.

In Japan, meanwhile, public sentiment would soon turn against the treaty, despite the U.S. and British concessions. The Japanese militarists' slogan became "5:5:3" and the resulting controversy played no small part in their ascension to power in 1934. At that point, a more belligerent Japanese government would demand, unsuccessfully, revision of the treaty to enable naval parity with the United States and Britain.

Japan would respond to the rejection of its demands by denouncing the treaty and embarking on a furious naval rearmament program. By the time another world war would erupt in the Pacific, U.S. and British defenses of its bases in the region would prove inadequate. Japan, on the other hand, would boast of a navy more powerful than the U.S. and British fleets combined.

Kellogg-Briand Pact

Naval disarmament was not the only way the United States weakened itself in the years after World War I. In 1928, the Senate ratified the Pact of Paris, also known as the Kellogg-Briand Pact, in which it formally condemned "recourse to war for the solution of international controversies."

First proposed by French Foreign Minister Aristide Briand as a bilateral treaty between France and the United States, the pact became, under the leadership of U.S. Secretary of State Frank B. Kellogg, a multilateral agreement against war originally signed by 15 nations and later by 47 more. Those nations signing the treaty agreed to peacefully settle all their conflicts, no matter how they had begun. The nations who ratified the treaty renounced war as an instrument of national policy.

But the Kellogg-Briand Treaty, as it became more popularly known, had one significant problem: It was completely unenforceable. The document provided no way to ensure that signatories abided by its dictates. Historian Samuel Eliot Morison later ridiculed the pact as "an attempt to keep the peace by incantation."

Cold Facts

The 1928 Kellogg-Briand Treaty stated, in part, that the countries who were party to the pact … "solemnly declare in the names of their respective peoples that they condemn recourse to war for the solution of international controversies, and renounce it as an instrument of national policy in their relations with one another."

Furthermore, they agreed that … "the settlement or solution of all disputes or conflicts of whatever nature or of whatever origin they may be, which may arise among them, shall never be sought except by pacific means."

Despite its high idealism, the treaty was pitifully ineffective. Within a dozen years, the world would again be enveloped in war.

The methods the United States and other nations employed to keep the peace in the 1920s, Morison observed, "would have been effective among nations that wanted peace. They were worse than useless in a world in which three nations—Germany, Italy, and Japan—wanted war." Disarmament and "incantation," Morison and others would later argue, only gave aggressor nations time to "plot, plan, and prepare for a war" while the United States and its allies retreated from many aspects of world affairs.

Feeding the World

Not everything the United States did in the postwar years was of an isolationist nature. During the 1920s, American diplomats were active in peace initiatives in the Far East, Mexico, and Central America. Many U.S. leaders, including some of the most vociferous political isolationists in the U.S. Senate, also supported American efforts to provide humanitarian relief in Europe and the Near East.

The government-financed American Relief Association provided famine relief to starving Russians in 1922 and 1923, saving as many as 11 millions lives. From 1919 to 1930, another American organization, the privately funded Near East Relief program, provided more than $115 million in direct and other assistance to refuges from Greece, Turkey, Armenia, Macedonia, and other parts of the region.

The United States was also exceedingly generous in the manner it handled the war debts of its World War I Allies, as well as reparations owed by Germany. The United States not only forgave a large portion of those war debts of the Allies, but assisted Germany in the repayment of its reparations. (Eventually, however, the Allies, as well as Germany, defaulted on their debts.)

For the most part, however, the United States remained distant from the world's political affairs. A succession of Republican presidents during the 1920s, Harding, Calvin Coolidge, and Herbert Hoover, kept the country aloof from world affairs, hoping that the country would never again be called upon to fight a war in Europe.

The Great Depression and Communism

In 1929, the Great Depression hit the United States and much of the industrialized world. By the early 1930s, the American economy would be in shambles. Discussing capitalism, Marx and Engels had once predicted a series of "commercial crises that by their periodic return put the existence of the entire bourgeois society on trial, each time more threateningly." The severity of the Great Depression suggested to some that the two men might have been more prescient than anyone had imagined.

To communists in Moscow and in the United States, the depression vindicated Marx's predictions about capitalism's demise. Politically, it was just the opportunity for which the American Communist Party had been waiting. The dire economic conditions—as many as a third of U.S. workers were unemployed during the worst depression years—persuaded some communists that their time had finally arrived. And they regarded the collapse of the U.S. economy as an opportunity—albeit a painful one—to finally persuade Americans of communism's superiority.

Cold Facts

The Great Depression was the worst and longest economic failure of the modern industrial era, a period that lasted from 1929 until about 1940. Caused by a combination of high debt, uneven income distribution, risky investments, and a slump in production and consumer spending, the Depression quickly spread throughout the industrialized world. It hit hardest those countries with economic ties to the United States.

During 1932, the Depression's worst year, 25 to 30 percent of the U.S. work force (12 to 15 million workers) was unemployed. By late 1932, stock prices had slumped to about 20 percent of their value before the October 1929 stock market crash. Manufacturing output in the United States had fallen by 54 percent from 1929 levels. By 1933, 11,000 of the nation's 25,000 banks had failed.

In 1932, the U.S. economy was in ruins. Manufacturing output had sagged to little more than half of its 1929 level. As many as 15 million workers were jobless—and many of those were World War I veterans desperate for the $1,000 bonus payments Congress had promised them in 1924. By law, the bonuses would not be fully paid to the 3.5 million World War I veterans until 1945. But frustrated and desperate for income, many began demanding that Congress pay them immediately.

Throughout the country, social unrest was brewing. In December 1931, communist activists staged a small hunger march on Washington, D.C., followed by 12,000 unemployed men who marched on the Capitol to demand jobless benefits. In March of 1932, unrest at a Ford Motor Company plant in Michigan resulted in the deaths of four workers. More than 50 were wounded.

In May, thousands of jobless veterans gathered at the Capitol to demand their bonus payments. Army Chief of Staff Douglas MacArthur and Secretary of War Patrick Hurley scornfully viewed the growing unrest as nothing less than a communist plot to overthrow the U.S. government. The veterans called themselves the "Bonus Expeditionary Forces," and they were overwhelmingly loyal American citizens who had fought honorably in the war and wanted nothing more than the early fulfillment of the government's promise made in 1924.

By June 1932, the ranks of disgruntled veterans had swelled to more than 20,000 men—some with their families—camped in ramshackle, makeshift shacks below the Capitol and in tents and shanties at a base camp along the Anacostia River. Hope appeared briefly in June when the House approved, over Hoover's veto threat, a $500 bonus payment. But the Senate dashed those hopes several days later and many of the veterans left Washington. About 2,000 to 5,000, however, stayed behind. And on July 28, violence broke out in a scuffle with Washington police officers. It was then that Hoover ordered the U.S. Army to "surround the affected area and clear it without delay."

Cold Facts

James W. Ford—an African American and the American Communist Party's vice presidential candidate in 1932, 1936, and 1940—was one of the Bonus Marchers arrested in Washington, D.C., in July 1932.

A Bonus Marcher with his wife and children camped near the U.S. Capitol in 1932.

(Courtesy of the Library of Congress)

Mounted soldiers led by Major George Patton charged through the camps with their sabers unsheathed and drove the veterans out, destroying their camps in the process. Adding insult to injury, MacArthur defied orders and ordered his men to pursue the veterans across the Anacostia River to their main encampment. Shortly thereafter, fire razed the camp. At day's end, the scattered and disheartened veterans were left victims of MacArthur's imaginary battle against domestic communism—the first time U.S. troops had attacked American citizens in their own capitol.

The Red Decade

Douglas MacArthur's fears about communism in the bonus marchers' ranks were unfounded. While there were real communist organizations operating in the United States, the Bonus Expeditionary Force was not among them.

Officially formed in 1921, the Communist Party of America had forsaken radical militancy and, instead, worked to develop a mass following by working with existing labor organizations. Throughout the 1920s, this strategy had achieved little success. In fact, some notable failures—unsuccessful strikes in New Jersey, Massachusetts, and New York—diminished the party's influence and standing within the unions.

The onslaught of the Great Depression, however, was cause for optimism among the communists. National despair and disillusionment with capitalism, the communists believed, would finally turn the country in their direction.

The highest hopes of the party—renamed the Communist Party of the United States—were invested in the 1932 election and its presidential nominee, William Z. Foster and his running mate, James W. Ford, the first black nominated for national office. The ticket attracted support from prominent writers and poets, including John Dos Passos, Sherwood Anderson, and Langston Hughes.

Quotes from the Cold

There is only one issue in the present election. Call it hard times, unemployment, the farm problem, the world crisis, or call it simply hunger—whatever name we use, the issue is the same .... [T]he Communist Party proposes as the real solution of the present crisis the overthrow of the system which is responsible for all crises.

—From a 1932 manifesto issued by the League of Professional Groups for Foster and Ford, comprised of 53 prominent American writers

Unlike 1919, this time there erupted no Red Scare. Despite the desperate times, the vast majority of Americans looked to the two major political parties for relief. Foster and Ford received a pitiful 102,000 votes and finished far out of the running—well behind the 22.8 million votes cast for the winner, Democratic nominee Franklin D. Roosevelt. By contrast, voters gave the more moderate Socialist Party more than 880,000 votes.

As President Roosevelt began enacting his New Deal initiatives to combat the depression, the communists attacked them, alternately, as *fascist* and *Nazi* programs. The *Daily Worker* labeled the National Recovery Administration—which enforced a collection of fair labor laws—as a "fascist slave program." The U.S. party's chairman, Earl Browder, charged that the New Deal was "the same as Hitler's program."

Cold Facts

Fascism is a totalitarian form of government in which individual rights are totally subordinated to the interests of the state. Unlike communism, facism permits private enterprise so long as it serves the purposes of the state. Fascist regimes, such as Italy's during World War II, are usually headed by a militaristic dictator and are characterized by intense nationalistic and patriotic fervor, as well as the persecution of ethnic minorities. **Nazism** was the fascist ideology espoused by Adolf Hitler and his National Socialist German Workers Party during the 1930s and 1940s. Intense anti-Semitism and a hatred of communism characterize Nazism.

For all their efforts to infiltrate and control the American labor movement, as well as unite the country's antifascist groups into a "popular front," the American communists would remain on the fringes of American politics.

The Least You Need to Know

- Soviet leader Lenin was eclipsed by Joseph Stalin, a skillful and brutal leader who would later dismantle Lenin's semicapitalist economic system in favor of a rigid, centralized economic system.
- In the 1930s, Stalin embarked on an ambitious five-year plan to industrialize the Soviet Union. He drove more than 25 million peasants from their farms. The subsequent famine killed as many as 25 million people.
- After World War I, the United States retreated into isolationism and drastically reduced its military might, which would prove one of the major causes of World War II.
- The Great Depression of the 1930s caused some Americans to question the long-term viability of capitalism.

Chapter 4

The Gathering Storm

In This Chapter

- Roosevelt fights the Great Depression
- America's reluctant approach to war
- Hitler gobbles up Europe
- Japan attacks Pearl Harbor
- The United States goes to war

The 1930s were turbulent years in the United States and around the world. First, the Great Depression spread from America to Europe and much of the world. At about the time that Americans elected President Franklin Roosevelt in hopes that he could lift the country out of the economic morass, Germans were electing a leader they hoped would end their years of suffering.

Like Roosevelt, Adolf Hitler promised better times. Unlike his American counterpart, Hitler was willing to start a European war to achieve his goal. While Hitler planned for war, Americans remained in relative isolation, refusing to involve themselves in the brewing conflict in Europe and in Asia.

By the time war erupted, it would be too late. Just like it had done in the years before World War I, the United States did not exert its considerable influence to prevent the outbreak of another war. By 1941, however, the country would be drawn into the fighting.

The New Deal

The country and its economy needed a shot in the arm, and President Roosevelt believed he had the right medicine. Declaring his intention to vigorously fight the depression—"wage a war against the emergency, as great as the power that would be given to me if we were in fact invaded by a foreign foe"—Roosevelt told the nation at his inauguration that "our greatest primary task is to put people to work."

The First Hundred Days

Putting Americans to work is what Roosevelt did. With dizzying speed, Congress enacted Roosevelt's proposals for a wide array of economic reforms and new government programs designed to stimulate the economy. Within days of taking office in March 1933, Roosevelt called the Congress into special session, for what he called the "Hundred Days," a period of unprecedented action that would last until June 16, 1933.

In that period, members of Congress established several new agencies designed to put Americans back to work in public works projects: the Civilian Conservation Corps, the Public Works Administration, and the Civil Works Administration. Roosevelt and Congress tried to strengthen the business climate with the National Recovery Administration, which devised codes for fair business competition, including abolishing child labor, limiting production, and establishing price controls, minimum wages, and maximum weekly work hours.

Roosevelt pushed through banking reforms designed to strengthen the nation's banking system and restore public confidence in financial institutions. Among other things, he signed into law the Emergency Banking Act, giving the government power to reorganize insolvent national banks. And at Roosevelt's behest, Congress passed other banking laws, including a broad banking reform measure, the Glass-Steagall Banking Act, that created the Federal Deposit Insurance Corporation, providing insurance for depositors.

Farmers got help in the form of the Agriculture Adjustment Administration, which controlled farm production and crop prices. Congress also passed legislation creating the Farm Credit Administration to provide loans for farmers, and the Farm Bankruptcy Act, which postponed farm mortgage foreclosures for five years.

Cold Facts

Before he took office, Franklin Roosevelt was the subject of an assassination attempt. Visiting Miami with the mayor of Chicago, Roosevelt was fired upon by Joseph Zangara, an unemployed bricklayer. The assassin's bullet missed the president-elect but hit the mayor, inflicting a mortal wound. Reflecting the frustration that many felt toward their government and its inability to address the Great Depression, Zangara said, "I do not hate Mr. Roosevelt personally. I hate all presidents … and I hate all officials and everybody who is rich."

The Second New Deal

This flurry of activity did reassure people that their federal government was taking the Great Depression seriously. For the first time, the U.S. government was becoming aggressively involved in virtually every aspect of the economy, ending the government's hands-off relationship with American business and industry. But the activity of the first Hundred Days did not end the Depression. The nation's economic problems were too deep and severe to be instantly cured by a handful of new agencies. To make matters more difficult for Roosevelt, the Supreme Court declared a number of the new recovery laws unconstitutional. That sparked what historians now call "the Second New Deal," a flood of new legislation increasing taxes for the wealthy and focusing on the specific problems of laborers and farmers.

In 1935, Congress enacted the National Labor Relations Act, establishing a series of fair employment rules and giving workers the right to organize into unions. That same year was born Social Security, a program providing retirement subsidies for workers, and unemployment insurance and welfare funds. Congress also passed regulations on utilities and subsidized rural electrification projects.

Quotes from the Cold

There is not a garbage dump in Chicago which is not diligently haunted by the hungry. Last summer in the hot weather when the smell was sickening and the flies were thick, there were a hundred people a day coming to one of the dumps, falling on the heap of refuse as soon as the truck had pulled out and digging in it with sticks and hands.

—Journalist Edmund Wilson writing in *The New Republic*, 1933

Critics

Although Roosevelt was re-elected in 1936 in a landslide, opposition to the New Deal was growing. Republicans and conservative Democrats in the South were worried about the vast new powers these programs gave to the federal government. Some critics alleged that the New Deal, despite the economic hard times, was undermining the nation's capitalist society. Government, they complained, was sticking its nose into virtually every nook and cranny of American business.

That criticism may have slowed the advance of new programs a bit, but it failed to stop Roosevelt's momentum. The president's overwhelming re-election victory, which significantly increased the Democratic Party's majorities in both houses of Congress, made it impossible for his opponents to overturn his New Deal initiatives. In the end, the New Deal advanced, and Roosevelt and the Congress continued enacting legislation to strengthen the economy (the Works Progress Administration, National Youth Administration, Fair Labor Standards Act, the Farm Tenant Act, and the Food Drug and Cosmetic Act).

The Legacy of the New Deal

The New Deal's legacy was immense. Franklin Roosevelt and his allies in Congress had permanently altered the relationship between the U.S. government and the American people. Government was now an integral part of the everyday lives of Americans. Many of the agencies Roosevelt created, as well as the laws he proposed, exist to this day.

In the end, however, the New Deal did not end the Great Depression. As the 1930s came to a close, the U.S. economy was still very sick. Only the advent of World War II would fully lift the country out of the economic morass.

America First

World events did not come to a standstill while the United States and its allies struggled to overcome the Depression. But you might not have known it from the way Congress and the Roosevelt administration acted. Isolation reigned supreme. Still haunted by the carnage of World War I, many members of Congress believed the best policy toward the growing unrest in Europe was to remain scrupulously above the fray.

The Neutrality Acts

Beginning in 1934, Congress began to pass a series of laws that built an imaginary wall around the United States. Germany and Italy might be threatening the peace of the world, but Congress believed that it could insulate the country from the brewing turmoil.

In the first instance, Congress wanted no more financial ties to its World War I Allies. It had lent considerable sums of money to European nations during the war and all of those countries, except Finland, had defaulted. To prevent a repeat of this distasteful situation, Congress passed the Johnson Act (named for its sponsor, Republican Senator Hiram Johnson of California), forbidding the sale in the United States of any bonds issued by countries that had defaulted on their World War I loans.

Next came news, from a special Senate investigating committee headed by Republican Senator Gerald Nye of North Dakota, that American businessmen, particularly munitions makers, had reaped fantastic profits during World War I. These businessmen, many in Congress suspected, had been largely responsible for whipping up public sentiment to enter the war. That prompted a series of neutrality acts.

Quotes from the Cold

To maintain a democracy of effort requires a vast amount of patience in dealing with differing methods, a vast amount of humility. But out of the confusion of many voices rises an understanding of dominant public need. Then political leadership can voice common ideals, and aid in their realization.

—Franklin D. Roosevelt, inauguration address, January 20, 1937

The first, passed in 1935, required the president, when confronted with a war anywhere, to prohibit the sale or transport of munitions to either side. When that legislation expired the following year, Congress renewed it and made it even stronger with the addition of a provision forbidding any direct or indirect loan to either side in a war.

As historian Richard M. Ketchum has noted in his book, *The Borrowed Years: 1938–1941* (Random House, 1989): "This piece of legislation meant that the United States would hold itself aloof from any collective security efforts and would even be unwilling to halt out-and-out aggression where aggression might occur. It also meant that this country was not going to come to the aid of its friends, no matter what kind of trouble they were in."

The third neutrality act, passed in 1937 in reaction to civil strife in Spain, extended the existing arms embargoes and loan restrictions to any involvement by the United States in a foreign civil war. But the act went a step further, allowing the president to stop shipments of nonmilitary goods to belligerents, unless the material was already paid for and would be shipped on foreign vessels.

Roosevelt Supports Neutrality?

In each case, Roosevelt signed the neutrality bills that Congress sent him, ostensibly placing him on the side of the congressional isolationists. Realistically, he could not have sustained a veto. Popular opinion and congressional sentiment was overwhelmingly on the side of isolation.

Cold Facts

Some of those around Franklin Roosevelt begged the president to act more decisively during the time that Congress, in full-throated isolationist tenor, seemed to be tying his hands. Roosevelt, they feared, was too passive and was waiting too long to begin pushing for a more aggressive U.S. role in world affairs. They longed for him to repeat the magic of the early New Deal days. In 1937, he complained to reporters that some were looking for him "to come forward with a hat and a rabbit in it." That, he told them, would not happen. "I haven't got a hat and I haven't got a rabbit in it."

Sometimes, the president pandered to the natural American isolationism. "I have seen war," he said, going on to describe its horrors. "I hate war." Yet, at other times, the president was conflicted, worried about the consequences if America remained too long on the sidelines. In a 1937 speech in Chicago, he warned his audience that if aggression prevailed in Europe, "let no one imagine that America will escape, that America may expect mercy, that this Western Hemisphere will not be attacked."

The Fascist Threat

Roosevelt was correct. The aggression in Europe didn't threaten Europe alone. The United States might find another war distasteful, but it would do no good for the isolationists to bury their heads and pretend the war would not eventually come to the United States. And what was the nature of the threat? By 1938, Hitler had amassed an enormous military force and was ready to conquer Europe. In March, he made his first move by annexing Austria in a near-effortless display of military might.

In September, worried British and French leaders met with Hitler in Munich to discuss Germany's territorial claims on the Sudeten area of Czechoslovakia, where 3.5 million Germans lived. Believing Hitler's promise that "this is the last territorial claim I have to make in Europe," Britain and France acquiesced to the German leader's claims.

Quotes from the Cold

My good friends, for the second time in our history, a British Prime Minister has returned from Germany bringing peace with honor. I believe it is peace for our time. … Go home and get a nice quiet sleep.

—British Prime Minister Neville Chamberlain in September 1938, after signing the Munich Pact with Hitler.

Britain, France, and the United States wanted to believe Hitler. But within six months, he proved the foolishness of their hopes when his military forces swept into Czechoslovakia, incorporating most of the country into his growing empire. By April 1939, Germany began to threaten Poland and other European nations. That same month, a disheartened Roosevelt privately told a group of newspaper editors that a general war in Europe appeared likely and the ultimate outcome was unclear.

Alliance with Stalin

War was much closer than Roosevelt imagined. For months, the British and French had been attempting to persuade the Soviets to join a formal alliance against Nazi Germany. At the same time, however, the Russians were engaged in secret talks with Germany. Throughout the late spring and early summer of 1939, Hitler and Stalin, through intermediaries, had undertaken negotiations for a nonaggression pact.

Despite a long and intense mutual antipathy, Stalin and Hitler had much to gain from a formal alliance. To Hitler, ending any chance of an Anglo-French-Russian pact seemed the best way to isolate Poland and the other European nations the German leader wanted to acquire. From Stalin's perspective, a pact with Hitler simply meant foreclosing another bloody war with Germany. And Stalin, of course, had another motive. In the words of biographer Alan Bullock, he wanted to share "not in the defense of an ungrateful Eastern Europe's independence, but in its partition." Like Hitler, Stalin wanted the spoils of war.

On August 23, 1939, in the Kremlin, German and Russian representatives signed the Nazi-Soviet nonaggression pact. That evening, in celebration, Stalin lifted a glass of champagne and proposed a toast to his new ally: "I know how much the German nation loves its Führer; I should therefore like to drink to his health."

Preparing for War

Despite the pact and what it portended for Hitler's future aggression, Roosevelt continued to bow to his country's isolationist sentiment. "We are not going to send armies to Europe," he promised. "But there are lots of things, short of war, that we can do to help maintain the independence of nations who, as a matter of decent American principle, ought to be allowed to live their own lives."

With that, Roosevelt began to gently coax the United States into greater assistance for the nations threatened by Hitler's armies. He asked Congress to begin beefing up the U.S. military, and it did, providing a 50 percent increase in appropriations for the army and navy over the two-year period that ended in June 1940.

Cold Facts

In 1933, as Adolf Hitler began strengthening Germany's military might, the United States Navy ranked seventeenth in size among all the nations of the world. It would be another six years before President Roosevelt would persuade a reluctant Congress to begin increasing the size of the U.S. fleet.

Congress was still reluctant. Roosevelt didn't get all that he requested. When, in January 1940, the president asked Congress to spend even more money for armaments, members were stingy, cutting his recommendation for 496 new military airplanes to just 57.

Finally, in July 1939, Roosevelt asked Congress to repeal the Neutrality Acts. But the Senate Foreign Relations Committee, voting 12–11, turned him down. Those in the majority refused to believe war would actually come to pass.

Hitler Takes Poland

On September 1, 1939, to the surprise of many in the U.S. Congress, war did come, when Germany—with Stalin's tacit support—attacked Poland. Two days later, France and Britain declared war on Germany. Three weeks after that, Roosevelt asked Congress to repeal the neutrality laws. "I regret that the Congress passed that Act," he said. "I regret equally that I signed that Act."

Stalin Takes Advantage

Stalin wanted new territory as much as he wanted peace with Hitler. The Soviet leader annexed eastern Poland, Estonia, Latvia, Lithuania (also known as the Baltic States), and portions of Romania. He also forced Finland to surrender territory.

Cash and Carry

Even in the face of Hitler's naked aggression and Stalin's opportunistic actions, Congress was recalcitrant. Roosevelt and his allies had to fight vigorously for a law that partially lifted the U.S. arms embargo against its European Allies. Now, Congress finally allowed the sale of armaments to U.S. Allies, but only on a "cash-and-carry" basis (similar to the policy for nonmilitary goods). In other words, as long as our ally paid for the military supplies up front and carried them home on its own ships, America would allow the sale.

America wasn't in the war yet, but this partial repeal of the neutrality act was a small step in that direction. Until Congress and the general public believed that the country was directly threatened by the growing European war, America would remain on the sidelines.

War Spreads

Throughout 1940, the war kept getting hotter. In April, Hitler invaded Denmark and then Norway. Next, the German army marched into Holland, Belgium, and France. Roosevelt responded by persuading Congress to spend another billion dollars for defense and set as a goal the construction of 50,000 new military airplanes a year.

In June 1940, Italy joined Germany's attack on France. Paris was in German hands within days. Now, it seemed that America's closest ally, Great Britain, might be the next target for Hitler's aggression.

With that, Roosevelt made his boldest move yet. On June 10, he declared that the United States would "extend to the opponents of force the material resources of this nation." Congress again stubbornly refused to appropriate money for direct aid, opting instead to increase its domestic defenses.

Roosevelt went ahead with the program, ordering the transfer to Britain of all available war material—airplanes, ammunition, and other supplies. And, in September, he negotiated a bold arrangement with Britain under which the United States "leased," for 99 years, 50 World War I destroyers.

Cold Facts

Roosevelt's 1940 decision to send U.S. military supplies to Britain alarmed his critics who feared that the Allies were destined to lose the war and the result would be a defenseless and vulnerable United States. Roosevelt was willing to make the gamble, deciding to "scrape the bottom of the barrel" and send Britain all available war supplies. Roosevelt's orders were carried out so completely that by late 1941, some American military units were forced to train with sections of telephone poles, pretending that they were artillery pieces.

By mid-September, with the Germans threatening to storm across the English Channel, public opinion began to turn, if only slightly, in favor of increased assistance for the Allies. Congress voted, narrowly, to institute a draft, and then began debating legislation to increase military assistance to Britain.

Cold Facts

Franklin Roosevelt technically didn't ask to be nominated by the Democratic Party for an unprecedented third term in 1940. But he didn't protest when the party asked him to continue serving as president. And the people agreed, not wishing to change presidents as their country drifted toward war in Europe. Challenged by Republican Wendell Wilkie, who ran on an isolationist platform, Roosevelt won decisively, beating his opponent by five million votes, and scored a landslide, a 449 to 82–vote victory in the Electoral College.

Lend-Lease

In March 1941, with Britain nearly broke, Congress vigorously debated, but eventually passed by an overwhelming margin, the Lend-Lease Act—legislation permitting the United States to lend military equipment, rather than money, to any nation whose defense the president deemed vital to U.S. security. The program also made U.S. shipyards available to Britain and other Allies.

The Lend-Lease program would make the United States, in Roosevelt's words, "the arsenal of democracy," while assuring its own security. To support the program, Congress initially appropriated $7 billion—a huge sum, considering the paltry amount it had previously committed to national defense. In all, the nation would spend more than $50 billion to arm its Allies during the war.

1941: Year of Decision

Given an unprecedented third term by the American people, Franklin Roosevelt accurately interpreted the election results as an affirmation of his policies toward the war in Europe. It was fortunate that he enjoyed the overwhelming confidence of the American people, for 1941 would prove one of the most daunting years ever experienced by an American president.

Quotes from the Cold

I know I will be severely criticized by the interventionists in America when I say we should not enter a war unless we have a reasonable chance of winning. … But I do not believe that our American ideals, and our way of life, will gain through an unsuccessful war.

—Charles Lindbergh, heroic aviator, in a speech delivered on April 24, 1941

Dedicated to helping the U.S. Allies defeat Hitler, Roosevelt could not stand by while German submarines sank ships carrying American-made munitions to Britain. By the summer of 1941, the United States was engaged in an undeclared war with Germany in the north Atlantic, where American ships alerted the British to sightings of German submarines.

Next, American troops occupied Greenland and Iceland so that American ships, in convoys, could safely ferry the supplies halfway across the Atlantic. Germans submarines—also called U-boats—did attack American ships, prompting Roosevelt and the Congress to arm American merchant ships. Thereafter, American naval vessels were ordered to "shoot on sight."

Hitler Attacks Russia

In June 1941, Hitler transformed the war in Europe. Despite his vicious air attacks on a better-armed Britain (thanks to America's Lend-Lease program), Germany had not been able to knock the British out of the war. With Yugoslavia, and Greece added to his list of conquests and Hungary, Bulgaria, and Rumania added to his list of allies, Hitler now turned on his erstwhile ally, Russia. In June, Hitler doublecrossed Stalin and invaded the Soviet Union.

Immediately recognizing the difficulty Hitler would have with a two-front war, Roosevelt and British Prime Minister Winston Churchill announced plans to extend the Lend-Lease program to their new ally, Joseph Stalin.

No More Neutrality

With the war in Europe widening and with German U-boat attacks increasing, in September Roosevelt asked Congress to repeal most of the provisions of the 1930s neutrality acts. This time, the president wanted authority to ship Lend-Lease supplies on armed merchant ships, escorted by naval vessels. Congress quickly approved the proposal, escalating the nation's undeclared war with Germany.

War in the Pacific

Strange as it may seem, it was not the events in Europe that would ultimately drag the United States into the war as a full belligerent. Instead, it would be the growing conflict in the Pacific that would decisively shift public opinion in favor of war.

Like Germany, Japan—now allies with the fascist governments of Germany and Italy—had designs on its neighbors. In 1937, it had invaded China. Now, after Hitler had conquered France and Holland, Japan took advantage of the situation by occupying those nations' colonies in the region—Indochina (Vietnam, Cambodia and Laos) and the Dutch East Indies. The United States, Britain, and the Netherlands responded by freezing all Japanese assets in their country, severing Japan's supplies of the rubber, scrap metal, oil, and aviation fuel vital to making war. Hoping to end the standoff, Japan and the United States entered into negotiations in the spring of 1941. But the talks soon turned sour in the face of Japan's increasingly militancy. By year's end, it was clear that the two nations were headed for armed conflict in the Pacific.

Pearl Harbor

On the morning of Sunday, December 7, 1941, the Japanese staged a daring and devastating attack on Pearl Harbor, headquarters for the U.S. Pacific fleet, on the island of Oahu, Hawaii. By day's end, more than 2,400 American soldiers and civilians were dead. The attack had destroyed 149 American planes. Numerous American ships and other vessels were sunk or badly damaged, including the battleships *Oklahoma*, *Tennessee*, *West Virginia*, and *California*.

The next day, Congress, at Roosevelt's behest, declared war on Japan. On December 11, Germany and Italy declared war on the United States. With that, more than 20 years of American isolationism—some of it having contributed to the outbreak of the war—came to an abrupt end. The United States was now embroiled in World War II.

Cold Facts

Only one member of Congress voted against the war declaration Roosevelt requested on December 8, 1941. Republican Representative Jeanette Rankin of Montana had also voted against the war in 1917, the only member of Congress to have voted against both world wars. In 1942, Rankin was defeated.

President Franklin D. Roosevelt signs the congressional declaration of war against Japan on December 8, 1941.

(Courtesy of the Library of Congress)

The Least You Need to Know

- President Franklin Roosevelt attacked the Great Depression with an ambitious series of government programs that he called "the New Deal."
- Despite the government's herculean efforts, the depression would not completely end until 1942, after the United States entered World War II.
- Most members of Congress and a majority of the American people believed their country could avoid becoming entangled in the unfolding conflict in Europe.
- President Roosevelt, not wanting to get too far ahead of public opinion, cautiously chipped away at the neutrality acts, gradually maneuvering the United States into greater participation in the defense of Europe while simultaneously beefing up U.S. defenses.
- Escalating German attacks on U.S. and British shipping in 1941 edged the U.S. closer to war in Europe.

Global Responsibility

After the bitter experience of World War I, the United States retreated into isolationism, believing it could insulate itself from the effects of the next war. World War II permanently dispelled that notion. Moreover, in the immediate postwar years, the United States was the world's leading superpower, and the only country with atomic weapons. The United States became the defender of the free world—a huge responsibility that, over time, Americans eagerly accepted. Despite the country's strong world position, however optimism and confidence was tempered by the outbreak of a nasty Cold War with the Soviet Union.

Chapter 5

The Good War

In This Chapter

- The Allies challenge Hitler
- The Atlantic Charter articulates the Allies' high ideals
- America and the Soviets fight Hitler
- The Allied summit meetings
- FDR, Churchill, and Stalin begin dividing postwar Europe

To many of those who fought in it or who supported the effort back home, World War II will forever be remembered as "the Good War." It seems such a contradiction in terms. How could war be good? "It was a 'just war,'" if there is any such animal," explained Studs Terkel in the introduction to his best-selling 1984 oral history, *The Good War* (Pantheon, 1984). It was a time when erstwhile allies, and later adversaries—the Soviet Union and the United States—became allies again, valiantly fighting the forces of Nazism, but for far different reasons. During and after the war, the United States—unlike the more passive role it had played in World War I—moved front and center in the Allied effort to crush Nazi Germany and, then, to dispose of Japan's war machine.

Determined not to repeat the mistakes of Wilson and his World War I Allies, President Roosevelt would insist on Germany and Japan's total surrender. And unlike those who had directed the previous war, Roosevelt, Stalin, Britain's Winston Churchill, and China's Chiang Kai-shek would work to agree upon the postwar order *before* the war ended. Alas, these leaders were not as successful in planning the new world as they had hoped. Much of the resulting acrimony over their agreements, in the United States and throughout Europe, would set the stage for the intense 45-year rivalry between the United States and the Soviets.

In this chapter, we explore the personal relationship between Roosevelt and Stalin, as well as the wartime relationship between the United States and the Soviet Union.

Roosevelt's Grand Alliance

Roosevelt later called them the "Four Policemen," the United States, Britain, the Soviet Union, and China—allies in the struggle against Nazi Germany and Japan and later, he hoped, the world's chief peacekeepers. Of the four wartime allies, the United States and Britain cooperated the most, but the other two were essential, if not always cooperative, partners.

Quotes from the Cold

We are all in the same boat now and it is a ship which will not and cannot be sunk.

—British Prime Minister Winston Churchill, the day of the Japanese attack on Pearl Harbor, on the phone to President Roosevelt

Cold Facts

After a week of back-and-forth communication among the 26 Allied nations, Roosevelt received word of a final agreement on the "Declaration by United Nations" on New Year's Day 1942. Churchill was a guest at the White House and Roosevelt personally delivered the good news. "I got out of the bath, and agreed to the draft," Churchill later quipped.

United Nations

The United Nations would be the postwar organization formed after World War II to maintain world peace. The name, however, came into being in January 1942, at the Washington, D.C., meeting of Allied nations. At that meeting, 26 nations agreed on their collective war goals, based primarily on the Atlantic Charter, a document created in August 1941 by Roosevelt and Churchill.

The Atlantic Charter articulated the high ideals the United States and Britain were prepared to defend. They would oppose the Axis (Germany, Italy, and Japan) in order "to ensure life, liberty, independence, and religious freedom and to preserve the rights of man and justice." Neither country would seek a separate peace. They would not fight to gain territory or to alter borders without the consent of the people of those countries affected. They would support self-government for all nations. And they promised to give all nations, "great or small, victor or vanquished," access to raw materials and commerce.

At the January 1942 conference, all 26 nations supported the aims of the Atlantic Charter, vowing to use all their resources to win the war. Roosevelt termed the new alliance of countries "the United Nations."

Western Front

The Alliance became the most successful and powerful international coalition in world history. But it was not perfect. Cracks in the coalition developed almost immediately. American leaders, political and military, wanted to launch a quick invasion of the European mainland, mostly to sap German strength on the eastern front with the Soviet Union. Churchill, on the other hand, warned of moving too quickly and argued forcefully for diversionary operations in southern Europe to buy time for the necessary build up and training of invasion forces. Stalin, of course, favored the American plan, needing relief for his beleaguered army.

Roosevelt also harbored unrealistic hopes for the role China would play in the war. While backing Nationalist leader Chiang Kai-shek's government, he would be repeatedly frustrated by Chiang's unwillingness to pour his government's full resources into the effort to defeat Japan. Chiang was also fighting an internal war with Communist forces led by Mao Zedong (Mao Tse-Tung is the old spelling). Both sides fought the Japanese, but also wasted precious resources on their internal conflict. Nothing, however, frustrated Roosevelt and Churchill more than their relations with Joseph Stalin.

Quotes from the Cold

It was all grandly conceived and finely executed. … The deed and spirit and the invigoration of a common human fraternity in the hearts of men will endure—and steel our will and kindle our actions toward the goal of ridding the world of this horror.

—Supreme Court Justice Felix Frankfurter to Franklin Roosevelt regarding the Atlantic Charter

Cold Facts

In addition to the United States and Britain, those nations whose representatives formed Roosevelt's Grand Alliance of United Nations were: Austria, Belgium, Canada, China, Costa Rica, India, Cuba, Czechoslovakia, Dominican Republic, El Salvador, Greece, Guatemala, Haiti, Honduras, Luxembourg, Netherlands, New Zealand, Nicaragua, Norway, Panama, Poland, South Africa, Soviet Union, and Yugoslavia.

Our Friendly Uncle Joe

The U.S.-Soviet relationship was a marriage of necessity after years of estrangement. The United States had recognized the Communist government in Moscow only in 1933, 16 years after it had come into being. Furthermore, many Americans were still angry over Stalin's collusion with Hitler.

However, Roosevelt was dedicated to the defeat of Hitler by any means, and this meant, for the war years at least, any enemy of Hitler was a friend of the United States. As one of Roosevelt's aides put it privately in the summer of 1941: "So long as Russia is preoccupying Hitler … we should and will do everything in our power to aid Britain. … Between them

Britain and Russia may frustrate Hitler's aim to rule the world." To Roosevelt, the value of his new alliance was nothing but pragmatism: "Put it in terms of dead Germans and smashed tanks."

Quotes from the Cold

The Japanese attack on Pearl Harbor caused many isolationists to reexamine their philosophy, as did one U.S. senator:

[Pearl Harbor] drove most of us to the irresistible conclusion that world peace is indivisible. We learned that the oceans are no longer moats around our ramparts. We learned that mass destruction is a progressive science which defies both time and space and reduces human flesh and blood to cruel impotence.

—Senator Arthur Vandenberg, a leading isolationist, quoted in *A Concise History of the American Republic* (Oxford, 1977)

It was no exaggeration to say that the Russians were, indeed, doing the heaviest fighting against the Germans. Roosevelt wrote to General Douglas MacArthur in May 1942 that "the Russian armies are killing more Axis personnel and destroying more Axis material than all other 25 United Nations put together."

Franklin and Joe

Roosevelt had few illusions about the brutality of Stalin's regime. But he regarded Hitler as a far more dangerous leader for one simple, if naive reason: Hitler wanted to rule the world, while Stalin appeared content to obtain and secure power with the Soviet Union's narrow sphere of influence. Roosevelt believed that Russian hostility toward the United States and its Allies was due primarily to ignorance. "I think the Russians are perfectly friendly," Roosevelt said. "They aren't trying to gobble up all the rest of Europe or the world. They didn't know us, that's the really fundamental difference."

The way that Woodrow Wilson had tried to isolate and humiliate the Russians after World War I had been counterproductive, Roosevelt believed. And he vowed to treat Stalin differently after the war. He would respect the Soviet Union's security needs so long as Stalin behaved himself by not trying to export communism around the world.

Quotes from the Cold

I know you will not mind my being brutally frank when I tell you that I think I can personally handle Stalin better than either your Foreign Office or my State Department. Stalin hates the guts of all your top people. He thinks he likes me better and I hope he will continue to do so.

—Roosevelt to Churchill, March 18, 1942

A New American Hero

For all his brutality, Stalin was a simple, gregarious man who made a strong positive impression on American officials during the war's early years. That favorable image gained some currency in the American press during the war, so much so that many Americans temporarily forgot their strong antipathy toward the Soviet Union and the leader who became known to many as "good old Uncle Joe." Of course, our good old uncle was a mass murderer of epic proportions. But this hardly mattered when his army on the eastern front was suffering most of the casualties of the war, keeping Hitler's army from throwing its full weight against Britain.

Quotes from the Cold

One can see in retrospect that by late 1942 the triumph of the democracies over Hitler had probably become inseparable from the triumph of Russian communism, an anomaly that was to be a major complicating factor in the conduct of the war and a source of endless troubles to come.

—David Eisenhower, *Eisenhower at War: 1943–1945* (Random House, 1986)

Communists and Conference Diplomacy

Although Roosevelt and Stalin wanted a cross-channel invasion by 1943, Churchill's wishes—and common sense—had prevailed. Allied forces simply would not be ready in time. But Roosevelt wanted America in the fighting, as much to raise U.S. morale as to relieve Stalin's forces on the eastern front.

The result would be Operation Torch, the Allied invasion across North Africa—and later into Sicily, Italy, and southern France—that would commence in the fall of 1942.

Quotes from the Cold

It is essential for us to bear in mind our Ally's [Russia] personality, and the very difficult and dangerous situation that he confronts. I think we should attempt to put ourselves in his place, for no one whose country has been invaded can be expected to approach the war from a world point of view.

—Franklin Roosevelt to Winston Churchill, 1942

Stalin's Bounty

Before he formally allied himself with Britain and the United States, Stalin wanted assurances that the two nations would honor the territory he had seized in 1939–40 during his brief alliance with Hitler. During those months, Stalin had seized the Baltic States, and portions of Poland, Romania, and Finland. Now he wanted to make sure that his new allies would let him keep them.

At first, the British were cool to the idea, but suddenly warmed when Stalin hinted that he might again seek a separate peace with Hitler. Initially, Roosevelt was amenable to Churchill's proposal to formally recognize most of Stalin's acquisitions. But when Secretary of State Cordell Hull vigorously opposed the idea, Roosevelt reversed course.

The best Roosevelt could offer Stalin were continued promises—insincere as they were—that Britain and the United States would open a second front sometime in 1942. Roosevelt knew that Churchill would never go along, but desperately wanting to keep Stalin in the Allied fold, he lied. When he finally learned the truth, Stalin was bitter over the betrayal.

Casablanca

Churchill continued fighting to foreclose the idea of a cross-channel invasion. To keep the focus on the Mediterranean theater, the British leader wanted the Allied forces to hopscotch their way northward into southern Europe, first into Sicily, then to Italy and, finally, into southern France. Next, Churchill wanted the Allies to stage an invasion of the Balkans from Turkey—primarily to keep the region out of Stalin's clutches. Finally, Churchill believed, the Allies might be ready to invade France by the late summer of 1943.

U.S. officials had little choice but to go along, knowing that a full-scale invasion of France was not possible before 1944. But Roosevelt also knew that the Russians could not be expected to continue waging the war virtually unaided. Waiting until 1944 to engage Hitler's armies was unthinkable.

At a conference between Roosevelt and Churchill at Casablanca, Morocco, in January 1943, the two leaders agreed to extend Operation Torch into Sicily and to escalate the Allied bombing of Germany. All the while, they would concentrate on amassing the fighting force required to cross the English Channel into German-occupied France.

Unconditional Surrender

At Casablanca, Roosevelt, for the first time, articulated the ultimate war aims of the Allied forces. Unlike World War I, the United States and its Allies would insist on Germany's "unconditional surrender." After the war, there would be no negotiating with the defeated Nazis. Moreover, Roosevelt believed that his call for Germany's unconditional surrender would keep Stalin within the Allied fold—especially after he received the disconcerting news about delaying the cross-channel invasion.

London Poles

The dispute over when to launch a cross-channel invasion wasn't the only sore topic among the Allies. The discovery in April 1943 of a mass grave of murdered Poles in the

Kaytn Forest, near Smolensk in the Soviet Union, sparked a furor in England. According to the Germans, the Russians had murdered 10,000 Polish soldiers, formerly prisoners in Soviet camps during Stalin's occupation of eastern Poland in 1939. (The allegations would later be proven, but the death toll was actually 20,000.)

In London, the Polish government-in-exile demanded a formal inquiry. Roosevelt and Churchill, however, wavered. Stalin broke off relations with the London Poles. And fearing that an investigation would anger Stalin and threaten the Allied coalition, Roosevelt and Churchill responded by questioning the veracity of the German reports.

Cold Facts

The U.S. Lend-Lease program did not provide military assistance only to Britain. Significant assistance was provided by the United States to the Soviet Union, including 13 million military boots, five million tons of food, 11,800 locomotives and railroad cars, 409,000 cargo trucks, and 47,000 jeeps.

Some U.S. officials saw the Polish massacre as evidence, not only of Stalin's ruthlessness, but of his territorial avarice—a desire to rule most, if not all, of Eastern Europe. William C. Bullitt, the former U.S. ambassador to the Soviet Union, advised Roosevelt to support Churchill's idea of a Balkan invasion in order to prevent the Soviets "from replacing the Nazis as the masters of Europe." Roosevelt rejected the advice, telling Bullitt: "I have a hunch that Stalin is not that kind of man." Roosevelt believed the Soviet leader "doesn't want anything but security for his country." And he doubted that Stalin would attempt to annex any more territory, express-ing confidence that he "will work with me for a world of democracy and peace." Although Roosevelt's decision against a Balkan campaign was sound—it might have driven Stalin back into Hitler's arms—history would prove him dreadfully wrong about the Soviets' territorial desires.

Quotes from the Cold

This war is not as in the past; whoever occupies a territory also imposes on it his own social system. Everyone imposes his own system as far as his army can reach. It cannot be otherwise.

—Joseph Stalin, 1944

Cooperating on Paper

Much of the map of Europe during the latter half of the twentieth century was decided during World War II. But it wasn't entirely the result of territory captured in battle. Rather, some of the postwar map was drawn during negotiations among Roosevelt, Stalin, and Churchill before the war ended.

The first of these "mapping" sessions was at Tehran, Iran, in November 1943. Here, for four days Roosevelt and Stalin, joined by Churchill, met for the first time. And despite their disputes over war strategy and the postwar world order, the three men enjoyed generally warm relations.

President Franklin Roosevelt and Soviet leader Joseph Stalin first met at the Tehran Conference in November 1943.

(Courtesy of the Library of Congress)

Operation Overlord

At Tehran, the "Big Three," as they became known, first worked to harmonize their war strategies against Hitler. Still hoping for an Allied invasion of the Balkans and possibly Italy, Churchill found himself outnumbered. With Stalin and Roosevelt in agreement, the British prime minister reluctantly approved a plan to launch the cross-channel invasion—now called Operation Overlord—no later than June 1, 1944.

Quotes from the Cold

I may say that I "got along fine" with Marshal Stalin. He is a man who combines a tremendous relentless determination with a stalwart good humor. I believe he is truly representative of the heart and soul of Russia; and I believe that we are going to get along very well with him and the Russian people—very well indeed.

—Franklin Roosevelt, in a national radio address following the 1943 Tehran Conference

The Baltics

When the discussions turned to postwar political matters, the going got rougher. The first matter was the disposition of the Baltic States (Lithuania, Latvia, and Estonia) that Stalin had seized during his alliance with Hitler. Roosevelt wanted these nations to choose freely whether they would join the Soviet Union. Stalin, of course, had no intention of relinquishing his bounty and told Roosevelt "there would be plenty of opportunities for such an expression of the will of the people." (There never would be an opportunity for the Baltic States to express their will—at least under Soviet rule.)

Poland

Next, the three men turned to Poland, but, again, failed to reach a consensus. They could not agree on the country's postwar boundaries. Stalin wanted a far-western border for Poland, one that ate into German territory. And he also wanted Russia to swallow up a large chunk of eastern Poland. Roosevelt, strangely, expressed no strong objections to Stalin's strong appetite for Polish territory. But he knew that such an outcome would surely enrage the exiled Polish government in London and would, in turn, spark protests among the sizeable Polish-American community.

Well before the discussion, the president informed Stalin that he would refrain from discussing Poland. And he largely remained silent. But to observers, Roosevelt appeared to give tacit support to the postwar Polish boundaries that Stalin proposed. Stalin would eventually get his way. For now, however, the Big Three postponed the discussion over Poland.

Cold Facts

At Tehran, Stalin demanded to know who would command the Allied invasion of France, now dubbed Operation Overlord. "It has not been decided," FDR answered. "Then nothing will come out of these operations," Stalin replied, urging that Roosevelt promptly name a commander.

Later, Roosevelt made the painful decision to pass over General George C. Marshall, the chief of staff of the U.S. Army. Marshall was Roosevelt's most valued military advisor and desperately wanted to command the Overlord forces. Roosevelt, however, gave the job to General Dwight D. Eisenhower. "I feel I could not sleep at night with you out of the country," Roosevelt told Marshall.

Germany

Stalin, Roosevelt, and Churchill also discussed how to constrain Germany's ability to rearm after the war. Roosevelt favored splitting the country into five self-governing states.

Churchill wanted only two, believing that a strong, more unified Germany could check against Stalin's desire to expand the Soviet empire. Stalin, fearing the rise of another fascist state near his western border, opposed any confederation of German states.

The Big Three wartime leaders: Soviet leader Joseph Stalin, U.S. President Franklin D. Roosevelt, and British Prime Minister Winston Churchill (left to right).

(Courtesy of the Library of Congress)

As the conference ended, not much had been decided. The decisions on the Baltics and Germany would be left, ostensibly, to the European Advisory Commission—an organization the Big Three had created to deal with intractable postwar issues.

Tehran Declaration

Before departing Iran, the three leaders issued a joint statement, notable for the lofty ideals about peace and democracy endorsed by Stalin. The three expressed determination that our nations shall work together in war and in the peace that will follow. Furthermore, they sought …

> the cooperation and active participation of all nations, large and small, whose peoples in heart and mind are dedicated, as are our own peoples, to the elimination of tyranny and slavery, oppression and intolerance. We will welcome them, as they may choose to come, into a world family of democratic nations.

Second Thoughts

The irony of Stalin—the brutal Bolshevik who had already gobbled up a good portion of Eastern Europe—endorsing democracy was not lost on some of Roosevelt's aides. After Tehran, one of Roosevelt's military advisors, Admiral William Leahy, remarked to presidential aide Harry Hopkins: "Well, Harry, all I can say is, nice friends we have now." Another Roosevelt advisor, Charles Bohlen, worried that Stalin's posture at Tehran suggested a disturbing picture of postwar Europe. "The Soviet Union would be the only important military and political force," he told the U.S. ambassador to the Soviet Union. "The rest of Europe would be reduced to military and political impotence."

In only a few short years, Bohlen's chilling prediction would be realized. While the Americans, the British, and the Soviets found it relatively easy to agree on how to fight their common enemy, they would not fare nearly as well in the debate over the postwar political questions. By the end of 1945, that "debate" would become the Cold War.

The Least You Need to Know

- The 26 nation Grand Alliance during World War II proved the most successful coalition of nations in world history.
- Leading the fight against Nazi Germany and Imperialist Japan were the United States, Great Britain, the Soviet Union, and China.
- Stalin and Roosevelt, who thought that he could trust the Soviet leader, developed a warm personal relationship at their several wartime conferences.
- In January 1943, at their Casablanca conference, Roosevelt and Churchill began laying plans for a cross-channel attack of Nazi-occupied France.
- At the first of several wartime conferences, Roosevelt, Churchill, and Stalin met at Tehran in November 1943 to begin drawing the map of postwar Europe, and Stalin—revealing plans to keep the Baltic States and Poland—gave his Allies reason to believe that he would try to dominate Eastern Europe after the war.

Chapter 6

Breaking Up Is Hard to Do

In This Chapter

- The Allies take back Europe
- Reversing the New Deal
- Roosevelt gets a fourth term
- The Yalta Conference and Eastern Europe's future
- Roosevelt dies in Georgia

The U.S.-Soviet wartime alliance was never very secure. Despite Franklin Roosevelt's hopes for an enduring postwar relationship with the Soviet Union, cracks in his Grand Alliance began to show even before the war ended.

While the United States and Britain would finally give Stalin his much-desired western front in June 1944, the Soviet leader would not be content to see Europe restored to peace and self-determination. Stalin saw the war as his opportunity to expand the Soviet Union's territory and to assure its security. In this chapter, we see how the struggles over the Soviets' role in postwar Europe set the stage for the Cold War.

From Normandy to Paris

While Roosevelt, Churchill, and Stalin were meeting in Tehran in the fall of 1943, the Americans were fully engaged in the war. American forces were

Cold Facts

By the end of June 6, 1944 D-Day, about 150,000 Allied troops, along with thousands of vehicles, munitions, and other supplies were on the European mainland. By late July, two million Allied troops and 250,000 vehicles had landed in France.

fighting their way onto the European continent from Northern Africa, to Sicily, to Italy, and finally to France.

D-Day

By June 1944, the Allies were ready to launch their attack across the English Channel. For months, they had been amassing troops in southern Britain—1.5 million in all, including 620,000 ground troops in 21 divisions. When they finally left the British coast, they were the largest invasion force ever assembled in history.

The invasion began on the morning of June 6, as American, British, and Canadian forces (aided by Polish, French, Italian, Belgian, Czech, and Dutch troops) stormed ashore along a 50-mile stretch of beach at Normandy in northwestern France.

Quotes from the Cold

They came ashore on Omaha Beach, the slogging, unglamorous men that no one envied. No battle ensigns flew for them, no horns or bugles sounded. But they had history on their side. They came from regiments that had bivouacked at places like Valley Forge, Stoney Creek, Antietam, Gettysburg, that had fought in the Argonne. They had crossed the beaches of North Africa, Sicily and Salerno. Now they had one more beach to cross. They would call this one "Bloody Omaha."

—Cornelius Ryan, *The Longest Day: June 6, 1944* (Simon and Schuster, 1959)

To Paris

In the days and weeks after D-Day, the fighting was tough, fierce, and sometimes hand-to-hand. Eventually, in late July, the Allies broke through as General Omar Bradley's First Army smashed the German lines. In August, General George Patton's Third Army completed the Allied encirclement of the German forces.

Those German troops that were not captured retreated toward Germany. Next, a separate Allied invasion along France's Mediterranean coast in mid-August opened up more ports and supply lines for the advancing troops.

On August 25, French forces, followed by the Americans, arrived in Paris, and were greeted by jubilant crowds celebrating their liberation from Nazi occupation. Within weeks, the Allies had driven German forces from most of France and Belgium.

For the Allied troops, liberating France was hard enough; pushing into Germany was an unexpected struggle. Hampered by strong German defenses, supply problems, and persistent rains, the Allied march toward Berlin halted, temporarily, at the German border. Another eight months of difficult fighting lay ahead.

America Turns Right

Silently, with no fanfare at all, the New Deal had died. As early as 1938, Congress had begun to repeal many of the economic reforms it had enacted just a few years earlier. Gone were the job-creating Civilian Conservation Corps, the Works Progress Administration, and the National Youth Administration. The war had created so many American jobs that these agencies now seemed superfluous.

Quotes from the Cold

There are moments that go beyond each of our poor little lives. Paris! Paris outraged! Paris broken! Paris martyrized! But Paris liberated!

—French General Charles De Gaulle upon Paris's liberation on August 25, 1944

Congress—more conservative and, thus, more hostile to expanded government—abolished or scaled back other New Deal agencies, including the National Resources Planning Board, the Farm Security Administration, and the Rural Electrification Administration.

Goodbye New Deal

By 1944, many Republicans and conservative southern Democrats regarded the New Deal not simply as a movement that had been made unnecessary by the economic boom of the war; they believed it had been a needless governmental intrusion into virtually every aspect of the American economy. More than ever, domestic opposition to Roosevelt and his policies were on the rise.

Despite the flagging popularity of his domestic programs, Roosevelt was still highly regarded as a wartime leader. A national public opinion poll in November 1943 revealed that while 56 percent approved of his handling of domestic problems, an overwhelming 70 percent favored his military and foreign policies.

The problem was, however, that many Americans regarded the war as virtually over. U.S. production of munitions was amply supplying Allied forces in Europe. The situation appeared so dire for Hitler's forces that many, including some of Roosevelt's advisors, believed the war might be over as early as the spring of 1944 despite the reality of more than another year of fierce fighting in Europe and the Pacific.

Returning to the United States from the Tehran Conference, the president admitted to being "let down" as he saw the country "laboring under the delusion that the time is past when we must make prodigious sacrifices—that the war is already won and we can begin to slacken off." Roosevelt had good reason to worry. Some prominent voices were already suggesting that wartime munitions plants could soon be converted for production of much-desired consumer goods.

Dr. Win-the-War

Yet Roosevelt was not about to abandon the war effort. In a Christmastime radio address in 1943, the president introduced the nation to "Dr. Win-the-War." Roosevelt argued that the New Deal had been necessary because the United States had been "an awfully sick patient." On December 7, 1941—the day of the Japanese attack on Pearl Harbor—Roosevelt said the country had suffered "a very bad accident—not internal trouble, but breaking several bones." Roosevelt continued:

> Old Doctor New Deal didn't know "nothing" about legs and arms. … So he got his partner, who was an orthopedic surgeon, Dr. Win-the-War, to take care of this fellow. … And the result is that the patient is back on his feet. He had given up his crutches. He isn't wholly well yet, and he won't be until he wins the war.

Second Bill of Rights

Despite his attempts to turn the nation's attention back to the war, Roosevelt was far from ready to shelve his New Deal. Looking ahead at the 1944 elections, he reasoned that a program of expanded government benefits, if not popular with a majority of Americans, might at least energize his Democratic base.

On January 11, 1944, delivering his annual State of the Union address over the radio from the White House—illness prevented him from giving the speech to a joint session of Congress—Roosevelt called for "a second Bill of Rights … an economic Bill of Rights." Roosevelt wanted the government to guarantee every person a job, a living wage, adequate housing, medical care, and education, and "protection from the economic fears of old age, sickness, accident, and unemployment."

Cold Facts

The National Resource Planning Board (NRPB), chaired by an uncle of Roosevelt, provided the basis for FDR's call for a federally guaranteed income for every American. "The need for socially provided income is in large measure a consequence of the imperfections in the operation of our economy." The NRPB estimated that a reasonable yearly national income would be about $100 billion, with government providing what the private economy could not. The NRPB's estimates proved fantastically conservative and demonstrated little faith in the potential of the American economy. By 1942, national income had already reached $137 billion. By 1950, it would be $241 billion and, by 1970, $800 billion.

While the speech was largely a tribute to the New Deal of the 1930s, it was a visionary and politically inspired address that challenged the United States to include all Americans in the economic expansion of the 1940s. But as Roosevelt expected, his plan, in the words of a biographer, "fell with a dull thud" in Congress.

The Fourth Term

Not since 1864, when Abraham Lincoln had been reelected during the Civil War, had the United States held a presidential election in wartime. The 1944 election would be such an occasion and Franklin Roosevelt wanted a fourth term.

Unlike 1940, Roosevelt did not play coy about his intentions. He would not wait for the Democratic National Convention to draft him. In fact, the only questions were: Was Roosevelt, at age 62, healthy enough to serve? Who would be his running mate? And who would the Republicans run against him?

Roosevelt's Health

Anyone who saw Roosevelt in 1944 could tell that he was a sick man. To aides who inquired how he was feeling, Roosevelt often replied "rotten" or "like hell." He looked haggard, gaunt, and unhealthy. A physical examination by Navy doctors in March 1944 revealed that he suffered from high blood pressure and heart disease.

To the world, his sickly appearance notwithstanding, Roosevelt tried to project the image of good health and vigor. And his doctors participated in the deception, pronouncing him healthy and able to serve as president for another four years.

Despite his attempts to control his weight and to alter his diet, it was quite evident that Roosevelt could not last long. Medication that would have controlled his blood pressure, and possibly prevented a stroke, would not be developed until the 1950s.

But Roosevelt could not bear the thought of stepping down with a war in progress. It simply did not seem the right time to change national leadership. As he told his son James, he must run again "to maintain a continuity of command in a time of continuing crisis."

Roosevelt's Running Mate

While Democratic Party leaders—especially southerners—would never refuse Roosevelt the nomination for a fourth time, they were not about to abide another four years of Vice President Henry Wallace, aptly described by one historian as "unapologetically liberal and unpredictably loony." Some of them even believed that Roosevelt might lose the election with Wallace as his running mate. Most of those who knew Roosevelt intimately believed that he would not serve out a fourth term. That meant whomever Roosevelt chose as vice president would become president. And that meant that the radical, unpredictable Wallace had to go.

When Roosevelt settled on the short, scrappy senator from Missouri, Harry S. Truman, the choice seemed an unlikely one. Truman had never graduated college and had served in the Senate only 10 years. But during his brief career in Washington, he had demonstrated not only loyalty to the New Deal, but a great degree of independence as he headed an investigation into military waste and abuse. Truman, from a border state, was also acceptable to conservatives and liberals.

Thomas Dewey

To challenge Roosevelt, the Republicans nominated Governor Thomas E. Dewey of New York, a dynamic young reformer who had the misfortune of challenging one of the most popular wartime leaders in American history. Dewey gamely went after Roosevelt, but had little in the way of issues to use against the incumbent.

With U.S. military triumphs in Europe and the Pacific, there was almost nothing regarding Roosevelt's handling of the war to criticize. With the country booming, he could not attack the president's stewardship of the economy. And while he might have legitimately faulted Roosevelt for his postwar plans, he did so at the risk of damaging the bipartisan consensus over foreign policy at a time when American soldiers were still fighting overseas.

Worst of all for Dewey, Roosevelt refused—until the latter days of the campaign—to seek votes like a traditional candidate. Instead of rallies, the president mostly limited his public appearances to military inspection events during which he could play the less-political role of commander-in-chief.

The best Dewey could do was to plead with voters to turn out the "tired old men" from the White House, a not-so-oblique reference to Roosevelt's age and health. But Dewey never had a chance. While the popular vote was relatively close—Roosevelt won by 2.3 million out of 47.9 million votes cast—he buried Dewey in the Electoral College, 432 to 99.

Yalta

Just three months after Roosevelt's re-election, Russian and Allied troops were approaching Berlin. The war was all but won. And Roosevelt left the United States again, this time for Yalta, in the Soviet Crimea, for his final meeting with Churchill and Stalin. For the first time, they would meet as all-but-certain victors.

Roosevelt certainly had no idea that, after his death, his actions at Yalta would be bitterly attacked by conservatives who believed he had delivered much of Eastern Europe, particularly Poland and Eastern Germany, into Communist domination. But he did know that most of the important decisions regarding territorial matters had already been made at Tehran and Casablanca. At Yalta, the Big Three would simply close the deal.

At the Yalta Conference in 1945, Roosevelt, Stalin, and Churchill decided, among other things, the fate of postwar Poland.

(Courtesy of the Library of Congress)

Sellout?

Although critics would later accuse him of selling out Eastern Europe, Roosevelt arrived in Yalta with very little power—short of a war with Russia—to affect Stalin's actions regarding Poland and Germany. Stalin already had Poland in his possession and his armies were then marching deep into German territory.

Quotes from the Cold

We really believed in our hearts that [the Yalta agreement] was the dawn of the new day we had all been praying for and talking about for so many years. We were absolutely certain we had won the first great victory for peace. … The Russians had proved that they could be reasonable and farseeing and there wasn't any doubt in the minds of the President or any of us that we could live with them peacefully for as far into the future as any of us could imagine.

—FDR advisor Harry Hopkins quoted by Robert Sherwood in *Roosevelt and Hopkins* (Harper, 1948)

At best, the president knew that he could extract only minor concessions from the Soviet leader. As one of Roosevelt's advisors told him at the time, it would be futile "to demand of Russia what she thinks she needs and most of which she now possesses."

Besides, Roosevelt had other important objectives at Yalta for which he needed Stalin's support. Other than resolving the status of postwar Poland and Germany, he hoped to persuade Stalin to enter the war against Japan, and then to secure his support for establishment of a permanent United Nations organization.

Cold Facts

After the negotiations over Poland at Yalta, Admiral William Leahy, one of FDR's top military advisors, complained that the agreement was "so elastic that the Russians can stretch all the way from Yalta to Washington without ever technically breaking it." Roosevelt could not muster the energy to disagree: "I know, Bill—I know it. But it's the best I can do for Poland at this time."

Quotes from the Cold

At Yalta, Roosevelt urged Stalin to ensure that the first postwar elections in Poland were fair and open, "beyond question." Roosevelt said they "should be like Caesar's wife. I did not know her but they said she was pure." To that, Stalin replied: "They said that about her but in fact she had her sins."

Poland

Long before Yalta, the Big Three had agreed to alter Poland's borders. In the words of historian James MacGregor Burns, the country "would be picked up like a carpetbag and set down a few hundred kilometers to the west." That point was assured. But who would govern this altered nation? Stalin favored the communist-dominated "Lublin" Poles, while Roosevelt and Churchill argued on behalf of the London Poles, the Polish government-in-exile.

Roosevelt, aware of his significant Polish constituency, argued for a unity government created by free elections. Stalin, however, wanted maximum control over Poland, regarding it as a buffer against future German aggression. Although Stalin eventually agreed to concessions regarding free elections and a unity government that would include the London Poles, it was evident that he would never relinquish control of his valued war prize.

Roosevelt may not have been able to affect Stalin's attitudes toward Poland. But his failure to communicate with Polish leaders and the American public about the realities he faced at Yalta made it only more likely that he and the Yalta accords would be vigorously attacked once the import of the conference became widely known.

Japan

Roosevelt's primary goal at Yalta was to ensure the Soviets' participation in the war against Japan. As Stalin had once longed for a second front in Europe to hold down his losses, the United States now desired the same kind of assistance from Stalin.

Here, Stalin knew that his negotiating position was strong. And he made the most of the situation, extracting from Roosevelt several concessions, including Soviet possession of the Kurile Islands and the southern region of Japan's Sakhalin Island; control of Outer Mongolia; and recognition of the Soviets' "pre-eminent interests" in Manchuria. In return, Stalin promised, in writing, that he would enter the war against Japan within two to three months after Germany's surrender.

Germany

Roosevelt, Stalin, and Churchill agreed to divide Germany into four zones of occupation to be controlled respectively by the United States, the Soviet Union, Great Britain, and France. The decision placed a divided Berlin in the Soviet zone and ensured that the Soviet Union would dominate East Germany for the next 45 years.

Roosevelt and Churchill—while sympathetic to Stalin's demands for war reparations from Germany—recalled the disastrous impact of reparations in the years after World War I. Stalin, however, was adamant and, after considerable debate, Roosevelt and Churchill compromised, allowing an Allied Reparations Commission to consider the Soviets' request for $10 billion in reparations.

United Nations

Like Poland's borders, the reality of a postwar international world body, the United Nations, was preordained by the time the Big Three arrived in Yalta. Representatives of the United States, Soviet Union, China, and Britain had met in 1944 at the Dumbarton Oaks mansion in Washington, D.C., to draft the organization's basic outline. At Yalta, the real question was the organization's structure and authority.

Stalin wanted 16 votes in the proposed general assembly, one for each of the Soviet Union's republics. Eventually, Roosevelt and Churchill agreed to two extra votes, one each for the Ukraine and White Russia. The Big Three also determined voting procedures for the new body, agreed on creation of a smaller Security Council, and called for an international conference to create a United Nations charter.

Cold Facts

On April 25, 1945, the United Nations Conference on International Organization convened in San Francisco. There, representatives of 50 nations modified the original Dumbarton Oaks proposals. On June 26, the delegates completed and signed the United Nations Charter. In July, the U. S. Senate voted, 89 to 2, to ratify the charter. By October of the same year, enough nations ratified the charter so that the United Nations was officially established.

Death in Warm Springs

Roosevelt returned home in late February full of optimism about what he had accomplished in Yalta. He looked forward to the United Nations organizing session scheduled for late April in San Francisco. And, further brightening his outlook was the rapidly collapsing position of Hitler's army in Germany and the solid progress of American forces in the Pacific war.

Report to Congress

Two days after his return to Washington, Roosevelt addressed a joint session of Congress about the Yalta Conference, telling the assembled members in a weakened, sometimes-faltering voice that while he was hopeful about Yalta's outcome, the ultimate results rested with "you here in the halls of the American Congress."

"Twenty-five years ago, American fighting men looked to the statesmen of the world to finish the work of peace for which they fought and suffered," Roosevelt said. "We failed—we failed them then. We cannot fail them again, and expect the world to survive again." Roosevelt said that he hoped Yalta would "spell the end of the system of unilateral action, the exclusive alliances, the spheres of influence, the balances of power, and all the other expedients that have been tried for centuries—and have always failed."

Troubles with Joe

However, the ink on the Yalta agreement was barely dry before acrimony erupted between Roosevelt and Stalin. Taking advantage of the ambiguity of the Yalta accords, Stalin was determined to install his communist allies in leadership positions in Poland. He refused to allow Western observers into the country.

Churchill was alarmed. "Poland has lost her frontier," he cabled FDR. "Is she now to lose her freedom?" Unless the Allies faced up to the "utter breakdown of what was settled at Yalta," Churchill believed he might be forced to reveal in Parliament the British-American "divergence" over Poland. Roosevelt knew Churchill was correct. "We can't do business with Stalin," he said privately of the man he had once trusted. "He has broken every one of the promises he made at Yalta."

Stalin was making trouble in other ways. When he suspected that U.S.-British talks with the defeated Germans in Italy were the first step toward a separate peace with Hitler, Stalin fired off an angry message to Washington, suggesting not simply a "misunderstanding but something worse." Roosevelt tried to reassure his Soviet counterpart, but was rankled by Stalin's decision to send representatives to the UN conference instead of leading the Soviet delegation himself. To Roosevelt, it appeared Stalin did not hold high hopes for the United Nation's success.

Still, Roosevelt was optimistic about U.S.-Soviet relations and the prospects for a quick end to the war. Sadly, the president who had taken the nation to war and had served as an outstanding wartime leader, would not live to see victory finally declared. On April 12, 1945, at his home in Warm Springs, Georgia, Roosevelt died of a cerebral hemorrhage.

Later that day, at the U.S. Capitol, as Vice President Harry Truman visited over drinks with House Speaker Sam Rayburn and other friends, a call came from the White House. After rushing across town, First Lady Eleanor Roosevelt confronted Truman with the tragic news. "Harry," she said, "the President is dead." Stunned, Truman finally said, "Is there anything I can do for you?" Mrs. Roosevelt replied: "Is there anything *we* can do for *you*. For you are the one in trouble now."

The Least You Need to Know

- Stalin finally got his second front on June 6, 1944, when Allied forces staged a massive invasion of the French coast at Normandy.
- During the war, conservatives succeeded in undoing sizeable portions of Franklin Roosevelt's New Deal programs, which Roosevelt defended, but deftly refocused the nation's attention and energies toward the final push to win the war.
- In 1944, the American public elected an ailing Roosevelt to a fourth term of office, reaffirming its support for his wartime policies.
- At the Yalta Conference, Roosevelt, Churchill, and Stalin formalized key decisions on the future of postwar Europe, and with grudging acquiescence, Roosevelt allowed Stalin to solidify his already firm grip on much of Eastern Europe, particularly Poland and East Germany.
- By April 1945, Roosevelt suspected that Stalin would not live up to his vague promises regarding autonomy for the nations of Eastern Europe, but Roosevelt died on April 12, 1945, before the end of World War II and before the official outbreak of the Cold War.

Chapter 7

Harry Gives 'Em Heck

In This Chapter

- Truman takes on the war
- Truman, Churchill, and Stalin meet at Potsdam
- America uses the bomb in Japan
- The beginning of the containment policy
- Churchill's "Iron Curtain" speech

Franklin Roosevelt was dead and the inexperienced, little-known vice president from Missouri, Harry Truman, was America's new wartime leader. It was Truman who would continue negotiating with Stalin and Churchill over the future of Eastern Europe. It was Truman who would decide whether to use the atomic bomb against Japan, a device he did not know existed until he became president. And it was Truman, in the face of Stalin's determination to dominate Eastern Europe, who decided how the West would respond.

A Plain-Speaking President

Perhaps since Abraham Lincoln, the American people had not seen a president quite like Harry Truman. Born into modest means on a farm in rural Lamar, Missouri, in 1884, Truman's family moved to Independence, Missouri, when he was six years old. Although he worked briefly on a railroad and in a bank, Truman had mostly worked as a farmer until his early 30s.

During World War I, Truman's National Guard unit went to France, where he led Battery D of the 129th Field Artillery, 35th Division. Returning home to Missouri at war's end, Captain Truman married his childhood sweetheart, Bess Wallace, and opened a clothing store in Independence.

Politics

While a postwar agricultural depression had cost Truman his business, his interest in local politics led him to run for political office in 1922, under the patronage of the corrupt Thomas Pendergast political machine. Voters elected Truman judge of the Jackson county court (an administrative position). Except for a two-year hiatus, Truman held that position until 1934, when he ran for the U.S. Senate, again with Pendergast's support.

Elected to the Senate, Truman proved himself an able and independent politician. He enthusiastically supported Franklin Roosevelt's New Deal programs, as well as his foreign and defense policies. Narrowly reelected in 1940, Truman gained respect by leading a prominent investigation into defense corruption and mismanagement as chairman of the Special Committee to Investigate the National Defense Program.

Presidency

Few men were as unprepared for the presidency and yet as innately qualified for the office as Harry Truman. While he had no college education and had been uninformed about almost every aspect of the war by Roosevelt, Truman entered office with attributes that would serve him well. He was scrupulously honest, decisive, highly intelligent, and well read, especially in history. Best of all, he was a man of extraordinary common sense.

Quotes from the Cold

Truman's native intelligence enabled him to grasp quickly the situation into which he was so suddenly thrown, and on which he had not been briefed by Roosevelt. … He kept a firm hand on the new Department of Defense and Foreign Service; and with more fateful decisions than almost any President in our time, he made the fewest mistakes. Truman was always folksy, always the politician, but nobody can reasonably deny that he attained the stature of statesman.

—Historian Samuel Eliot Morison, *The Oxford History of the American People, Volume Three*, (New American Library, 1972)

Summit in Potsdam

Asked by a newspaperman what it felt like to be president on his first day in office, Truman replied: "Did you ever have a bull or a load of hay fall on you? If you ever did, you know how I felt last night." For Truman, the deteriorating relations with the Soviet Union would soon represent that load of hay.

On May 8, 1945, the Allies had accepted Germany's unconditional surrender. The European war was finally over. But the Cold War was just beginning as the Allies now struggled to agree on the map and administration of postwar Europe.

At the Potsdam Conference, held in a suburb of war-ravaged Berlin from July 17 to August 2, the victorious Big Three once again took up the thorny postwar issues, particularly the status of Germany and Poland.

Cold Facts

Just weeks after taking office, Harry Truman was persuaded that Joseph Stalin was flouting the Yalta accords, particularly in Poland, where he had imposed Soviet control and had imprisoned leaders of the government-in-exile who returned from London. In a fit of pique, Truman summoned the Soviet Foreign Minister, Vyacheslav Molotov, to complain, bluntly, that the Soviets had broken their word. Shaken by the lack of diplomacy in the new president's words, Molotov replied, "I have never been talked to like that in my life." Truman brusquely responded, "Carry out your agreements and you won't get talked to like that."

Most of these decisions had been "settled" at Yalta. And at Potsdam, Truman, Churchill, and Stalin were expected to begin implementing them. That notion soon proved mistaken. Now concerned with consolidating his power in Eastern Europe, Stalin was in no mood for greater cooperation with his Allied partners, especially if that meant restrictions on his activities in the Soviet-occupied regions.

Deep Divisions

From the beginning, deep divisions between the United States and the Soviets were evident. Truman wanted to discuss free elections to reorganize the governments of Rumania and Bulgaria. Stalin, however, was more interested in discussing German reparations and a final settlement of Poland's western border, as well as elimination of the London-based Polish government-in-exile.

Cold Facts

According to a Gallup poll taken in the summer of 1945, more than half the American people expected the Soviet Union to continue cooperating with the United States after the war.

Such bickering with Stalin prevented any major new decisions at Potsdam. Truman and Churchill protested Stalin's decision to give the Polish administrative control of Eastern Germany, but Stalin was unyielding. The Soviets wanted to share control of the Black Sea straits with Turkey, while Truman insisted on guarantees that the straits would remain open to international vessels.

Those were the relatively minor issues. The major questions were even more difficult to resolve.

Quotes from the Cold

I knew at Potsdam that there is no difference in totalitarian or police states, call them what you will, Nazi, Fascist, Communist, or Argentine Republics.

—President Harry Truman, in a letter to his daughter Margaret in 1947

Agreement

The predominant issue at Potsdam was postwar Germany. At Yalta, the Big Three had agreed to split the country into four zones, but at Potsdam they could not agree on where to go next. The United States and Britain wanted to quickly put the country back on the road to unification, realizing that a united but disarmed Germany was vital to Europe's economic recovery. The Soviets and France, understandably, feared a resurgent Germany. They favored keeping the country divided and impotent.

President for not even four months, Harry S. Truman meets Joseph Stalin in Potsdam, Germany, in July of 1945, where the Big Three discussed the status of Germany and Poland.

(Courtesy of the Library of Congress)

The best the conferees could do on this question was to establish guidelines for a new representative government for the country, disarm its military, and outlaw the Nazi Party. Thereafter, matters relating to the whole of Germany would be referred to an Allied Control Council, represented by each of the four powers that occupied the divided nation.

On reparations and Germany's borders, the Allies compromised. The United States and Britain accepted the Oder-Neisse line as the country's eastern border, while the Soviets settled for 25 percent of Germany's equipment from the western zones—in addition to virtually everything in the Russian zone—as its share of reparations.

Ultimately, as far as Germany was concerned, the Potsdam Conference was a failure. The Allied Control Council never worked as expected. And the ambiguous wording of the Potsdam Declaration almost guaranteed that the Soviets would not feel bound by its provisions in the early days of the Cold War.

Quotes from the Cold

The result of the futile and senseless German resistance to the might of the aroused free peoples of the world stands forth in awful clarity as an example to the people of Japan. The might that now converges on Japan is immeasurably greater than that which, when applied to the resisting Nazis, necessarily laid waste to the lands, the industry, and the method of life of the whole German people. The full application of our military power, backed by our resolve, all mean the inevitable and complete destruction of the Japanese armed forces and just as inevitably the utter devastation of the Japanese homeland.

—From the Potsdam Declaration, July 26, 1945

Ultimatum

There was something that the Big Three could agree upon—defeating Japan. On July 26, the three leaders (the defeated Winston Churchill had been replaced by Prime Minister Clement Attlee) issued an ultimatum to Japan: unconditional surrender or complete destruction. "The time has come," the Big Three declared, "for Japan to decide whether she will continue to be controlled by those self-willed militaristic advisers whose unintelligent calculations have brought the Empire of Japan to the threshold of annihilation, or whether she will follow the path of reason." What Japan did not know, but what Stalin suspected, was that the United States had the means to back up its threat against Japan.

The Bomb

Since 1939, scientists had known about fission, the process of creating enormous amounts of energy by splitting an atomic nucleus. How to harness and magnify this energy into an explosion of enormous proportions had been the subject of intensive research in the United States since August 1942, when nuclear weapons research had been reorganized as a U.S. Army program.

Manhattan Project

The highly secretive so-called Manhattan Project first focused on finding adequate supplies of the two isotopes believed necessary for building a nuclear bomb, uranium-235 and plutonium-239. The project was an enormous leap of faith, for it was not yet clear that a massive nuclear explosion envisioned by scientists was even possible.

Ultimately, however, the intensive research proved successful. Working at the remote White Sands Missile Range near Alamogordo, New Mexico, scientists discovered how to produce the components for the device. By the spring of 1945, they had designed and developed a workable nuclear bomb.

For Truman, development of the bomb could not have come too early. In the Pacific, U.S. forces would soon begin their final assault on the Japanese mainland. But the island hopping already required had been a bloody, deadly business. The U.S. fierce assault on the small but strategic island of Iwo Jima in February had claimed the lives of almost 7,000 U.S. personnel.

The Japanese, despite the inevitable defeat they faced, were refusing to surrender. And the terrifying prospect of months of additional fighting—much of it hand-to-hand—loomed large in the minds of Truman and his military advisors. The bomb, with its awesome, destructive force, was thought to be the surest way to force Japan's early surrender and save untold American lives.

Quotes from the Cold

"We have discovered the most terrible bomb in the history of the world. It may be the fire destruction prophesied in the Euphrates Valley Era, after Noah and his fabulous Ark."

—President Harry S. Truman, to his diary on June 5, 1945

Cold Facts

When deciding where to drop the first atomic bombs, U.S. military planners chose the Japanese cities of Hiroshima and Nagasaki because neither city had been previously bombed. This made it easier to accurately assess the destructive impact of the bombs.

Hiroshima and Nagasaki

On July 16, 1945, as the Big Three prepared to begin their meeting at Potsdam, U.S. scientists at Alamogordo successfully tested the world's first nuclear bomb. Within a month, on August 6, the U.S. Air Force dropped a similar device on Hiroshima, Japan, and, three days later, on Nagasaki. Together, the two bombs would kill more than 100,000 Japanese civilians and bring to an end, upon the Japanese surrender on August 14, the deadliest war in human history.

The Biggest Stick

It was not the Japanese who were foremost in Truman's mind as he had departed Potsdam in late July. It was the Russians and his growing displeasure over their duplicity—as well as his growing confidence that the United States, with atomic weapons at its disposal, could now force Stalin to abide by his agreements.

Cold Facts

American estimates of those killed in the two atomic explosions over Japan in 1945 were placed at just over 100,000. Japanese officials disputed that number, claiming that 240,000 lives were lost.

Truman also believed that the awesome power of "the bomb" would persuade Stalin to keep his hands off Japan. As he returned to the United States by ship, Truman later said he had determined to never again "take chances on a joint setup with the Russians." Stalin and the other Russian leaders, he had concluded, understood only raw power. And now, Truman and other U.S. leaders would conclude that the bomb would be an effective weapon to neutralize Stalin in Europe.

Cold Facts

Historians believe that more than 55 million people were killed during World War II—25 million soldiers and other military personnel and 30 million civilians. Russia sustained the heaviest losses. In all, more than 20 million Russians—civilian and military—died during the war. By contrast, the United States lost 407,000 soldiers in the war, 292,000 of them in battle. (In most wars, a significant percentage of the deaths are non-combat deaths.)

In the 1950s, under President Dwight D. Eisenhower, this strategy would be called "massive retaliation"—using the threat of nuclear attack to alter the behavior of the communist rulers in Russia and China. In a manner of speaking, the United States would say to its adversarial neighbors, "If you steal my car, I will burn down your house."

The problem with this strategy, as historian Stephen Ambrose has noted, "was that even as early as 1945 it bore little relation to reality." Atomic bombs were not yet powerful enough to deter the Russians, who were working on their own bomb. Furthermore, the United States simply did not have enough bombs to make good on its threats. "These truths were only gradually realized by the politicians," Ambrose noted, "but they colored the military situation from the beginning."

Stalin Emboldened

Far from being cowed by the bomb, the Soviets appeared emboldened. And the U.S. ambassador to the Soviet Union believed that he understood why, speculating that "the

Quotes from the Cold

Atomic bombs are meant to frighten those with weak nerves.

—Joseph Stalin, September 17, 1946

Russian people have been aroused to feel that they must again face an antagonistic world. American imperialism is included as a threat to Russia."

In response to these perceived threats, Stalin increased his repression of Romania and Bulgaria. He refused to hold the free elections he had promised in Eastern Europe. He annexed a portion of eastern Germany into Poland, and pulled Korea into the Soviet orbit in the face of Western efforts to reunify the divided country. He also refused to participate in two institutions the United States hoped would hasten Europe's economic recovery, the World Bank and the International Monetary Fund.

Quotes from the Cold

In our possession of this weapon, as in our possession of other new weapons, there is no threat to any nation. The world, which has seen the United States in two great wars, knows that full well. The possession in our hands of this new power of destruction we regard as a sacred trust. Because of our love of peace, the thoughtful people of the world know that trust will not be violated, that it will be faithfully executed.

—President Harry S. Truman, October 27, 1945

Privately, Truman adopted a hard line. "Unless Russia is faced with an iron fist and strong language, another war is in the making," he told his aides. "Only one language do they understand—'how many divisions have you?' … I'm tired of babying the Soviets."

Kennan's "Long Telegram"

In February 1946, many Americans finally came to understand that the Soviet Union was no longer their loyal and dependable ally. The first blow to this image was Stalin's speech in which he blamed the outbreak of World War on "monopoly capitalism," a system that he said must be supplanted by communism to prevent another war. A week later, alarmed Americans were further disheartened to learn that 22 people had been arrested in Canada for trying to steal nuclear weapons information on behalf of the Soviets.

Inside the Truman administration, the outlook for U.S.–Soviet relations was even gloomier. On February 22, the State Department received from Moscow a telegram written by George F. Kennan, the minister-counselor in the U.S. embassy. Kennan warned that the "USSR still lives in antagonistic 'capitalist encirclement' with which in the long run there can be no permanent peaceful coexistence."

Kennan had concluded that "at [the] bottom of [the] Kremlin's neurotic view of world affairs" was a "traditional and instinctive Russian sense of insecurity." Thus, he observed, "they have learned to seek security only in patient but deadly struggle for total destruction of rival power, never in compacts and promises with it."

To Kennan, the Soviet Union was "a political force committed fanatically to the belief that with [the] U.S. there can be no permanent *modus vivendi*, that it is desirable and necessary that the internal harmony of our society be disrupted, our traditional way of life be destroyed, the international authority of our state be broken, if Soviet power is to be secure."

The following year, in an anonymous article published in *Foreign Affairs*, Kennan set forth what would later become known as the *containment* approach to the Soviet Union, a policy that would guide American foreign policy for the next four decades. The United States, he argued, should meet Soviet expansionism "with unalterable counter-force at every point where they show signs of encroaching upon the interests of a peaceful and stable world."

Cold Words

Containment was the Cold War defense policy of the United States and its allies—first articulated by diplomat George F. Kennan in 1946—aimed at preventing the Soviet Union from extending its reach into Western Europe.

Iron Curtain

Two weeks after Kennan's "Long Telegram" reached the State Department, former British Prime Minister Winston Churchill traveled with Truman to Fulton, Missouri, for a speech at Westminster College. There, Churchill gave tenor and tone to the new Cold War about which most Americans were only vaguely aware:

> From Stettin in the Baltic to Trieste in the Adriatic, an iron curtain has descended across the continent. Behind that line lie all the capitals of the ancient states of Central and Eastern Europe. Warsaw, Berlin, Prague, Vienna, Budapest, Belgrade, Bucharest and Sofia; all these famous cities and the populations around them lie in what I must call the Soviet sphere, and all are subject, in one form or another, not only to Soviet influence but to a very high and in some cases increasing measure of control from Moscow.

Quotes from the Cold

I do not believe that Soviet Russia desires war. What they desire is the fruits of war and the indefinite expansion of their power and doctrines. … I am convinced that there is nothing they admire so much as strength, and there is nothing for which they have less respect than for weakness, especially military weakness.

—Winston Churchill at Fulton, Missouri, March 5, 1946

By accompanying Churchill to the speech, and applauding his remarks, Truman had tacitly endorsed Churchill's grim view of the world. With that, the Cold War was officially declared.

President Harry S. Truman with former British Prime Minister Winston Churchill, who declared in March 1946 that "an iron curtain has descended across the [European] continent."

(Courtesy of the Library of Congress)

The Least You Need to Know

- When Franklin Roosevelt died in April 1945, the responsibility for concluding the war in Europe and the Pacific fell to Harry Truman, a man with little foreign affairs experience and little intimate knowledge of Roosevelt's military strategies.
- At the Potsdam Conference, outside Berlin in July and August 1945, President Truman first began to realize that the Soviet Union could not be trusted to keep its vague promises regarding autonomy for the nations of Eastern Europe.
- While the atomic bomb ended the war in the Pacific, American leaders believed, mistakenly, that nuclear weapons would check Soviet aggression in Europe.
- By late 1945 and early 1946, Truman and his advisors knew of the deep and intractable divisions in the U.S.-Soviet relationship.
- With his famous "Iron Curtain" speech in March 1946, Winston Churchill announced to the world the beginnings of the Cold War.

Chapter 8

Cooperating for Peace

In This Chapter

- The UN is born
- Truman resolves to protect Western Europe
- The Marshall Plan
- America saves Berlin

By 1947, the Cold War was on, but it had not yet taken form. No one really knew how the United States and the Soviet Union would coexist in the new world order created by World War II.

Europe was still smoldering from the fires of war. Many of its major cities lay in ruins. Its economy was shattered. Refugees roamed the continent in search of a home. Millions were starving.

Back home, Americans were justifiably proud for having liberated much of Europe from Nazi domination. But what next? Hitler was gone, but misery and suffering persisted.

Unlike the post-World War I years, this time the United States would not retreat into isolation. Most, but not all, members of Congress finally acknowledged how much their country's interests were intertwined with Europe's. U.S. leaders vowed to participate fully in world affairs.

But continued participation in the affairs of Europe also meant conflict with the Soviet Union. In this chapter, we look at the widening rift between the

United States and the Soviet Union and how the world, particularly the United States, grappled with the aftermath of war.

Nations United

In the aftermath of World War I, the United States had forsaken a leading role in securing the postwar peace. World War II persuaded many Americans of the foolishness of their isolation. Before his death, Franklin Roosevelt had resolved that the country would not make that mistake again. And Harry Truman shared Roosevelt's passion for an active U.S. role in maintaining world peace.

Indeed, Truman's first decision as president on April 12, 1945, was to insist—President Roosevelt's death notwithstanding—that the San Francisco Conference on the United Nations would proceed as planned. A U.S. delegation would fully participate in the deliberations.

On April 25, 12 days before Germany would surrender to the Allies, Truman spoke by phone from the White House to the assembled delegates. "You members of the conference are to be the architects of the better world," he said. They were not, he said, charged with settling postwar disputes such as reparations or boundaries. Instead, he told them, they were charged with the vital work of establishing "the essential organization to keep the peace. … We can no longer permit any nation, or group of nations, to attempt to settle their arguments with bombs and bayonets."

Trouble over Poland

Despite the high hopes for international cooperation embodied in Truman's words, difficulties with the Soviets soon emerged. Only two days into the conference, the Russians demanded admission of delegates representing the Soviet-backed Lublin Polish government.

Truman did not want Poland represented at the conference until its government had been organized along the lines of the Yalta accords (that is, in accordance with Stalin's vague promises for free elections). With that in mind, Secretary of State Edward Stettinius rejected the Russian proposal. A vitriolic fight over the issue was averted when delegates compromised and agreed to admit Poland once the conference's organizing powers recognized its new government.

The Russians went along, but grudgingly. Soviet Foreign Minister Molotov bitterly complained that the United States had invited the pro-Nazi government of Argentina to the conference while it protested the seating of Poland's delegates.

Some of those who suspected that the Soviets might be reluctant to trust their postwar security concerns to the United Nations might also have questioned the United States' motives. It appeared to some that Stettinius had invited the Argentine delegation only because he needed their vote to maintain hemispheric unity.

It seemed, in the words of *Time* magazine, "a straight power game" in Latin America "as amoral as Russia's game in Eastern Europe." As Cold War historian John Lewis Gaddis noted, that judgment appeared to be sound. In May, Secretary of War Henry Stimson, in a private conversation, argued forcefully for a U.S. sphere of influence, much like the Soviets enjoyed in their back yard. "I think that it's not asking too much to have our little region over here, if she [Russia] is going to [begin] building up friendly *protectorates* around her."

Quotes from the Cold

I told [the press in San Francisco] we would have real difficulties with the Soviet Union in the postwar period. This came as a great shock to many of them. At one meeting, I explained that our objectives and the Kremlin objectives were irreconcilable; they wanted to communize the world, and we wanted a free world.

—Averell Harriman, U.S. Ambassador to the Soviet Union

Cold Words

A **protectorate** is a nation or state that surrenders part of its sovereignty to another nation. Usually such states give up control over their foreign policy while retaining considerable say over domestic affairs.

Despite the apparent double standard, the Russians were not likely to arouse any American sympathy for their conduct in Poland. And it did their cause no good when news came in early May that Soviet officials had arrested 16 Polish underground leaders who had been promised safe passage to Moscow to discuss joining the Lublin government. The arrests prompted harsh criticism by some in the American press who concluded that the Soviets were worried about only their parochial interests, not the success of the United Nations.

Russian Bashing

Criticism of the Soviets wasn't limited to the press. Some in the American delegation regarded the conference as little more than a forum to attack the Russians. Present in San Francisco was the U.S. ambassador to the Soviet Union, Averell Harriman, who warned the U.S. delegation that the Soviets were willing "to chisel, by bluff, pressure, and other unscrupulous methods to get what they wish." Moscow, he charged, wanted "as much domination over Eastern Europe as possible."

Quotes from the Cold

We the peoples of the United Nations, determined to save succeeding generations from the scourge of war, which twice in our lifetime has brought untold sorrow to mankind, and to reaffirm faith in fundamental human rights, in the dignity and worth of the human person, … have resolved to combine our efforts to accomplish these aims.

—From the Charter of the United Nations, June 26, 1945

Attending as the chief Republican delegate was Senator Arthur Vandenberg of Michigan, who detested the agreements Roosevelt had made at Yalta and wanted to use the San Francisco Conference to stir up international hostility toward the Soviets. "I have great hope," he confided to a friend, "that we can here mobilize the conscience of mankind against the aggressor of tomorrow."

Meanwhile, back in Washington, some prominent officials in Truman's administration had little confidence in the UN's ability to address the world's problems. "A future war with Soviet Russia," lamented one high-ranking State Department official, "is as certain as anything in this world."

Agreement

One of the more important aspects of the new United Nations was its Security Council—ostensibly an attempt by the United States, the United Kingdom, the Soviet Union, and China to continue serving, in Roosevelt's words, as the "Four Policeman." France was added to the council and the UN's founders charged it with the tall order of keeping world peace.

To do this, the UN Charter established a military staff committee represented by the military chiefs of each permanent member Security Council. Its aim was to assume strategic control of the Security Council's military operations. (Despite the high hopes for this part of the UN's operation, the committee would never direct a military operation during the Cold War.)

Over the objections of many smaller nations, veto power for the permanent council members was included in the final charter. In other words, the Security Council could not approve any resolution that was not supported by all of its permanent members—the United States, USSR, Britain, France, and China. In a compromise, however, other delegates demanded a General Assembly and an Economic and Social Council, organizations in which smaller nations would play a larger role.

On June 26, 1945, all 50 nations assembled in San Francisco voted to ratify the United Nations charter. On October 24, after a sufficient number of nations had ratified the charter, the UN was officially born.

Doubts

As the U.S. delegates had departed San Francisco, some—particularly the Republican delegates—took with them serious reservations about the ability of the United States to cooperate with the Soviet Union, with or without a United Nations organization.

More importantly, after the public dispute over Poland and its Russian-controlled government, the opinion of many Americans toward the Soviets had begun to change. By May 1945, public opinion polls had revealed rising doubts about Russia's willingness to cooperate with the United States. For the first time, a majority of Americans blamed the Russians more than the British for deteriorating relations among the Big Three.

The Truman Doctrine

In early 1947, the United States faced its first postwar "showdown" with the Soviet Union. In February, British officials informed the Truman administration that it would no longer provide military support for the pro-Western governments of Greece and Turkey. In the words of historian H.W. Brands, "before dropping this self-assumed burden, they offered Washington first refusal."

From Athens, U.S. diplomats sent word that the British withdrawal would almost certainly mean the collapse of the Greek government. One of Truman's advisors warned that the outcome of a Greek-Turkish collapse might be that "the whole Near East and part of North Africa" were "certain to pass under Soviet influence."

Truman reacted swiftly. Without consulting its leaders, he sent to Congress an urgent request for $400 million in aid to prop up the governments of Greece and Turkey. Republicans were initially cool to the idea, but Truman had one important ally: Senator Vandenberg, the Republican chairman of the Senate Foreign Relations Committee. Once a fierce isolationist, Vandenberg had become an internationalist during the war. He was now more than willing to support Truman, so long as the president sold the idea to the American people.

The only way to persuade the Republican-controlled Congress to shed its instinctive isolationism, Vandenberg advised, was to "make a personal appearance before Congress and scare the hell out of the American people." On March 12, 1947, Truman went before joint session of Congress and did just that. In a strongly worded speech, he gave the world a new Hitler. His name was Stalin. Without naming him, Truman made it clear it was the Soviet leader who threatened the two nations.

Quotes from the Cold

The overriding task that seemed to confront American policy in Europe was to provide an incentive for the Europeans to look at the situation [in Greece] in the broadest possible terms rather than in narrowly nationalistic, or even partisan, focus.

—Harry Truman, *Years of Trial and Hope,* Vol. II (Doubleday, 1956)

Quotes from the Cold

The seeds of totalitarian regimes are nurtured by misery and want. They spread and grow in the evil soil of poverty and strife. They reach their full growth when the hope of a people for a better life has died. We must keep that hope alive.

—President Harry Truman, speech to Congress, March 12, 1947

In joining the United Nations, Truman said, the United States had acted to insure freedom for all nations. "We shall not realize our objectives, however, unless we are willing to help free peoples to maintain their free institutions and their national integrity against aggressive movements that seek to impose upon them totalitarian regimes."

He painted a picture of a world teetering toward communist domination. In articulating a set of principles—later known as the "Truman Doctrine"—the president then declared: "I believe that it must be the policy of the United States to support free peoples who are resisting attempted subjugation by armed minorities or by outside pressures."

In May, both houses of Congress overwhelmingly approved Truman's plan and, thus, set the nation on a determined and idealistic crusade against communism—one that would eventually stretch from Europe to Africa to Latin America to Southeast Asia.

In March 1947, President Harry Truman articulated his Truman Doctrine, vowing U.S. support for "free peoples who are resisting attempted subjugation."

(Courtesy of the Library of Congress)

It is not entirely clear that the communist threats to Greece and Turkey were as dire as Truman portrayed them. But, as H.W. Brands notes, "these questions faded into irrelevance once Greece became a proving ground for American resolve."

Nonetheless, the Truman Doctrine was a turning point in U.S. foreign policy, not simply because Truman had identified the Soviet empire as a totalitarian threat to the rest of the world, but because the United States had, for the first time, intervened on behalf of nations threatened by communism.

Marshall Has a Plan

One reason Greece and Turkey were on the ropes was that Europe was an economic and political basket case. War had left the continent destitute. People were starving. Governments were on the verge of collapse.

Back in the United States, however, the economy was booming. War had lifted the United States out of the Great Depression. Unemployment had been virtually abolished as the effort to defeat Germany and Japan required the labor of every able-bodied American—most directly in the military or in production of military supplies and munitions.

The Lend-Lease program had not only helped win the war, it had conquered the Depression—so much so that American leaders now worried about what would happen when those shipments of American goods stopped crossing the seas. Would the Depression return? Would the returning soldiers find work? With Europe flat on its back, who would buy American goods?

Another Depression?

Those questions dogged a coordinating committee of the U.S. State, War, and Navy departments in early 1947. After a study, the committee concluded that "under present programs and policies, the world will not be able to continue to buy United States exports at the 1946–47 rate beyond another 12 to 18 months." The result, the committee suggested, might be another depression.

To further assess the problem, Truman sent Will Clayton, the undersecretary of state for economic affairs, to Europe in May 1947. His report shocked American officials. The condition of the European economy was even worse than they had imagined.

Quotes from the Cold

Europe is steadily deteriorating. ... Without further prompt and substantial aid from the United States, economic, social, and political disintegration will overwhelm Europe.

—Under Secretary of State for Economic Affairs Will Clayton, May 27, 1947

Clayton predicted that, short of massive American assistance, the continent might completely fall apart. "Aside from the awful implications which this would have for the future peace and security of the world," Clayton wrote, "the immediate effects on our domestic economy would be disastrous: markets for our surplus production, gone, unemployment, depression, a heavily unbalanced budget on the background of a mountainous war debt. *These things must not happen.*"

Americans had other concerns about Europe. Communism was not universally unpopular in Western Europe. In fact, some communist parties had begun to attract considerable popular support because of their fierce wartime resistance to the Nazis. After the war, communists won elections in Italy, France, and Belgium—a situation that further alarmed U.S. officials.

Therefore, what Will Clayton proposed in May 1947 seemed to provide the perfect answer to the two questions that most troubled the Truman administration: How to save the U.S. economy, and how to slow or stop communism in Western Europe. Clayton's plan was fairly simple: A massive program of economic assistance to the governments of Western Europe. It would be a grant program toward the purchase of U.S. products. In effect, the U.S. government would buy the goods and services of American businessmen and farmers for shipment to Europe.

Marshall's Embrace

When Clayton's proposal reached the desk of Secretary of State George C. Marshall, the former army general embraced it immediately. So did Truman. One week later, on June 5, 1947, Marshall unveiled the plan in a commencement speech at Harvard University.

After laying out the dire nature of the problem—"a very serious situation is rapidly developing which bodes no good for the world"—Marshall proposed "substantial additional help" for the nations of Europe. He did not suggest an amount, although Clayton had proposed $20 billion over three years. And he did not propose how the aid program would be administered. That he would leave to the Europeans. But, he added, "the program should be a joint one, agreed to by a number, if not all, European nations."

Cold Facts

Because of his vision in promoting the European Recovery Program, more commonly called "The Marshall Plan," George C. Marshall was awarded the Nobel Peace Prize in 1953.

Marshall's speech was a high-minded call for Americans to give one more measure of badly needed assistance to their European allies. "It is logical that the United States should do whatever it is able to do to assist in the return of normal economic health in the world, without which there can be no political stability and no assured peace," he told the Harvard graduates. "Our policy is directed not against any country or doctrine but against hunger, poverty, desperation, and chaos."

In 1947, Secretary of State George C. Marshall, retired army chief of staff and general of the Army, championed the Marshall Plan for the economic recovery of Europe.

(Courtesy of the Library of Congress)

Europe's Embrace

As Marshall made clear, the United States would extend assistance to any European nation—even Germany and the Soviet Union—that agreed to participate in the program. Western European leaders responded warmly to Marshall's proposal and promptly convened a conference to discuss how to administer the program.

Predictably, Stalin declined Marshall's offer, rejecting entanglement with the proposed Western European alliance, fearing that the plan's vision for greater economic freedom might undermine his authority over Eastern Europe. Stalin then coerced the governments of Eastern Europe to reject the plan. And a Soviet spokesman later denounced the proposal as a "plan of world expansionist policy carried on by the United States."

Quotes from the Cold

We welcome the inspiring lead given to us and the peoples of Europe by Mr. Marshall. His speech at Harvard will rank, I think, as one of the greatest speeches made in world history.

—British Foreign Secretary Ernest Bevin, June 13, 1947.

Congress Approves

The public did not immediately embrace the Marshall Plan. In fact, because of scant press coverage, most citizens had never even heard of it. A national poll in July 1947 made that fact clear and prompted the Truman administration to embark on a massive campaign to educate the public. Marshall and other administration officials fanned out across the country to sell the plan, and administration officials recruited private groups to pressure Congress for its passage.

Cold Facts

The $13 billion the United States spent on the Marshall Plan would be equal to approximately $100 billion in today's dollars.

Quotes from the Cold

Few presidents have had the opportunity to sign legislation of such importance. … This measure is America's answer to the challenge facing the free world today.

—President Harry Truman, April 3, 1948, upon signing the Marshall Plan legislation.

Truman formally presented the plan to Congress in December 1947, asking members to spend $4 billion in the first year. Still suffering from vestiges of isolationism, Republicans initially were wary of the proposal, complaining of its high cost and arguing that it could spark inflation.

Those doubts dissolved in February 1948, however, when the Czech government fell in a Soviet-backed communist coup. Members of Congress, fearing the beginning of a communist wildfire in Europe, approved the bill within weeks.

Truman signed legislation creating the European Recovery Program in April 1948. Over the next three years, it would provide more than $13 billion in American assistance to 16 European countries.

Stalin's bitter rejection of the Marshall Plan had played no small part in the bill's success. His hostility made it easier for Truman to sell the plan to Congress—first, because it appeared to be an answer to Stalin's communist designs on Europe and, second, because no one wanted to provide economic assistance to a communist-controlled government.

Yet, Stalin's adamant refusal to participate also heightened tensions in the burgeoning Cold War. The two countries were drifting further and further apart, viewing each other not so much with suspicion, but dread and outright animosity.

Legacy

By helping push Western and Eastern Europe more deeply into opposing camps, the Marshall Plan paved the way for the North Atlantic Treaty Organization (NATO) and the Atlantic alliance. By the end of 1951, the plan's emphasis would shift from economic assistance to military aid. The Economic Cooperation Administration—the government agency that directed the Marshall Plan—would become the Mutual Security Administration.

While the plan did not single-handedly rescue Europe's economy, it did help immensely. During the period 1948 and 1951, the United States spent about 10 percent of its entire federal budget on the European Recovery Program. During that period, the economies of Western Europe began to recover; some expanded by as much as 25 percent. The plan contributed greatly to the renewal of Europe's chemical, engineering, and steel industries. Europe's near-certain slide to abject poverty—as well as an American depression—had been averted.

Cold Facts

Congress required that all items shipped to Europe under the Marshall Plan be clearly labeled, "For European Recovery—Supplied by the United States of America." Later, when the program shifted its emphasis to military assistance, the label was changed to read: "Strength for the Free World—From the United States of America."

The Berlin Airlift

More so than Poland, the struggle over Germany was now the open wound of East-West relations in the late 1940s. The Big Three had never been able to agree on the status of the war-ravaged nation after the Nazi war machine collapsed in 1945. The United States and Britain, recognizing Germany's importance to Western Europe's economic recovery, argued for quick reunification. Stalin, however, had other notions. In a span of 25 years, Germany had twice invaded his country. The most recent war had claimed the lives of 20 million Russians. He was understandably fearful that reunified Germany would again threaten Russia.

Since the war's end, the Allies continued to occupy four zones in Germany. The United States, along with Britain and France, supervised the western and southern regions; the Soviets had the east to themselves. Berlin, although deep in the Russian zone, was also a divided city, sliced into four occupation sectors.

A peaceful agreement on Germany's future seemed impossible, given the Allies' widely divergent views. Not only did Russia want Germany to remain weak and divided, Stalin was still insisting on war reparations, particularly from the more industrialized western zones. But U.S. and British leaders were adamantly opposed to Stalin's

Quotes from the Cold

The Russians were obviously determined to force us out of Berlin. They had suffered setbacks recently in Italy, in France, and in Finland …. The European Recovery Program was beginning to succeed. The blockade of Berlin was international Communism's counterattack.

—Harry Truman, *Years of Trial and Hope*, Vol. II.

demands, fearing a repeat of the political upheaval over German reparations following World War I.

It was the Marshall Plan, instituted in the spring of 1948, that once again moved the German question to center stage. When the United States offered the nations of Europe economic assistance, West German officials eagerly participated. But East Germany, coerced by Stalin, declined. That decision put West Germany, with U.S. assistance, on the road to economic recovery.

By mid-1948, the United States, Britain, and France moved toward unification of their occupation zones, a move that would transform the western zones into a single political entity. Next, the Allies instituted currency reforms that began yielding remarkable economic results. The potential reunification of West Germany bothered Stalin immensely, but it was the currency reforms—and the economic transformation they promised—that spurred him to action.

Blockade

On June 24, 1948, in an attempt to drive the Allies from Berlin, the Soviets shut off all rail, highway, and water traffic in and out of the former German capitol. Except by air, there was no way for the 2.5 million residents of the city to leave. The trucks, trains, and barges that normally delivered food and fuel supplies suddenly halted. The city's food supplies would last no more than a month. Within six weeks, West Berlin would be out of coal.

Faced with another potential confrontation with the Soviets, Truman remained calm. He resisted the belligerent advice of some advisors who suggested that the Allies storm their way into Berlin by armored convoy. Instead, Truman ordered a massive airlift to supply the city.

Quotes from the Cold

I have a terrible feeling … that we are very close to war.
—Harry Truman, writing in his diary, September 13, 1948.

As a very public warning to the Soviets, the president boldly dispatched two squadrons of B-29s to Germany. While these were the same planes that had dropped the atomic bombs on Japan, Stalin did not know that these particular aircraft were not so equipped. But the implied threat that they represented could never have been far from his mind.

Airlift

Truman was determined that U.S. troops would remain in Berlin, despite the fact that Allied forces were vastly outnumbered by the Soviets—6,500 Allied troops versus 18,000

Soviet troops, and other 300,000 in the eastern German zone. "We'll stay in Berlin—come what may," Truman vowed. He knew the airlift might lead to war, but it was a chance he was willing to take to demonstrate his country's resolve.

For almost a year, the Allies kept Berlin supplied with round-the-clock flights. Hundreds of planes landed each day. Sometimes a cargo plane flew into the city every four minutes. The Berlin airlift proved a remarkable success. In all 1.7 million tons of supplies were delivered by air into the city from late June 1948 until May 12, 1949, when the embarrassed Russians finally lifted their blockade.

The Marshall Plan and the Berlin crisis had finally forced a resolution of the German question. In August 1949, the Federal Republic of Germany (West Germany) held elections for the government of the now-unified western zones. Several months later, in October, the one-party, Soviet-dominated German Democratic Republic was born. Germany, like the rest of Europe, was now divided into opposing camps.

The Berlin crisis was nothing other than a defeat for Stalin. He had wanted the Allies out of Berlin. Instead, he got a unified and vital West Germany that was strongly supported—economically and militarily—by the United States and Britain. "Berlin," wrote General Lucius Clay, the American military governor of occupied Germany, "had become a symbol throughout Europe of western determination to resist Communist expansion."

The Least You Need to Know

- The United States was a leading sponsor of the international conference that created the United Nations in 1945.
- In ennunciating the Truman Doctrine in 1947, Harry Truman declared that "it must be the policy of the United States to support free peoples who are resisting attempted subjugation by armed minorities or by outside pressures."
- Under the Marshall Plan for the recovery of Europe, the United States spent more than $13 billion to help restore the decimated economies of 16 countries.
- The Berlin Airlift in 1948–49 was the first postwar confrontation between the United States and the Soviet Union—a crisis that ended when Stalin terminated his blockade of the former German capitol.

Chapter 9

It's a Bad, Bad World

In This Chapter

- The NATO alliance is born
- The "fall" of China to communism
- Truman takes a beating over China
- A sobering assessment of the Soviet threat

Americans were now fully aware that the Soviet Union was no longer their nation's ally. Europe was split into two camps, east and west. But were Americans and their leaders fully aware of the threat the Soviet Union posed to Western Europe? Some of Harry Truman's national security advisors believed they were not. And while it was increasingly apparent that the United States and its European allies regarded the USSR as a threat to the peace and security of Western Europe, there was no concerted, agreed-upon plan to stop further Soviet aggression.

Meanwhile, trouble was brewing in Asia, where the Chinese Communists, led by Mao Zedong, were steadily gaining ground against the Nationalist government of U.S. ally Chiang Kai-shek. To Harry Truman's more partisan political opponents in Congress, it appeared that the President, while vigilant against the communist threat in Europe, wasn't paying enough attention to the problem in Asia.

This chapter discusses the creation of the North Atlantic Treaty Organization as well as the new communist threat in China.

NATO Versus the Soviets

To Harry Truman and his advisors, Soviet-style communism appeared to be on the march in Europe. Besides the Berlin blockade and Stalin's hostility toward the Marshall Plan, there was ample reason for concern.

Russian Push?

In early 1948, the Communist Party in Hungary forced the resignation of Premier Ferenc Nagy and seized control of the country's government. By early 1949, the government was not only communist controlled, but also completely subservient to the Soviets. Moreover, it was, as Truman noted in his memoirs, "the first seizure of a government by Communists which was openly supported by Russia since the fighting had stopped in Europe."

Next, it was Czechoslovakia's turn. The country fell into the Soviet orbit in February 1948, after a campaign of political agitation by the communists. And in Poland, the Sovietization of that government was completed by 1949 when Soviet Marshall Konstantin Rokossovsky became minister of defense and commander in chief of the Polish army.

"To the people in Europe, who were just beginning to take courage from the Marshall Plan," Truman later wrote, "these Communist moves looked like the beginning of a Russian 'big push.'"

Further evidence of Soviet mischief was the internal communist threats in Greece and Turkey (suspected by many to be supported by the USSR), as well as the activities of Cominform (the Communist Information Bureau), organized in 1947 to facilitate exchanges of information among the communist parties of Europe.

The Brussels Treaty

Western Europe's first unified response to these developments was the Brussels Treaty, signed in 1948 by several Western European countries. The treaty—agreed to by the United Kingdom, Belgium, France, Luxembourg, and the Netherlands—obligated its member nations to assist each other militarily in the event an "armed attack."

On March 17, 1948, the day the Brussels Treaty was signed, Truman spoke of the communist menace in a St. Patrick's Day speech in New York. "Since the close of the hostilities [of World War II], the Soviet Union and its agents have destroyed the independence and democratic nature of a whole series of nations in Eastern and Central Europe." In another speech that day, Truman said: "Free men in every land are asking: 'Where is this leading? When will it end?'"

Quotes from the Cold

If any of the [nations who are parties to the Brussels Treaty] should be the object of an armed attack in Europe, the other [nations] will, in accordance with the provisions of Article 51 of the Charter of the United Nations, afford the Party so attacked all the military and other aid and assistance in their power.

—Article 4 of the Treaty of Economic, Social, and Cultural Collaboration and Collective Self-Defense (The Brussels Treaty), March 17, 1948.

North Atlantic Treaty

Truman did not answer those questions directly, but he did take bold moves to associate the United States with the new European alliance. In July 1948, the U.S. State Department entered into secret negotiations with the Brussels Treaty powers in hopes of forming a "North Atlantic Pact" that would include the United States and its allies in Europe.

As Truman later argued, the Marshall Plan had delivered economic relief to Europe, but "the constant threat of unpredictable Soviet moves resulted in an atmosphere of insecurity and fear" in Western Europe. "Only an inclusive security system could dispel those fears."

On April 4, 1949, representatives of 12 signatory nations signed the North Atlantic Treaty in Washington, D.C. "In this pact," Truman told the foreign ministers, "we hope to create a shield against aggression and the fear of aggression—a bulwark which will permit us to get on with the real business of government and society, the business of achieving a fuller and happier life for all our citizens."

Quotes from the Cold

The Parties agree that an armed attack against one or more of them in Europe or North America shall be considered an attack against them all and consequently they agree that, if such an armed attack occurs, each of them … will assist the Party or Parties so attacked by taking … such action as it deems necessary, including the use of armed force, to restore and maintain the security of the North Atlantic area.

—Article Five of the North Atlantic Treaty

Truman submitted the treaty to the Senate on April 12, and while it was warmly received by most, support for America's new, formal defense alliance with Europe was not unanimous. Republican Senator Robert Taft of Ohio, a leading isolationist, argued that the treaty violated the spirit of the United Nations charter.

Cold Facts

The 12 original signatories of the North Atlantic Treaty were Great Britain, France, Italy, the Netherlands, Belgium, Luxembourg, Norway, Denmark, Portugal, Iceland, Canada, and the United States. Greece and Turkey joined in 1952, and the Federal Republic of Germany (West Germany) in 1955.

Cold Facts

The first supreme military commander of NATO was General Dwight D. Eisenhower, appointed by Truman in December 1950.

"The Atlantic Pact moves in exactly the opposite direction from the purposes of the [UN] Charter and makes a farce of further efforts to secure peace through law and justice," Taft told the Senate. "It necessarily divides the world into two armed camps."

Of course, as far as Truman and his supporters were concerned, the world—or Europe, at least—was already divided into opposing camps. The North Atlantic Treaty simply stated how the Allies would react to further Soviet aggression. On July 21, 1949, the Senate ratified the treaty, 82 to 13. By August 24, enough nations had ratified the treaty to bring the North Atlantic Treaty Organization (NATO) into being.

The treaty was significant not simply because it formalized America's role as a permanent participant in the peace and security of Western Europe, but because it marked the official end to the nation's historic isolationism. It was the first peacetime military alliance between the United States and another country since the Franco-American Alliance of 1778.

By itself, the treaty's words meant little. To give it the backbone it needed, Truman argued that the United States had to help the nations of Europe not just economically, but militarily. In October 1949, Congress authorized $1.3 billion for the Mutual Defense Assistance Act, legislation extending various types of economic assistance to its allies in Europe.

The Trouble with China

In September 1949, Truman stunned the American public with some disturbing news. He announced that the Soviet Union had recently detonated an atomic bomb. Since the end of World War II, America's sole possession of the bomb had been regarded as the most effective deterrent to another world war and had firmly secured the nation's status as the world's most powerful military force.

It was a distinction that had comforted an American public still weary from the turmoil and sacrifice of nearly four years of world war. Truman's staggering announcement, however, changed the essence of the Cold War and reordered America's worldview. It was no longer a war of words waged primarily with strong rhetoric and competing economic assistance. A new militaristic Cold War had dawned.

Some Americans believed that a military showdown between the United States and the Soviets was now inevitable. Those fears appeared more justified than ever in January 1950 when Truman announced that the nation would respond to the Soviet bomb test by developing a hydrogen bomb—a device vastly more destructive than any existing atomic weapon.

Victory for Mao

Still reeling from the news about the Soviets' atomic test, Americans were far more aroused in October 1949 when Mao Zedong's Communist forces in China finally drove General Chiang Kai-shek's Nationalist army from the mainland and onto the island of Taiwan, known then as Formosa.

For years, China had held a special place in the hearts of many church-going Americans who regarded the nation as the world's most fertile field for Christian evangelism and Chiang as a devout Christian. American churches and Christian organizations had supported missionaries in China for generations and had developed a deep and lasting affection for the country and its people.

Thus, many Americans were shocked and heartbroken by the Communist victory and largely unaware that Chiang actually ruled a corrupt and undemocratic regime destined to fall of its own weight—although its collapse was greatly hastened by an effective, intense, and ideologically driven communist opposition.

Truman and his State Department knew the truth and understood that the president could have turned the tide in China's civil war only by massive military intervention. That would have meant making the country a U.S. protectorate—something that even Chiang's most ardent supporters opposed.

Chiang

In truth, U.S. efforts to save China had been far from paltry. Since the end of World War II the United States had given $3 billion in economic and military assistance to the Nationalist government with little to show for it. The Communists routed Chiang's poorly trained and unmotivated troops over and over.

Quotes from the Cold

[Nationalists in China failed because] the almost inexhaustible patience of the Chinese people in their misery [had] ended. They did not bother to overthrow this government. There was really nothing to overthrow. They simply ignored it throughout the country.

—Secretary of State Dean Acheson, 1950

Additional U.S. aid to China would have been wasted. "There is no evidence," Acheson accurately told Senate Foreign Relations Committee Chairman Tom Connally in March 1949, "that the furnishing of additional military materiel would alter the pattern of current developments in China."

Chinese Nationalist leader Chiang Kai-shek enjoyed the support of the United States, but could not keep his country from falling to his communist opponents in October 1949.

(Courtesy of the Library of Congress)

The China Lobby Challenge

That Chiang was a corrupt leader in charge of an inept army was obvious to anyone with a passing knowledge of China. Truman's political enemies, however, saw China's woes in a far different light. Foremost among those critics was *Time* publisher Henry Luce, born in China to missionary parents, who argued that the Communist victory was a result of American irresolution, not Chiang's perfidy. "At no time in the long chronicle of its failure [in China] had [Truman's administration] displayed a modest fraction of the stamina and decisiveness which had checked Communism in Europe," *Time* said in a vitriolic broadside against the Truman administration in August 1949.

Republicans Attack

Congressional Republicans exploited the developments in China with a relentless assault on the Truman-Acheson foreign policy. Leading Republicans echoed Luce's charge that while Truman and Acheson were preventing Communist expansion into Western Europe, they had, in the words of New Jersey Republican H. Alexander Smith, "left the back door wide open in Asia."

In the Senate, California Republican William Knowland, whose intense devotion to Chiang earned him the mocking title "Senator from Formosa," led a vigorous Republican attack on Truman and Acheson. Truman's policies, he charged, had "accelerated the spread of communism in Asia" so much that "gains for communism there have far more than offset the losses suffered by communism in Europe."

Chiang's corruption and inept leadership notwithstanding, Knowland charged that the "debacle solely and exclusively rests upon the administration which initiated and tolerated it." Truman and Acheson, he suggested, were guilty of "appeasement," as well as "aiding, abetting and giving support to the spread of communism in Asia."

The charismatic communist leader Mao Zedong defeated the Nationalist government in China in 1949, setting in motion a vigorous, partisan political debate in Washington over "who lost China."

(Courtesy of the National Archives)

The China Hands

Further compounding the political damage were allegations—partly true—that some U.S. Foreign Service officers had systematically disparaged and undermined Chiang while expressing their admiration and support for the Communists—thereby abetting the Nationalists' defeat. However, the truth was that U.S. disillusionment with Chiang was nothing new, nor was it limited to a small group of Foreign Service officers.

U.S. disillusionment dated back to early 1942 when General Joseph Stilwell arrived to oversee military operations in the China-Burma-India Theater. Given the task of repelling Japanese aggression in China and Southeast Asia, Stilwell quickly concluded that Chiang was far more interested in preserving his crumbling regime—that is, fighting the Chinese communists—than in stopping Imperialist Japanese aggression.

Quotes from the Cold

[Harry Truman's State Department is] guided by a left-wing group who obviously have wanted to get rid of Chiang [Kai-shek], and were willing at least to turn China over to the Communists for that purpose.

—Senate Republican leader Robert Taft, in 1950, arguing that the United States could have prevented the communist victory in China

Unable to persuade Chiang to provide the troops needed to oppose Japan, a frustrated Stilwell finally suggested that communist forces should be enlisted for the fight. Supporting Stilwell were a handful of respected State Department China experts—men such as John Patton Davies, John Stewart Service, and John Carter Vincent—who shared an intensive disdain for Chiang and urged U.S. pressure to force him to reform.

Taft, Knowland, and other conservatives thought it even more appalling that the "China hands"—as they became known—had expressed respect for Mao's Communist disciples, particularly their austere manner and espousal of self-government. In October 1944, at Chiang's insistence, Roosevelt finally recalled Stilwell. In late 1945—more than a year after President Franklin Roosevelt dispatched Major General Patrick Hurley to China to persuade Chiang to unify the Nationalist and Communist forces against Japan—this newest general resigned and blamed his failure on the China hands.

Quotes from the Cold

[T]he professional Foreign Service men sided with the Chinese Communist armed party and the imperialist bloc of nations whose policy was to keep China divided against herself .... [The China hands] continuously advised the Communists that my efforts in preventing the collapse of the National Government did not represent the policy of the United States."

—Major General Patrick Hurley, U.S. envoy to China, in a 1945 letter to President Truman

Who Lost China?

The fall of China was a call to arms for the conservative Republicans. Frustrated by their inability to regain the White House after 17 years in political exile, they sensed the makings of a potent campaign issue. Chiang's Nationalist Government, they alleged, did not fall because of economic and political forces beyond the control of U.S. policy makers; liberal Democratic foreign policy experts, sympathetic to communism, had "lost" China and thereby jeopardized U.S. national security.

In light of world developments, the allegation seemed plausible. Less than five years after the end of World War II, Russia had, indeed, made substantial gains throughout the world. A "Red Tide," it seemed, was consuming the nations of the world. And Truman's refusal to dispatch a military mission to bolster Chiang's exiled regime served only as further proof to the Republicans that Democrats could no longer be trusted to stop the march of communism across the world stage.

Quotes from the Cold

Communist governments—many of them led by men trained in Moscow—are in command of nations ruling almost 800 million people. [The result] is that the West finds it has lost more than 1 billion people from its sphere in less than 60 months.

—*U.S. News & World Report,* 1950

Quotes from the Cold

This the year, when the feverish fear of Communism is fanned higher by elections; when the men who legislate our futures think less of a hundred million votes in Asia than of a thousand votes in the Fourth Ward; when any gesture of conciliation to end the cold war is smeared as a surrender by an opposition whose dearest ambition is to pin the Communist label on our chief of state.

—*The New Republic,* January 16, 1950

But the demagoguery was not confined to the Republican Party. Some conservative Democrats, aware of their constituents' alarm over the communist victories, also fanned the flames. Speaking to a veterans group in January 1950, U.S. Representative John F. Kennedy of Massachusetts said Truman should send troops to Formosa and blamed him for Chiang's failure in China. "What our young men had saved, our diplomats and our president frittered away." The nation, he said, must now prepare to "vigorously … hold the line in the rest of Asia."

Alger Hiss

If the "loss" of China was a call to arms for Republicans, the conviction in January 1950 of Alger Hiss, a former State Department official charged with perjury for lying about his Communist Party activities, gave them even more ammunition against Truman. Although not among the country's top diplomats, Hiss was well regarded by his colleagues and was among the advisors President Roosevelt had consulted at the Yalta conference in early 1945. It was at Yalta, conservatives alleged, that Roosevelt had sentenced millions of eastern Europeans to communist slavery by acceding control over their nations to the Soviet Union.

Hiss's perjury conviction (the three-year statute of limitations on his alleged espionage activities had expired) vindicated Republican Congressman Richard Nixon and other members of the House Committee on Un-American Activities (HUAC) who exposed Hiss's alleged communism during the committee's wide-ranging investigation.

The Hiss conviction gave Truman's foes yet another opportunity to buttress their argument that a decade of treachery and treason by liberal Democrats had reaped a whirlwind of communist gains throughout the world. Hiss, they alleged, was the thread that connected the "fall" of China to the "giving away" of Eastern Europe.

Cold Facts

In the wake of the communist victory in China, South Dakota Republican Karl Mundt, a former House Un-American Affairs Committee member, wondered aloud about "what influence Alger Hiss might have had in writing a pro-Soviet foreign policy toward China." He suggested that Hiss had engineered "that most calamitous of all decisions at Yalta by which we agreed to give to the Russians control of the Communists in China." To Mundt and other conservatives, the Hiss case suggested a State Department crawling with Communists.

To be sure, Acheson's subsequent public defense of Hiss—the brother of a close family friend—only made matters worse for Truman and increased the Republicans' antipathy toward the secretary of state. It did not help that only six days after Hiss's conviction, authorities in England arrested German-born Klaus Fuchs—a noted physicist who had worked on the Manhattan Project—for passing atomic secrets to the Soviets. Arrested in connection with Fuchs were two New Yorkers, Ethel and Julius Rosenberg, who were later executed for treason.

"How much more are we going to have to take?" Republican Homer Capehart of Indiana asked the Senate on February 9. "Fuchs and Acheson and Hiss and hydrogen bombs threatening outside and New Dealism eating away at the vitals of the nation! In the name of Heaven, is this the best America can do?"

NSC Memorandum 68

In some respects, the dispute over China was not the worst of Truman's troubles in the spring of 1950. In April, at Sectary of State Acheson's direction, National Security Council staff members had produced a sobering assessment of the nation's military strength. The paper, known as NSC Memorandum 68 (NSC-68), concluded that the Soviets posed a very real threat to world peace and would become only more menacing by 1955 when they could amass a nuclear arsenal of up to 200 bombs.

"We must realize that we are now in a mortal conflict," a Defense Department official somberly informed Truman. "Just because there is not much shooting as yet does not mean that we are in a cold war. It is not a cold war; it is a hot war. The only difference between this and previous wars is that death comes more slowly and in a different fashion."

Quotes from the Cold

The Soviet Union is developing the military capacity to support its design for world domination. The Soviet Union actually possesses armed forces far in excess of those necessary to defend its national territory. These armed forces are probably not yet considered by the Soviet Union to be sufficient to initiate a war which would involve the United States. This excessive strength, coupled now with an atomic capability, provides the Soviet Union with great coercive power for use in time of peace in furtherance of its objectives and serves as a deterrent to the victims of its aggression from taking any action in opposition to its tactics which would risk war.

—NSC-68, April 1950

Truman's aides believed that to keep pace with Soviet military expansion the United States would have to spend as much as $50 billion a year for nuclear and conventional weapons—an amount at least three times the current military budget. However, as alarming and significant as it was, NSC-68 was deeply flawed. It exaggerated the Soviets' current and potential military might and assumed the worst about their plans for world conquest.

In 1950, however, the peril of Soviet expansionism was hardly a matter for debate. The only question was how would Truman react to the explosive report. Reluctant to call for a dramatic military buildup, he hesitated. As one biographer noted, "He would make no drastic moves until he knew more."

Without a looming international crisis to influence public opinion and spur Congress to action, Truman seemed to understand the sheer folly of proposing such a drastic increase in military spending. But the communist invasion of South Korea in June 1950, as Dean Acheson later remarked, would change everything.

The Least You Need to Know

- In response to increased Soviet-inspired communist activity throughout Europe, the United States and eleven other nations formed the North Atlantic Treaty Organization in 1949, a mutual defense alliance that has lasted to the present.
- In 1949, communism emerged triumphant in Asia, when Chinese communists led by Mao Zedong finally defeated the Nationalist government of Chiang Kai-shek.

- Republicans in Congress angrily blamed the Democratic administration of President Harry Truman for the "loss" of China.
- In April 1950, National Security Council Memorandum 68 (NSC-68) helped harden U.S. attitudes toward the Soviets by concluding that the USSR posed a serious threat to world peace, and it called for drastic increases in defense expenditures.

Chapter 10

The Global Policeman

In This Chapter

- Korea: the Cold War's first battleground
- Republicans challenge Truman's Korean policies
- Douglas MacArthur and American reversals in Korea
- Truman fires MacArthur
- The domestic political fallout over Korea

The heated and politically charged debates over the Korean War, and who was responsible for it, would have long-lasting implications for the way American leaders fought the Cold War. For more than 20 years afterwards, American presidents and other political leaders would be guided by the political and diplomatic fallout over Harry Truman's military decisions in the summer and fall of 1950.

The next president, Dwight D. Eisenhower, would view Truman's troubles over Korea as evidence that Americans had no stomach for fighting another war in Asia. President Lyndon Johnson, however, would learn different lessons from Korea. Truman's distasteful experiences would be part of the reason Johnson would eventually conceal the extent of the Vietnam War from Congress and the American people. The Korean experience, however, would also persuade Johnson that he needed formal congressional assent for his military actions—something he would obtain by deception with the 1964 Gulf of Tonkin Resolution.

In this chapter, we examine the Korean War—the first proxy war of the Cold War era.

The Korean Complaint

In the early morning hours of June 25, 1950, Communist North Korea staged a surprise invasion of the Republic of Korea. Encountering little resistance from the poorly trained, ill-equipped South Korean military, Soviet-backed communist forces surged south across the thirty-eighth parallel—the arbitrary border created by the United States and the Soviet Union at the end of World War II—and headed for Seoul. Within days, the capitol fell and a devastated South Korean army fled in full retreat. In the United States, Truman administration officials viewed the situation with alarm and concluded the invasion was a Soviet-backed operation designed to test Truman's mettle.

A New Cold War

The communist attack suddenly turned Korea into the first major battleground of a newer, more dangerous Cold War. Only 11 months earlier, when Truman had ordered U.S. troops removed from Korea, the Joint Chiefs of Staff and the State Department had not viewed the region as an area of strategic importance.

By the time of the invasion, however, the political turmoil of the previous year had raised the stakes in Asia considerably. Truman and Secretary of State Acheson knew that the entire world would be watching their response. Failing to respond decisively to communist aggression in Asia would undoubtedly expose Truman to charges from Republicans that he had allowed two Asian nations (China had gone communist in 1949) to fall into communist hands within the span of only nine months. Had Truman wavered or refused to assist South Korea in the critical days following the invasion, it would have irreparably damaged his presidency and may have spelled an end to Democratic control of the Congress.

Quotes from the Cold

By God, I'm going to let them have it.

—Harry Truman in June 1950, upon learning of the North Korean invasion of South Korea

Police Action

Truman quickly directed General Douglas MacArthur, commander of the U.S. occupation forces in Japan, to supply South Korea with weapons and ammunition. He sent the U.S. Seventh Fleet to Taiwan with orders to protect Chiang Kai-shek's forces from a possible Chinese attack.

On June 30, after an urgent request from MacArthur, Truman made one of the most fateful decisions of his second term. After intense discussions with his advisors—and over strenuous opposition from the Joint Chiefs of Staff—the president committed ground, air, and naval forces to the United Nations' effort to defend South Korea. By the end of July, more than 47,000 U.S. troops were committed to the war in Korea. At a press conference announcing the decision, Truman agreed with a reporter who asked if the effort was a "police action."

The war in Korea. U.S. Marine ground units engage Chinese troops in the mountains of North Korea as a U.S. plane drops napalm on an enemy concentration.

(Courtesy of the Library of Congress)

Cold Facts

Unlike his successors, Harry Truman would make no effort to conceal the extent of the U.S. military involvement in Asia. However, his unilateral decision to inform only congressional leaders, not to consult them, would have broad implications for the nation's future involvement in the political and military affairs of Southeast Asia. Relying on varying interpretations of Truman's precedent, rarely would another president feel compelled to consult members of Congress before committing the United States to the armed struggle against communism in Asia, particularly in Vietnam.

Grumbling at Home

The first signs of domestic trouble over Korea first appeared on June 30, 1950, when Truman met with congressional leaders, not to consult, but to inform them of his decision to send U.S. troops to South Korea. Republican Senator Kenneth Wherry aggressively challenged the president and wanted to know, recalled one Truman aide, "if the President was going to advise the Congress before he sent ground troops into Korea." Truman matter-of-factly responded that "I just had to act as Commander-in-Chief, and I did."

Quotes from the Cold

If a burglar breaks into your house, you can shoot him without going down to the police station and getting permission. You might run into a long debate by Congress, which would tie your hands completely. You have the right to do so as Commander-in-Chief and under the UN Charter.

—Senate Foreign Relations Committee Chairman Tom Connally, to Harry Truman in the days following the Korean invasion

Should the need arise for a full-scale military action, Truman assured the congressional leaders, he would consult the Congress.

Truman may have had the constitutional right to dispatch U.S. troops unilaterally to Korea. But because he declined to make congressional leaders partners in his decision, the Republicans would feel no obligation to share the blame if the conflict went badly. Indeed, they would attack him mercilessly at the first opportunity.

As it turned out, that opportunity came early. Republican leaders were seething, not only over the way Truman had excluded them from his decision, but because of administration policies that they feared had encouraged the North Koreans to believe that the United States would not challenge an attack on South Korea.

Secretary of State Acheson had seemed to say as much in a widely heralded speech to the National Press Club the previous January. While he forcefully articulated a North Pacific perimeter that the United States would defend against communist aggression (a line running along the Aleutian Islands southward to Japan to Okinawa to the Philippines), he had curiously omitted South Korea. That glaring omission, Republicans later charged, was an open invitation to aggression.

But the Republicans often had shared the same opinions about Korea. Heavily influenced by the military isolationists who had once strongly opposed direct U.S. involvement in Europe during World War II and offered mild support for fighting communism in Asia, many Republican leaders were instinctively opposed to sending troops into Asia. Thus, in the early days of the conflict, while much of the nation rallied to Truman's support, most Republicans remained on the sidelines.

Cold Facts

Many of the Republicans who would later blame Truman for having ignored the communist threat in Korea until it was too late had themselves opposed American intervention. For example, Republican Senator William Jenner of Indiana complained that it was "just downright idiotic" for the State Department to place so much emphasis on Korea. Robert Taft, a leading Republican senator from Ohio, advised his colleagues not to be "stampeded into war" over Korea. Senator Eugene Milliken of Colorado summarized the Republican view of the Korean situation when he said that Republican lawmakers were "unanimous" in believing the communist invasion "should not be used as a provocation for war." The nation, he said, had no obligation to fight with South Korean soldiers.

Congress Falls in Line

Within days, however, the winds of public opinion swept through Capitol Hill. After months of attacking the president for having abandoned the fight against communism, Republicans realized they could offer Truman only their grudging support. "The general principle of the policy is right," Taft admitted.

Congress promptly ended its debate over whether to allow Truman to reinstate the draft. A unified House and Senate not only gave the president that authority, but handed him power to call up the National Guard and reservists. Both houses also authorized a $1.2 billion military aid program with provisions allowing Truman to spend up to $460 million to assist South Korea. The Senate unanimously approved both measures.

Cold Facts

Immediately following the Korean invasion, Robert Taft—as the ideological leader of the Republican Party's isolationist wing—gave his Republican colleagues the rhetorical framework for their political opposition to Truman's Korean policies: Truman's show of force was late in coming, Taft said. Had such a policy been in place before the invasion "there never would have been such an attack by the North Koreans. In short, this entirely unfortunate crisis has been produced, first, by the outrageous, aggressive attitude of Soviet Russia, and second, by the bungling and inconsistent foreign policy of the administration" that had, among other things, acquiesced to communism in China. Furthermore, Taft argued, the post-World War II decision to divide Korea at the thirty-eighth parallel was evidence of an unfortunate Roosevelt-Truman policy of cooperation with the Soviet Union.

More Domestic Attacks

Throughout the summer of 1950, as U.S. troops fought communist forces in the mountains and hills of South Korea, a political war broke out in Washington and across the country. With the fall congressional elections just months away, the Republican attacks on Truman intensified. In Iowa, a group of Republican Party chairmen from 12 states demanded the resignations of Secretary of State Acheson and Secretary of Defense Louis Johnson for "demonstrated ineptitude."

Speaking to 1,800 cheering American Legionnaires in Green Bay, Wisconsin, Republican Senator Joseph McCarthy also called for Acheson's head. "The Korea deathtrap," he said, "we can lay to the doors of the Kremlin and those who sabotaged rearming, including Acheson and the President, if you please."

Cold Facts

Near the end of World War II, the United States decided to occupy the southern end of Korea, primarily out of fear that the Soviet Union—which had just entered the war against Japan—might seize control of the entire nation. Korea was divided into north and south sectors at the thirty-eighth parallel in order to maintain U.S. control of the capitol of Seoul. Although the Soviet Union withdrew its troops in 1948, the USSR and China emerged as major allies of the North Korean regime.

The "American Caesar"

For almost three months, U.S. troops struggled to prevent the powerful, well-supplied communist forces from driving them off the Korean peninsula. Throughout the early days of the conflict an embarrassing series of setbacks and retreats served only to intensify Republican attacks on Truman.

Inchon

With the November election less than seven weeks away, General Douglas MacArthur launched a military counterstrike that changed the course of the war and finally put communist forces on the defensive. On September 15, American forces staged a daring amphibious landing at the Yellow Sea port of Inchon, 30 miles from the South Korean capitol of Seoul.

The invasion was a remarkable success. By September 26, Seoul was liberated. By month's end, the North Korean army had retreated to the thirty-eighth parallel and MacArthur began lobbying the administration for permission to cross into North Korea and vanquish the communist forces.

To the Yalu

As the fall congressional campaigns of 1950 went into full swing, so did the war in Korea. U.S. forces fared so well that MacArthur gained Truman's permission to attempt a total rout of communist forces. In October, he finally took the battle into North Korea in hopes of reunifying the two countries under the South Korean government.

The mission, however, was a disaster. In November, as American troops approached the Chinese border at the Yalu River, some 300,000 Chinese troops struck back with a vengeance and forced a humiliating and hasty U.S. retreat.

General Douglas MacArthur commanded U.S. forces in Korea during the first two years of the Korean War.

(U.S. Army photo courtesy of the Harry S. Truman Library)

By January, communist troops pushed MacArthur's beleaguered forces back below the thirty-eighth parallel and once more controlled Seoul. Only months earlier, MacArthur had boldly predicted the war would end by Christmas. Now, it was clear that the conflict was far from over. Weeks earlier, a UN victory seemed assured. Even that was now in doubt.

The Chinese attack caught Truman and his advisors by surprise. Responding quickly, the administration declared a national emergency, increased draft calls, imposed wage and price controls, and asked Congress to quadruple defense spending. Yet the last thing Truman had wanted was a direct conflict with Communist China.

Quotes from the Cold

Gentlemen, we're not retreating. We are just advancing in a different direction.

—Marine Corps General Oliver Smith, after the Chinese counter attack in November 1950.

Truman hoped to end the war—quickly—and was willing, therefore, to abandon the forcible reunification of the two Koreas. Reluctantly, the United States prepared to accept the prewar status quo of a divided Korean peninsula that was one-half communist.

MacArthur, however, saw the Chinese intervention as a perfect opportunity to take the battle directly to China and end the conflict, not by negotiation as Truman wanted, but with a decisive military victory. The general urged Truman to bomb and blockade Mainland China, offering a proposal to bring Chiang Kai-shek's nationalist army into the fight by equipping them to lead a ground offensive against the Chinese.

Just as troubling were MacArthur's dire reports from the field concerning the condition of his troops. To the Joint Chiefs of Staff came official reports that MacArthur's army suffered from fatigue and low morale—an assessment that later proved erroneous.

The fact was that MacArthur's troops were down, but far from out. Under the able leadership of Lieutenant General Matthew Ridgway, the new commander of the Eighth Army, they reversed their retreat and regained the initiative. By late January, U.S. forces were again on the offensive.

Truman Versus MacArthur

Despite having almost forfeited the American position in Korea with his reckless military strategy, General MacArthur continued urging an even more aggressive strategy on Truman.

Shifting Blame

Embarrassed that his promise to have U.S. troops home by Christmas had collapsed under the weight of the strong and unexpected Chinese offensive, MacArthur publicly tried to shift the blame to Washington and Truman.

In December of 1950, he had first argued that his army's inability to resist the Chinese was the result, not of his own military missteps, but of limitations—"without precedent"—imposed on him by Washington. He complained that U.S. officials would not allow him to bomb Chinese bases in Manchuria and pursue enemy planes across the Chinese border.

Quotes from the Cold

While General MacArthur was fighting the Pentagon, General Ridgway was fighting the enemy.

Dean Acheson, *Present at the Creation,* (W.W. Norton, 1969)

Fearing that a direct confrontation with China might bring the Soviet Union into conflict and precipitate another world war, Truman would not allow MacArthur to take the country into direct conflict with China. "I should have relieved General MacArthur then and there," Truman later said. "The reason I did not was that I did not wish to have it appear as if he were being relieved because the offensive failed." Instead, on December 6, Truman ordered that no military official publicly discuss anything but the most routine foreign policy matters without first consulting his superior.

MacArthur ignored Truman's order. On March 15, he escalated his dispute with the president by informing a news organization that he opposed the administration's decision to stop the Eighth Army's advance at the thirty-eighth parallel. The general ventured further into forbidden territory when he erroneously stated that his mission was "the unification of Korea"—a matter of policy and one that Truman had expressly rejected.

Ultimatum

Nine days later, MacArthur did it again. In the words of Acheson, the general "perpetrated a major act of sabotage." While U.S. officials composed a cease-fire proposal, MacArthur unilaterally issued an inflammatory ultimatum to the Chinese, threatening to widen the war.

In the United States, MacArthur's Republican supporters enthusiastically echoed the general's call to expand the war. Senator Robert Taft complained that Truman had "refused to fight that war with all the means" at his command.

MacArthur's hostile and threatening declaration torpedoed Truman's carefully crafted cease-fire initiative. Furious at the flagrant disregard for his December 6 order, Truman again resisted the urge to fire the general and, instead, issued a stern warning.

The final straw came in early April when House Republican Leader Joseph Martin released a March 20 letter from MacArthur in which the general endorsed Martin's view that the Nationalist Chinese forces should be enlisted. MacArthur declared that "we must win. There is no substitute for victory."

Quotes from the Cold

[Communist China] must by now be painfully aware that a decision of the United States to depart from its tolerant effort to contain the war to the areas of Korea, through an expansion of our military operations to his coastal areas and interior bases, would doom Red China to the risk of imminent military collapse.

—General Douglas MacArthur's unauthorized ultimatum to the Chinese government, March 1951

Quotes from the Cold

It seems strangely difficult for some to realize that here in Asia is where the communist conspirators have elected to make their play for global conquest, and that we have joined the issue thus raised on the battlefield; that here we fight Europe's war with arms while the diplomats there still fight it with words; that if we lose the war to communism in Asia the fall of Europe is inevitable, win it and Europe most probably would avoid war and yet preserve freedom. As you point out, we must win. There is no substitute for victory.

—General Douglas MacArthur to House Republican Leader Joseph Martin, March 1951

Acheson saw the letter as "an open declaration of war on the administration's policy." As Truman later said: "The time had come to draw the line. MacArthur's letter to Congressman Martin showed that the general was not only in disagreement with the policy of the government but was challenging this policy in open insubordination to his Commander in Chief." Truman had no choice but to relieve MacArthur of his command, which he did on April 11, 1951.

Harry Takes a Beating

MacArthur's firing sparked an unprecedented display of popular furor. Angry citizens inundated the White House with more than 250,000 telegrams of protest. A Gallup poll revealed that almost 70 percent of voters supported MacArthur. Across the country, flags were flown upside down or at half-mast. In some places, Truman and Acheson were burned in effigy.

Quotes from the Cold

MacArthur's contempt for half measures and a brokered truce, his determination to punish the evil men who had disturbed the peace—peace, in American eyes, being the normal relationship between nations—struck a chord deep within [the American people]. His moral challenge, his vow to crush wickedness, appealed to what they regarded as their best instincts. The fact that they could not respond to it saddened, even grieved, them, and they felt untrue to themselves.

—William Manchester, MacArthur's biographer, *American Caesar: Douglas MacArthur 1880–1964* (Little, Brown, 1978) on MacArthur's belligerent strategy to widen the Korean War

"Impeach Him"

On Capitol Hill, Republicans were privately gleeful and publicly outraged. They were gleeful because Truman, they believed, had once again fumbled the ball in Asia. Publicly, they were more than ready to milk the public's wrath.

"Impeach him," rolled off the tongues of many Republicans, despite the fact that Democrats still controlled the Congress and could block any move to oust the president. That did not stop Truman's critics from demanding his removal. In a Senate speech the morning of MacArthur's dismissal, Republican William Jenner of Indiana even suggested that Truman was a Soviet agent.

Among those who attacked Truman was Republican Senator William Knowland of California, who observed that "Mao Zedong in Peking and Josef Stalin in Moscow must have received great satisfaction" from Truman's decision.

Quotes from the Cold

I charge that this country today is in the hands of a secret inner coterie, which is directed by agents of the Soviet Union. They have formed a popular front government like that in France in the '30s and we know how France was taken from within .... We must cut this whole cancerous conspiracy out of our government at once. Our only choice is to impeach President Truman and find out who is the secret invisible government, which has so cleverly led our country down the road to destruction.

—Republican Senator William Jenner, April 1951

"Party of Betrayal"

Republican Senator Joseph McCarthy of Wisconsin used the occasion to launch an attack, not just on Truman, but the Democratic Party. "Unless Democrats in the Senate and House—after all, they are in control—stand up and let themselves be counted as being against treason they will forever, and rightly, have labeled their party as the party of betrayal."

In most cases, however, Republicans assailed Truman, not so much for firing MacArthur, but for his unwillingness to follow MacArthur's advice to take the United States into direct military conflict with Communist China. Typical was the critique of California Senator Richard Nixon:

> I believe that rather than follow the advice of those who would appease the Communists ... what we should do is to do what we intended to do when we went into Korea, and that is to bring the war to a successful military conclusion by taking the necessary steps in implementation of the resolution passed by the United Nations, to the effect that Communist China was an aggressor.

Nixon and others were essentially urging Truman to launch a full-scale assault on China in the calculated belief that the Soviet Union would not enter the fight.

Hero's Welcome

As the nationwide vilification of Truman continued, MacArthur returned home to a hero's welcome. On April 19, eight days after his dismissal, the defrocked general stood at the podium in the chamber of the House of Representatives. In perhaps one of the more bizarre public events in U.S. history, the elected representatives of the American people cheered an insubordinate general who had challenged the constitutional principle of civilian control of the foreign and military policies of the United States.

The MacArthur worship—journalist William S. White called it "a politico-military cult"—was not confined to the halls of Congress. All across the country, millions of Americans seemed ready to endorse the foreign policy of an unelected general.

Standing before a joint meeting of Congress, MacArthur defiantly articulated his own foreign policy. Decrying the Truman administration's refusal to fight the Chinese, MacArthur indirectly accused his critics of appeasement. "Like blackmail," said MacArthur, such an attitude "lays the basis for new and successively greater demands until, as in blackmail, violence becomes the only other alternative. Why, my soldiers asked of me, surrender military advantages to an enemy in the field? I could not answer."

Quotes from the Cold

The world has turned over many times since I took the oath at West Point, and the hopes and dreams have all since vanished, but I still remember the refrain of one of the most popular barracks ballads of that day which proclaimed most proudly that old soldiers never die; they just fade away. And like the old soldier of that ballad, I now close my military career and just fade away, an old soldier who tried to do his duty as God gave him the light to see that duty.

—Douglas MacArthur, from his speech to Congress, April 19, 1951

Republican Praise

As MacArthur staged his triumphant return to the United States, Republicans rushed to praise the general and his policies. "I have long approved of General MacArthur's program," Robert Taft said. Said Senator William Jenner: "MacArthur has bought us another, perhaps final chance, to destroy the Administration's pro-Communist, pro-Socialist foreign policy." But this praise for MacArthur was more predicated on an appreciation of the general as a political club with which to pound Harry Truman than as a valuable foreign policy advisor.

Quotes from the Cold

We cannot win the next election unless we point out the utter failure and capacity of the present [Truman] Administration to conduct foreign policy and cite the loss of China and the Korean war as typical examples of their very dangerous control. We certainly can't win on domestic policy, because every domestic policy depends entirely on foreign policy.

—Republican Senator Robert Taft, letter to a friend, July 1951

Despite the Republicans' professed agreement with MacArthur's desire to take the battle to the Chinese, no one had offered a formal congressional resolution that embodied that policy. As *Time* magazine, generally supportive of MacArthur, astutely observed: "Though Republicans in Congress considered MacArthur a godsend to the party, there were few who publicly endorsed all his proposals."

Harry's Silence

Throughout the entire episode, President Truman was strangely silent. Only occasionally did he rise to defend his foreign policy and the decision to fire the popular general. For weeks, his Republicans critics dominated the debate and inflicted serious and lasting political wounds on Truman and his party.

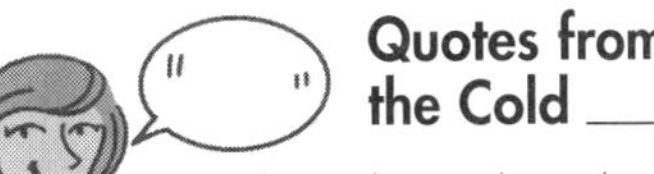

Quotes from the Cold

Nothing but a bunch of damn bull ….

—Harry Truman's private critique of General MacArthur's speech to Congress, April 1951

Senate Hearings

Truman's position did recover slightly during a seven-week Senate inquiry into MacArthur's dismissal. During joint hearings of the Senate's Armed Services and Foreign Relations committee a different image of MacArthur began to immerge. He was strangely uninformed or uninterested in world affairs and expressed confused and contradictory opinions about the nature and objective of Soviet communism. Worst of all, the Joint Chiefs of Staff and Defense Secretary George C. Marshall each contradicted MacArthur's claims that they supported his military strategy for Korea.

But MacArthur's fading fortunes provided no great political boost for Truman. The crisis had arrived on the heels of an embarrassing showing by Democrats in the 1950 congressional elections—Republicans gained five Senate and 28 House seats—and an election year that had seriously and deeply weakened Truman's standing with the American public. Piled on top of other perceived mistakes in China and the damaging attacks on the loyalty and competence of Truman's State Department, the MacArthur episode made the weight of negative public opinion almost unbearable.

By 1952, Americans were weary of the Korean War (a conflict, in stalemate, that would continue for two more years). They also harbored serious and lasting doubts about the Democratic foreign policies—doubts that were only confirmed by MacArthur's dismissal.

The Least You Need to Know

- In June 1950, communist North Korea invaded the Republic of Korea (South Korea), and President Harry Truman responded by sending U.S. troops to defend South Korea.
- Truman's political opponents attacked him for having invited the outbreak of war in Korea, accusing him of paying too little attention to the threat of communism in Asia.

- Invading Chinese troops sent U.S. forces in Korea into a full-scale retreat in November 1951 after General Douglas MacArthur's army attempted a rout of communist forces near the Korea-China border.
- In April 1951, after repeatedly defying President Truman's orders not to publicly complain about U.S. policy in Korea, the president fired General MacArthur.

Living in the Cold War

It was not bad enough that we had the Soviet Union as a mortal enemy. During the Cold War's early days, Americans were fighting with each other. Joe McCarthy saw communists behind every curtain—and many Americans believed him. After McCarthy and the Red Scare of the early 1950s, American leaders took great pains to prove their anticommunist credentials—and the United States paid the price in places such as Cuba and Vietnam.

During these years, relations with the Soviet Union grew only more tense and distrustful. By the early 1960s, that deteriorating relationship brought the two powers to the brink of nuclear war. The Cold War almost became deadly hot.

Chapter 11

The Senator from Wisconsin

In This Chapter

- Joseph McCarthy's campaign against communism in the U.S. government
- Republican leaders support McCarthy; Truman and the Democrats fight back
- The Red Scare in the U.S. House
- Richard Nixon fights communism
- Eisenhower runs for president

The early 1950s were times of great uncertainty and fear in the United States. Soviet communism loomed large in Europe, although Truman's containment policies appeared to have halted its advance. In Asia, meanwhile, communism was on the march. The Soviet-backed North Koreans had attacked the American-backed South Koreans, prompting a strong U.S. military response. By mid-1950, Americans would again be at war, just five years after the end of World War II. In China, meanwhile, Americans were still reeling over the victory of Mao's communist forces.

Republicans and a few conservative Democrats, needing a scapegoat, decided to blame Harry Truman. They charged that while he and Secretary of State Dean Acheson had stopped communism's march in Europe, they had forgotten to lock the "back door" in Asia.

The political consequences would be devastating for Truman and the Democratic Party in the 1950 and 1952 elections. But this wasn't the end of Truman's woes. In 1950, there erupted a political controversy about the impact of domestic communism in the United States. Joseph McCarthy, Richard Nixon, and others would gain considerable public acclaim for their efforts to expose communist infiltration in the U.S. government.

In this chapter, we explore the affects of "McCarthyism" and its related ills.

McCarthyism

After being denied the White House for almost 20 years, the Republicans were frustrated and angry. Like any political party in their circumstances, they were eager to find an issue that would put them back in power. Unwittingly, Harry Truman had handed it to them in 1949 and 1950.

First came news in the late summer of 1949 that the Soviets had exploded an atomic bomb, ending America's distinction as the world's only nuclear power. That was followed by news of the "loss" of China to communism. For this, Truman took a beating at the hands of Republicans in late 1949 and appeared vulnerable to charges that he had not done enough to prevent the communist victory in China.

That alone, however, wouldn't be enough to destroy Truman and the Democrats. To do this, it would have to be proven that the communist victory in China was not only the result of negligence, but of willful support by officials at the highest levels of the American government.

In February 1950, into the national limelight strode Senator Joseph R. McCarthy, a man consumed with political ambition and who provided the Republican Party with the explosive charges it needed to destroy Harry Truman and his party.

Explosive Charges

A 41-year-old Republican from Wisconsin, McCarthy had served in the Senate since 1946. His was an undistinguished career. He had never really made his mark in the Senate—until, that is, he discovered the potent power of the American fear of communism. On February 9, 1950, McCarthy spoke to a Republican women's club in Wheeling, West Virginia, telling them he had a list of 205 names "known to the Secretary of State as being members of the Communist Party who nevertheless are still working and shaping policy in the State Department."

McCarthy had no evidence to substantiate his allegations. His story changed constantly and many Washington insiders knew him as nothing more than a womanizing drunkard who had faked a war record and won his Senate seat in 1946 by unfairly suggesting that his Democratic opponent was a communist sympathizer. None of that, however, mattered to the press, a gullible and receptive public, and a Republican Party hungry for a potent issue to usher them back into power.

Cold Facts

Joseph McCarthy had no list of 205 State Department employees who belonged to the Communist Party. In fact, as time went on, the number of names kept changing. What he really had was a three-year-old congressional document with 108 case studies in which no communists were identified in the government. The report had actually absolved these employees of disloyalty. But that didn't stop McCarthy from later claiming to have a list of 57 "card-carrying Communists" who were working in the State Department in February 1950.

Hoping to examine McCarthy's evidence, the Senate directed its Foreign Relations Committee to appoint a special investigative subcommittee and named Maryland Democrat Millard Tydings, chairman of the Armed Services Committee, to lead the inquiry. After examining McCarthy's "evidence," however, the utter bankruptcy of the charges became apparent. By July, the subcommittee. split down partisan lines, declared McCarthy's charges "perhaps the most nefarious campaign of untruths in the history of our Republic."

Quotes from the Cold

The Democratic label is now the property of men and women who have … bent to the whispered pleas from the lips of traitors … men and women who wear the political label stitched with the idiocy of a Truman, rotted by the deceit of a[n] Acheson.

—Joseph McCarthy, 1950

Quotes from the Cold

[W]ith nothing, Senator McCarthy plunged headlong forward, desperately seeking to develop some information which, colored with distortion and fanned by a blaze of bias, would forestall a day of reckoning …. Were this a campaign founded in truth it would be questionable enough; where it is fraught with falsehood from beginning to end, its reprehensible and contemptible character defies adequate condemnation.

—Conclusion of the Senate committee investigating Joseph McCarthy's charges in 1950

McCarthy, however, benefited from Truman's stubborn refusal to change his executive order of 1948 that prohibited release of personnel files to Congress. For three months, McCarthy and the Republicans waged a campaign of relentless attacks on Truman and suggested that his refusal to release the files was proof that they contained incriminating evidence. To many Americans, that charge seemed plausible. By the time of the subcommittee's scathing report, McCarthy's charges of a partisan Democratic cover-up had gained credence with the public.

Wisconsin Senator Joseph R. McCarthy sparked a partisan firestorm in 1950 with his sensational allegations of communism in the U.S. State Department.

(Courtesy of the Library of Congress)

Defending Joe

The silence of most Senate Democrats and as well as the public support of Senate Republicans, who perceived a political windfall for their party in the 1950 elections, also enhanced McCarthy's credibility. Conservatives such as Homer Capehart and William Jenner of Indiana, Bourke Hickenlooper of Iowa, Karl Mundt of South Dakota, and Chiang Kai-shek disciples William Knowland of California and Styles Bridges of New Hampshire, all rushed to McCarthy's defense on and off the Senate floor.

Cold Facts

Although Joseph McCarthy was unable to provide conclusive proof of his charge that communists had infiltrated the U.S. State Department, opinion polls in 1950 showed that almost half of the American public believed him.

More helpful was the support he received from influential Republican leaders. Senate Republican Whip Kenneth Wherry tried to associate the rise of communism in Asia and with the communists McCarthy claimed to have discovered in the State Department. "Is it any wonder that an administration which harbors so many radicals at home is tolerant of the spread of socialism and its twin brother communism abroad?" Wherry asked.

Robert Taft, the most prominent Senate Republican and a possible presidential candidate in 1952, also supported

McCarthy's reckless behavior. Although McCarthy had not yet identified one communist in government, Taft later said that he told him to "keep talking and if one case doesn't work out, he should proceed with another one."

Angry at the Republican attempts "to sabotage bipartisan foreign policy," Truman had condemned McCarthy and his supporters as the Kremlin's "greatest asset." But an indignant Taft rushed to McCarthy's defense, praising him as "a fighting Marine who risked his life to preserve the liberties of the United States."

Hearings

The Tydings Committee hearings were not the only proceedings to examine McCarthy's explosive charges. From 1951 to 1952, a Senate committee headed by a noted anticommunist senator, Pat McCarran of Nevada, held hearings and later claimed that some of McCarthy's charges were credible. One of the alleged communists that McCarthy had identified, McCarran's committee said, was "a conscious, articulate instrument of the Soviet conspiracy." Actually, the man was noted China expert and sometimes State Department consultant who was a loyal American.

Quotes from the Cold

> It is easy to make light of McCarthy today, when even conservatives use the word "McCarthyism" to mean unfair political smear tactics—but the harsh fact, which must never be forgotten, is that … Joe McCarthy literally terrorized Washington and much of the nation.
>
> —Clark Clifford, *Counsel to the President: A Memoir,* (Random House, 1991)

However, the facts mattered little to those who wanted to prove what, for political or personal reasons, they had already decided. In McCarthy's reckless charges, Republicans saw a path back to political power. Others, some of them Democrats, simply rode his coattails because fighting communism was popular and it played upon the public's deep dread of domestic communist plots. Furthermore, the supposed presence of domestic communists at the highest levels of the U.S. government helped many Americans rationalize the great gains communism was making in China and elsewhere in Asia.

The Army-McCarthy Hearings

When the Republicans won the White House (Dwight D. Eisenhower was elected president) and control of the Congress in 1952, McCarthy became chairman of the Committee on Government Operations. It was not a particularly powerful or influential committee. But McCarthy saw potential in the committee's Permanent Investigations Subcommittee, which had the power to subpoena witnesses, and soon appointed himself chairman.

Beginning in 1953, McCarthy waged a series of high-profile, sensational hearings into communist infiltration in the U.S. government. His committee's activities culminated in 1954, with an investigation of alleged spying and sabotage within the Army Signal Corps at Fort Monmouth, New Jersey. McCarthy accused Army Secretary Robert T. Stevens and his aides of hiding the activities at Fort Monmouth.

Army officials responded by accusing McCarthy, his chief counsel, and a committee staff member of threatening army officials in hopes of gaining preferential treatment for a former committee consultant who had been drafted. To sort out the various charges, the Senate established a special committee to conduct hearings on the matter.

Quotes from the Cold

For 36 days, from April until June [1954], the Army-McCarthy hearings offered the nation an unparalleled spectacle. In their grip on the media, in their circus atmosphere, and in the emotions they churned up, they resembled the 1925 Scopes "monkey" trial.

—Richard M. Fried, *Nightmare in Red* (Oxford, 1990)

Although McCarthy was cleared of those charges, the televised proceedings showed a defensive, reckless, and evasive side of the Wisconsin senator that most Americans had never seen. "The hearings," journalist Richard Rovere concluded, "established before most of the nation the fact that McCarthy himself was an enemy of the established order." Nothing drove home the point better than McCarthy's dramatic televised confrontation with Joseph Welch, the army's special counsel, whom McCarthy accused of harboring a leftist attorney, Fred Fisher, in his Boston law firm.

Cold Facts

As chairman of the Permanent Investigations Sub-Committee of the Senate Committee on Government Operations, Senator Joseph McCarthy investigated the State Department's information program, its Voice of America, and its overseas libraries, which included books by people McCarthy believed to be communists. The State Department overreacted and removed 40 titles from its libraries around the world, including *The Selected Works of Thomas Jefferson,* edited by Philip Foner, and *The Children's Hour* by Lillian Hellman.

Welch's indignant retort destroyed what little credibility McCarthy had left: "Until this moment, Senator, I think I never really gauged your cruelty or recklessness. … Little did I dream you could be so cruel as to do an injury to that lad." Unbowed, McCarthy persisted with his attacks on Fisher. Welch responded: "You have done enough. Have you no sense of decency, sir, at long last. Have you left no sense of decency."

As many as 20 million people had watched the hearings. Most observers agreed that McCarthy was finished.

The Un-American Affairs Investigations

Joe McCarthy wasn't the first or the only member of Congress to milk the nation's great fear of communism (don't forget the Red Scare of 1919). He was just the best. But a close second in that fear-mongering department was the notorious House Committee on Un-American Affairs (HUAC).

Established in 1938, the committee was ostensibly established to monitor the activities of foreign agents. With the advent of the Cold War, however, the committee's focus changed dramatically. Its members may not have been the most responsible or honorable public servants, but they were good politicians who recognized the public's fear of communist *subversion*, and they exploited those fears with a vengeance.

Cold Words

Subversion is a plan or activity aimed at undermining or overthrowing a government or other institution.

Loyalty Investigations

HUAC's reckless behavior was not just the result of the Republicans' hatred of Harry Truman. Truman bore some responsibility for the climate of fear that gripped the nation in the years after the war. Two events prompted the president's actions. The first was the discovery in 1945 of classified government information at the offices of *Amerasia* magazine, a publication that sympathized with the Chinese communists. Next, in 1946, a Canadian commission released information suggesting that Soviet agents were operating in Canada. One of them, the commission said, had stolen nuclear secrets.

Those revelations prompted Truman to action. In early 1947, he ordered investigations into the loyalty of more than three million U.S. government employees. By 1950, those regarded as "security risks"—including alcoholics, homosexuals, and debtors—were being fired from their jobs because they were thought to be susceptible to blackmail. Fears of communist subversion spread like wildfire and HUAC was more than willing to fan the flames.

Cold Facts

During the 1950s, the House Un-American Activities Committee distributed millions of pamphlets to the American public, entitled: *One Hundred Things You Should Know About Communism.* One example of the information imparted: "Where can Communists be found? Everywhere."

The Hollywood Ten

In September 1947, HUAC turned its attention to communist influence in Hollywood. The committee summoned 41 witnesses, demanding of them information about communist sympathizers in the entertainment industry. During the committee's hearings in

October 1947, 10 hostile witnesses refused to answer the committee's intrusive and unconstitutional questions about their political views and activities. All were leftists or former communists who believed their political beliefs were no business of the nation's political leaders. These hostile witnesses—nine writers and one director—were later charged with contempt of Congress and served brief prison terms.

The "Hollywood Ten," as some later called them, were writers Alvah Bessie, Herbert Biberman, Lester Cole, Ring Lardner Jr., John Howard Lawson, Albert Maltz, Samuel Ornitz, Adrian Scott, and Dalton Trubo, and director Edward Dmytryk. Other Hollywood figures, however, backed HUAC's work and were far more eager to cooperate with the committee by discussing their political views and sometimes accusing others of communist leanings. Those who cooperated included studio heads Louis B. Mayer and Jack Warner, writer Ayn Rand, and actors Gary Cooper, Robert Montgomery, Ronald Reagan, and Robert Taylor.

The prison time meted out to the Hollywood Ten was not the worst of their punishment inflicted by the committee. A group of studio executives, supportive of the committee's witch hunt, drew up a blacklist guaranteeing that all but one of them would be refused work by American movie studios for most of the 1950s. They would live much of their lives under a cloud of suspicion. Their only crime: refusing to answer questions about their political activities or philosophies.

The Nixon Version of McCarthy

Before Joseph McCarthy there was Richard Nixon. Many people think of Nixon as a corrupt man, the first president to resign, or the leader who boldly paved the way to renewed relations with the Peoples Republic of China. But before all of that, Nixon's main claim to fame was his "success" in the fight against domestic communism.

Nixon was elected to Congress from California in 1947, accusing his incumbent opponent, Congressman Jerry Voorhis, of being "soft" on communism. Appointed to HUAC, Nixon distinguished himself for the fervor he brought to the job of weeding out subversives from American life.

The Hiss Case

Alger Hiss had been a senior State Department official during the 1940s, during the Roosevelt administration. He had accompanied Roosevelt to Yalta. He had participated in the creation of the United Nations and had even served temporarily as secretary-general of the San Francisco conference that created the UN. He was later the chief State Department advisor to the U.S. delegation to the UN.

In August 1948, Whittaker Chambers, an editor at *Time* magazine, stunned HUAC with his testimony that he had been part of a communist cell in the 1930s that had included several government officials. Chambers alleged that Hiss was one of those officials. Hiss vehemently denied the charges and sued Chambers for libel. Chambers later raised the stakes when, during a pretrial hearing, testified—in contradiction to his statements before HUAC—that the cell had also conducted espionage. Hiss, he charged, had stolen government documents.

Quotes from the Cold

I've always believed that Hiss was a victim of the "Red Scare" and of Nixon's political rapacity. It is a national outrage that this essentially decent man went to prison as a consequence of the demagoguery of Nixon and the ignominious House Committee on Un-American Activities.

—Former U.S. Senator George McGovern, 1996

Several committee members regarded Hiss's denials as persuasive. "We've been had! We're ruined," one Republican HUAC member cried. But Nixon, chairman of the subcommittee investigating the matter, believed Chambers. He arranged for Chambers and Hiss to confront each other and relentlessly probed inconsistencies in Hiss's testimony.

Nixon won Chambers' trust. And Chambers rewarded him handsomely with five rolls of microfilm that he had hidden in a hollowed-out pumpkin on his farm. The "pumpkin papers" were explosive. The documents they contained were later identified as classified papers of the departments of State, Navy, and War. Some of them appeared to bear notations in Hiss's handwriting. Hiss, it was charged, had not only belonged to the Communist Party, but had spied for the Soviet Union in the 1930s.

After a Justice Department investigation, Hiss was indicted for perjury (the statute of limitation for treason had expired). The first trial ended without a conviction, but Hiss was eventually convicted of lying under oath in January 1950. He served three years and eight months of a five-year prison sentence. Despite the evidence that pointed to Hiss's guilt, historians continue to disagree about the facts of the case.

The Hiss case was a fault line of partisan bitterness between Democrats and Republicans in the early 1950s. That Hiss had been in Roosevelt's State Department and had advised FDR at Yalta served as proof to Republicans that the Democrats had jeopardized American security by harboring communist agents. Democrats, on the other hand, viewed the case as evidence Republican eagerness to smear Roosevelt and Truman for political gain.

"Alger" Stevenson

His success in the Hiss case propelled Nixon into the United States Senate in 1950. During that election, Nixon actively engaged in more redbaiting, questioning the patriotism of his Democratic opponent, Helen Gahagan Douglas. For her adherence to Harry

Truman's China policy, Nixon had dubbed her "the Pink Lady." In turn, she named him "Tricky Dick," a moniker that stuck.

In 1952, Republican presidential nominee Dwight D. Eisenhower chose Nixon as his running mate. Considered a fierce and effective anticommunist, Nixon was also well-known for his expertise in the art of the smear. Only the year before, it was Nixon who had proved a skillful practitioner in the art of exploiting the fallout over Truman's dismissal of General MacArthur.

Truman's secretary of state, Dean Acheson, drew much of the partisan fire from Republicans during the Truman years.

(Courtesy of the Harry S. Truman Library)

Avoiding the wild and extreme rhetoric of Republicans such as McCarthy and Jenner, Nixon had carefully played to his strength as an expert on domestic communism. "The happiest group in the country," Nixon had said, "will be the communists and their stooges. … The president has given them what they always wanted—MacArthur's scalp."

As Eisenhower's running mate, Nixon was more than willing to serve as the campaign's hatchet man. While Eisenhower largely took the high road and promised to clean up "the mess in Washington," Nixon traveled low. In an August newspaper interview, he issued veiled accusations about Truman's patriotism. "The most devastating thing that can be said about the Truman record is that he has lost 600 million people to the communists."

Later in the campaign, Nixon struck at Truman even harder. In October, Nixon charged that Truman, Acheson, and Adlai Stevenson—the governor of Illinois and the 1952 Democratic presidential nominee—were "traitors to the high principles in which many of the nation's Democrats believe." Days later in Los Angeles, he ridiculed Stevenson's patriotism when he said that the Democratic candidate "holds a Ph.D. degree from Acheson's College of Cowardly Communist Containment."

Quotes from the Cold

If the record itself smears, let it smear. If the dry rot of corruption and communism, which has eaten into our body politic during the past seven years, can only be chopped out with a hatchet, then let's call for a hatchet.

—Richard Nixon, 1952 campaign speech

Nixon was not alone in his assaults on Truman. Eisenhower, although less personal, was not above attacking Stevenson and Truman over communism and Far East policy. He and his advisors understood the widespread public discontent over the stalemated Korean War and made it their most prominent issue in the campaign's homestretch.

Cold Facts

During the 1952 presidential election, Republican supporters of Dwight D. Eisenhower focused on the three "phonetic Ks": alleged corruption in the Truman administration, the spread of communism—especially Truman's "loss" of China—and what they considered the disastrous war in Korea.

In Philadelphia in early September, Eisenhower delivered a hard-hitting speech in which he charged that "seven years after victory in World War II this Administration has bungled us perilously close to World War III." Blaming Truman for having "grossly underestimated" the communist threat, Eisenhower claimed that "we are in that war because this administration abandoned China to the communists … [and] announced to all the world that it had written off most of the Far East as beyond our direct concern."

On Election Day 1952, the voters finished the repudiation of Harry Truman and the Democratic Party that had begun in 1950. Not only did they elect Eisenhower as the first Republican president in 20 years; they did so in a landslide, while handing his party control of the House and Senate, if only by slim margins.

While voters did not speak with one voice—Democratic congressional candidates actually won more 350,000 more votes nationwide than Republicans—they demonstrated that the turmoil and upheaval in Asia and in the State Department was a potent political weapon for Eisenhower's party. While Truman had also suffered from mounting concerns about the nation's economy and charges of corruption in his administration, nothing hurt him and his party more than two years of relentless, vituperative attacks on their foreign policy, as well as their personal patriotism.

The Reluctant Mr. Eisenhower

Like many politicians of the era, President Eisenhower detested Joseph McCarthy and his tactics. But he was often no more willing to challenge McCarthy than anyone else, fearing that he would be branded soft on communism. During the 1952 presidential campaign, after conservative allies of McCarthy had attacked General George C. Marshall and questioned his patriotism, Eisenhower acted cravenly. When he campaigned in McCarthy's home state of Wisconsin, he deleted from his prepared speech language defending Marshall, who had been his mentor and friend.

Once he was president, Eisenhower again pulled his punches. Behind the scenes, he tried to undermine McCarthy by encouraging his opposition in the Senate and discouraging Republican Party officials from inviting him to party gatherings. Publicly, however, Eisenhower refused to denounce McCarthy and his demagoguery. In some ways, he shared McCarthy's goals, but detested his tactics. He also worried that by attacking McCarthy directly he would afford the Wisconsin senator a wider forum for his views and might also spark a destructive inner-party war. "I will not get into the gutter with that guy," he told his friends. Later, he remarked privately, "I just won't get into a pissing contest with that skunk."

As the most respected American of his time, the victor of World War II, and a man with unassailable credentials as a patriotic American, Eisenhower might have been the only man alive who could have challenged McCarthy early on and won. That he shrunk from this responsibility—for party unity or to preserve his own popularity—was in the words of historian James T. Patterson, "a major moral blot on his presidency."

The Least You Need to Know

- With his reckless charges about communists in government, Senator Joseph McCarthy waged war on civil liberties during the early 1950s.
- Many Republicans supported McCarthy's crusade out of their frustration over being exiled from the White House for almost 20 years.
- McCarthyism was only an extension of the anticommunist crusade that had begun with the Red Scare in 1919 and was revived in the mid-1940s with the investigations of the House Un-American Affairs Committee (HUAC).
- Future president Richard Nixon rose to prominence as a HUAC member, exposing the alleged communist and Soviet ties of former State Department official Alger Hiss during dramatic hearings in 1948.
- President Eisenhower detested Joseph McCarthy and his tactics but did not publicly condemn him for fear of giving McCarthy a larger platform for his views.

Chapter 12

Hollywood Sees Red

In This Chapter

- Hollywood propaganda during World War II and the Fifties
- Cold War films of the Fifties
- How television portrayed the Cold War
- TV news and the Cold War

The Cold War wasn't fought only in military and diplomatic circles. Hollywood and a new medium, television, joined the battle in the 1950s. During World War II, the American film industry had played an important role in building and maintaining public support for the war effort. Now that the war was over, the movie studios—some of them coerced by Washington politicians—enlisted in the Cold War.

Our old ally Russia, embodied by "Uncle Joe Stalin" became a sinister adversary, vilified in films throughout the 1950s. Popular television programs, as well as TV journalists, also played their part in fomenting American animosity toward the Soviets and the Chinese.

In this chapter, we learn about the way the popular culture, particularly movies and television, influenced American public opinion during the early years of the Cold War.

The Old Versus New Propaganda Film

During World War II, Hollywood loved Russia. Movie studios, prompted by Washington, turned out numerous movies, documentaries, and other propaganda pieces aimed at reassuring Americans that their new ally in the fight against Hitler could be trusted, even admired.

First came the government-sponsored propaganda. A 1942 film series produced by the U.S. Army, "Why We Fight," was directed by noted director Frank Capra and included the film, *The Battle of Russia.* It employed documentary footage of the battles of Moscow, Leningrad, and Stalingrad to portray the valor of the Red Army.

Russian Films

Early in the war, some Russian films were actually imported and edited or adapted for American consumption. For example, Oscar-winning director Lewis Milestone put his touch to the film *Our Russian Front* in 1942, designed to portray Russian soldiers as dependable, courageous allies. The film featured battle footage from Russia and was narrated by actor Walter Huston.

Paramount Studios brought the Russian film, *Stalingrad,* to the United States in 1943, releasing it under the new title, *The City that Stopped Hitler—Heroic Stalingrad.* Other Russian films brought to the United States during the war included these:

- *Heroes Are Made* (1942)
- *Guerilla Brigade* (1942)
- *Mashenka* (1942)
- *Red Flyer* (1942)
- *Natasha* (1943)
- *In the Rear of the Enemy* (1943)
- *Moscow Sky* (1944)
- *Zoya* (1944)
- *The Great Earth* (1944)
- *Girl No. 217* (1944)
- *Jubilee* (1944)

Quotes from the Cold

I, a Red guerilla, swear to my comrades in arms that I shall be brave, disciplined and merciless to the enemy. To the ends of my days I shall remain faithful to my country, my party, and my leader Stalin.

—Advertising for the 1942 film *Guerilla Brigade*

The films were selected, wrote the authors of *Red Scared! The Commie Menace in Propaganda and Popular Culture* (Chronicle, 2001), for their "ability to inculcate in Western eyes sympathy for the Russian plight, along with admiration for the doughtiness and hardy spirit of the Soviet people, thereby helping to sell the British and American publics on the Russian War Relief program, and its ilk."

Hollywood Propaganda

The U.S. movie industry was not content to allow the Russians to dominate the pro-Russian propaganda market. During the war, Hollywood turned out numerous pro-Russian movies, including …

- *Miss V from Moscow* (1942), the story of a female Soviet agent in occupied Paris who aids a downed Allied pilot by infiltrating the German Gestapo.
- *The Boy from Stalingrad* (1942), the story of a group of small-town boys who defeat the invading Germans.
- *The Three Russian Girls* (1944), a love story that portrays the valor of Russian soldiers.
- *Song of Russia* (1943), about a love affair between an American conductor and a Soviet peasant woman.
- *The North Star* (1943), a film about the wartime heroism of the workers in a Russian collective farm after their rural village—named North Star—is attacked by the Germans.

Perhaps the most notable, and eventually the most fiercely attacked, Hollywood contribution to the pro-Soviet war effort was *Mission to Moscow* (1943), adapted from the book of the same title by former U.S. Ambassador to the Soviet Union Joseph Davies. In the book, Davies had portrayed Stalin in a favorable light. The movie, however, burnished the Soviet dictator's image even more, characterizing Stalin as a humanitarian and statesman. "I believe, sir," the Davies character says to Stalin in the movie, "that history will record you as a great benefactor of mankind."

Cold Facts

In 1947, the House Un-American Activities Committee investigated the production of the Warner Brothers' movie, *Mission to Moscow*. Committee members demanded to know of studio chief Jack Warner why he had given the American public such a distorted, favorable image of Joseph Stalin. Warner denied that he had produced his propaganda film after coercion from President Roosevelt. Later, however, he claimed that Roosevelt had asked him to produce the movie. "I considered FDR's request an order," he wrote in 1965. The movie's screenwriter, Howard Koch, was later blacklisted largely because of his work on the film.

Hollywood Joins the Cold War

Hollywood got on the Cold War bandwagon in 1947 when the Motion Picture Alliance for the Preservation of American Ideals, invited the House Un-American Activities Committee (HUAC) to Los Angeles. The committee left no doubt where it stood in the Cold War, insisting that "coexistence is a myth and neutrality is impossible … anyone who is not *fighting* communism is *helping* communism." In all, about 1,500 actors, writers, directors, and other movie industry employees joined the committee, including John Wayne, Gary Cooper, Walt Disney, and Cecil B. De Mille.

During the war, Hollywood producers had not promoted the kind of pro-communist propaganda that HUAC members suspected. Like most government officials and journalists, movie producers had simply expressed their admiration for America's strong ally in the fight against Adolf Hitler. After all, it was Franklin Roosevelt and Harry Truman who enjoyed friendly personal relations with Stalin, not the movie producers.

None of this made much difference to the most strident and politically motivated HUAC members who saw the political advantage of stoking the public's fears about communist infiltration of the movie industry. HUAC member John Rankin of Mississippi was particularly strident on this point. He charged that communist conspirators who hoped to "overthrow the government" had established "headquarters in Hollywood," which was "the greatest hotbed of subversive activities in the United States."

This was not a view widely shared, even by some of HUAC's best friends in Hollywood. "I do not believe," actor Ronald Reagan told the committee, "the communists have ever at any time been able to use the motion-picture screen as a sounding board for their philosophy on their ideology." But what Hollywood soon became—intimidated by HUAC and its supporters—was a sounding board for the ideology of America's cold warriors.

Quotes from the Cold

Don't smear industrialists … don't smear the free enterprise system …. Don't smear success. Don't give your character—as a sign of villainy, as a damning characteristic—a desire to make money. … Don't ever use any lines about "the common man" or "the little people." It is not the American idea to be either "common" or "little."

—Ayn Rand, *Screen Guide of Americans* (1950), instructions for screenwriters, directors, and producers distributed widely by the Motion Picture Alliance

Cold War Films

Throughout the late 1940s and early 1950s, Hollywood produced a number of Cold War–inspired films. As described in the book, *Red Scared! The Commie Menace in Propaganda and Popular Culture*, and elsewhere, they included …

- *Conspirator*, a 1949 story about a woman, played by Elizabeth Taylor, who learns that her husband is a communist agent.
- *The Whip Hand*, released in 1951, is the bizarre story of Nazi scientists working for the communists to produce biological weapons in a secret lab in the backwoods of Wisconsin.
- *Invasion, U.S.A.*, from 1952, depicts the United States being overrun by Soviet troops after an atomic bomb attack.
- *Big Jim McLain* was a 1952 film starring John Wayne and James Arness as HUAC investigators. It became the most successful anticommunist film of the 1950s.
- *Pickup on South Street* was a 1953 film about an American man who is targeted for assassination by the Russians after he unknowingly steals a roll of microfilm that is meant for a Soviet agent.
- *Anastasia*, the 1956 Oscar-winning film that starred Ingrid Bergman and Helen Hayes. Bergman plays a woman who believes she is the long-lost, exiled grand duchess of Russia, daughter of the late Czar Nicholas.

Quotes from the Cold

The movie and television industries weren't the only ones to support the Cold War against the Soviet Union. Many American newspapers and magazines enthusiastically entered the fray, some of them turning their pages over to alarmist theories about the Red Menace. The following was typical:

> Many factors make Detroit a focal point of communist activity. Not the least of these is its geographical location. Only a narrow river separates the city from Canada, a foreign country. Ignoring the formalities of legal entrance, Red agents can shuttle back and forth, as rumrunners did during Prohibition days.
>
> —James Metcalfe in "Could the Reds Seize Detroit?" *Look* magazine, August 3, 1948

TV and the Cold Warriors

The burgeoning medium of television quickly got into the Cold War act in the early 1950s. Indeed, television may have exerted a greater influence on popular opinions about the Cold War and the Soviet Union than motion pictures.

In 1950, only 9 percent of American homes had a television. Three years later, 45 percent American families owned a TV. And by 1955, that number had jumped to 64.5 percent. That year, 10,000 people a day were buying their first television sets. It was clear that this new medium would soon supplant motion pictures, newspapers, and magazines as the most influential medium.

Eager to Please

The television networks, probably because their businesses were regulated to a great extent by the federal government, were eager to please Washington officials. They promptly joined the Cold War effort.

In August 1951, the NBC and CBS networks—hoping to make a patriotic statement about American technological prowess—erected large color television screens in West Berlin to counter Soviet influence at the World Festival of Youth in East Berlin.

The networks also worked closely with government officials in the early 1950s when they aired civil defense education programs. To reassure the American people of U.S. nuclear superiority, the Pentagon welcomed live network coverage of atomic tests in the Nevada desert.

During this period, official government statements were rarely challenged or countered. Controversy, in the words of one historian of Cold War culture, "had become a code word for trouble (rather than an inevitable feature of democratic dialogue) [and] official views were rarely and insufficiently challenged on television."

For example, two radio programs that, during the 1940s, had provided their listeners with lively debates on various issues, were deemed too controversial for television in the early 1950s. Network heads apparently thought that American democracy was too fragile to continue airing ABC's *America's Town Meeting* and NBC's *American Forum of the Air*. Both shows were dropped in the early 1950s.

Quotes from the Cold

If a citizen has to be bored to death, it is cheaper and more comfortable to sit at home and look at television than it is to go outside and pay a dollar for a [movie] ticket.

—President Dwight D. Eisenhower, avid TV watcher, 1953

As historian Stephen J. Whitfield observed, during this period "television thus fit—and contributed to—the proclivity to hang a giant Do No Disturb sign over the nation." In 1958, CBS commentator Edward R. Murrow called this mentality "a built-in allergy to unpleasant or disturbing information. … Television in the main is being used to distract, delude, amuse, and insulate us."

The Dulles Network

Typical of television's fawning, favorable treatment of government officials and their announcements was U.S. Secretary of State John Foster Dulles. During his seven years in President Eisenhower's cabinet, the television networks gave Dulles free airtime on 18 different occasions so that he could discuss his views of various foreign policy matters.

Not only did the networks afford him extraordinary coverage, they allowed him considerable control over the way they portrayed him. Film of his press conferences had to gain

State Department approval before it could be aired. Because the networks often had no bureaus in the regions Dulles discussed in his speeches and press conferences, little of a contradictory nature ever found its way into the homes of American TV viewers.

Because the television networks were so generous, non-analytical, and one-sided in their presentation of Dulles's views, the result was that American viewers viewed the world largely through his eyes. As television historian Erik Barnouw has noted, "A filmed press conference excerpt, or a newsman's report 'from a reliable source [often Dulles],' or a filmed statement by Dulles from a lectern at the edge of an airstrip, *became* the news." On these occasions, reporters rarely bothered to seek analysis or reaction from other sources about Dulles's policy pronouncements.

Cold Facts

Wisconsin Senator Joseph McCarthy was a beneficiary of television's early unwillingness to view U.S. government officials with adequate skepticism. The fact that McCarthy was a United States senator was often the only evidence the television networks—and other news mediums, for that matter—ever required before they aired his reckless charges about individuals that he alleged were communist agents.

Talking Head Journalism

Dulles did more than dominate the American airwaves with his constant presence. He actively discouraged television coverage of the internal and foreign affairs of communist nations such as the Soviet Union and China. In 1956, Dulles rejected a Chinese offer to exchange journalists. When China said it would allow U.S. reporters into the country provided the United States admitted Chinese journalists, Dulles declined.

CBS Cowed

William Worthy of the *Baltimore Afro-American* ignored the ban, and went to China, where he filed shortwave radio reports from Bejing that were picked up and aired by CBS. However, it did not take long for one of Dulles's aides to intimidate the president of CBS. After speaking with the State Department official, William Paley not only pledged that his viewers would thereafter be denied an independent view of Chinese politics; he also muzzled correspondent Eric Sevareid, who had wanted to criticize what historian Stephen J. Whitfield called "the administration's effort to maximize American ignorance." When CBS commentator Edward R. Murrow discussed the issue on his program, CBS rebuked him.

Murrow

Few television journalists of the era possessed Edward R. Murrow's courage and stature. His weekly *See It Now* program was the most popular public affairs program on television in the 1950s.

Despite his considerable courage, Murrow waited several years, until the spring of 1954, to take on Joseph McCarthy and the reckless way the Wisconsin senator had "attacked" communism in the federal government. During that time, other journalists had confronted McCarthy, including columnists Drew Pearson and Walter Lippmann and radio commentators Erik Sevareid, Howard K. Smith, Quincy Howe, and Elmer Davis, but television had not yet exposed his vicious demagoguery.

Cold Facts

Edward R. Murrow was one television journalist in the 1950s not intimidated by the federal government's Cold War effort to manipulate public information about world affairs. In 1956, Murrow interviewed Chinese leader Zhou En-lai (Chou En-lai, old spelling) on his *See It Now* program. The following year, he interviewed Marshal Tito, the communist leader of Yugoslavia. In 1957, CBS's *Face the Nation* again broke ranks when it interviewed Soviet leader Nikita Khruschev for an hour.

In March 1954, Murrow launched a full-scale attack on McCarthy during a 30-minute broadcast of *See It Now.* The CBS broadcaster filled his Sunday-night program with a series of damaging, embarrassing film clips that showed the Wisconsin Republican at his partisan worst. It was a brilliant move. Murrow did not so much attack McCarthy as allow McCarthy to attack himself. There on display was, as one Murrow biographer described it, a "litany of McCarthy's excesses."

While Murrow did not single-handedly destroy McCarthy, he did help turn the tide of public opinion against him. Within weeks, the Senate would begin the Army-McCarthy hearings that would be McCarthy's downfall. "Murrow's contribution to the defeat of the demagogue," wrote Murrow's biographer Joseph E. Persico, "was that he had had the courage to use television against McCarthy. He had taken a young medium, skittish over controversy, and plunged it into the hottest controversy of that era."

The Least You Need to Know

- During World War II, Hollywood helped the federal government craft a favorable image of the Soviet Union and its soldiers, who were fighting as allies of the United States against Nazi Germany.

- Once the Cold War began, Hollywood stoked Cold War fever by producing numerous films that raised fears of subversive domestic activities by pro-Soviet agents in the United States.
- The new medium of television was also a loyal soldier in the Cold War during the 1950s, reporting—unfiltered—many official foreign policy pronouncements by government officials.
- In one of the most significant departures from television's pro-Cold War role, CBS broadcaster Edward R. Murrow attacked Senator Joseph McCarthy on his television program, *See It Now*, in 1954.

Chapter 13

Early Life in the Shadow of the Bomb

In This Chapter

- John Foster Dulles and the new Cold War
- Eisenhower, Dulles and the "New Look" strategy
- Scrapping Truman's containment policy
- Joseph McCarthy's downfall

Life had changed for the American people. Our new president, Dwight D. Eisenhower, came into office vowing to end the Korean War and radically alter the country's military policies. Instead of massive expenditures for more and more troops, weapons, and supplies, Ike and his Secretary of State, John Foster Dulles, would introduce a "New Look" at national defense. That meant, in large part, greater reliance on U.S. nuclear superiority to coerce our adversaries into peaceful behavior.

It was a time of some anxiety over the ever-present threat of war with the Soviet Union, but it was also a carefree period. The 1950s were largely marked by unprecedented economic expansion and unbridled optimism about the nation's future.

"In that era of general good will and expanding influence," wrote journalist David Halberstam in *The Fifties* (Villard, 1993), "few Americans doubted the essential goodness of their society." But perhaps they should have. Some, of course, did and what they saw was a nation deeply divided along racial lines. Black citizens were denied basic civil rights and liberties, including voting and equal access to schools, jobs, public accommodations, and public transportation.

It was a time of great stability, but also a period of breathtaking social, political, and economic transformation. In this chapter, we examine the early years of President Eisenhower's administration.

The Devil and John Foster Dulles

Eisenhower's appointment of John Foster Dulles as secretary of state in 1953 surprised no one. Virtually every Republican in Washington regarded Dulles as the logical choice. Of Dulles, Eisenhower said to a friend: "There's only one man I know who has seen *more* of the world and talked with more people and *knows* more than he does, and that's *me.*"

Foreign Affairs Pedigree

A deeply religious and extremely conservative Presbyterian with a strong sense of moral virtue, Dulles was born in 1888 into the rarified world of international diplomacy. His grandfather, John Foster, had served as secretary of state to President Benjamin Harrison. His uncle Robert Lansing had held the same position under Woodrow Wilson. "Foster has been training for this job all his life," Eisenhower told his chief of staff.

A successful Wall Street lawyer, Dulles had years of foreign policy experience to his credit, earned during service in the state departments of presidents Wilson, Roosevelt, and Truman. In fact, he had negotiated virtually all of the postwar international treaties, including the United Nations charter.

Cold Facts

John Foster Dulles was not universally admired. Some of his critics thought him a pompous, humorless man, prone to pontificating. Some of them described his manner as "Dull, Duller, Dulles."

His critics, however, thought that Dulles viewed the world simplistically, in mostly black-and-white terms. Others thought him moralistic and self-righteous. To Dulles, however, two forces—good and evil—were struggling for world domination. America, he believed, had only noble aims and stood for freedom and justice. Conversely, the communist Soviet regime, aided by its clients in China, personified evil.

Containment Equals Appeasement

Despite having served three Democratic presidents, Dulles now believed that Truman's containment policies smacked of appeasement, believing the United States should never compromise in the name of peace with the Soviets or their puppet states. Dulles believed that General Douglas MacArthur had said it best when he maintained that there was "no substitute" for victory. Containment, Dulles maintained, meant that "we are not working, sacrificing, and spending in order to be able to live without this peril—but to be able to live with it, presumably forever."

President Dwight D. Eisenhower (center) surrounded by two of his foreign policy advisors: Secretary of State John Foster Dulles (left) and U.S. Ambassador to the Soviet Union Charles Bohlen (right).

(Courtesy of the Library of Congress)

The *Life* Article

In a celebrated article for *Life* magazine in May of 1952, Dulles argued that the only proper response to Soviet communism "is for the free world to develop the will and organize the means to retaliate instantly against open aggression by Red armies, so that [if an attack] occurred anywhere, we could and would strike back where it hurts, by means of our choosing." What Dulles meant, of course, was that the United States should consider using its nuclear arsenal in the fight against communism. But it was not enough, Dulles maintained, to simply secure the good behavior of the Soviets by means of a nuclear threat. Dulles wanted the free world, led by the United States, to undertake "the political offense" against communism by exchanging a containment policy for "liberation" of the "captive peoples" in the Soviet orbit.

Cold Facts

John Foster Dulles's younger brother Allen headed the Central Intelligence Agency (CIA) during the Eisenhower years and during the first year of John F. Kennedy's presidency.

Although Dulles made it clear he did not expect the United States to enforce his liberation policy with military might, he left many wondering exactly what other means the country might use to liberate the "captive" nations.

New Look and Massive Retaliation

A new national security and defense policy adopted in October 1953, less than 10 months into the new administration, characterized Eisenhower's posture toward the Soviet Union. Called by many, the "New Look" policy, it aimed to bolster the effectiveness of the U.S. military's response to communism while simultaneously reducing its cost.

In a dramatic speech to the Council on Foreign Policy in January 1954, Dulles explained that the administration envisioned a more effective and economical system of mutual security that placed "more reliance on deterrent power, and less dependence on local defensive power." That meant that the United States would no longer base its expensive containment policy on military forces spread throughout the globe, but would, instead, withdraw much of its foreign ground forces in favor of "massive retaliatory power."

Nukes Not Troops

Dulles was saying that if the Soviet Union invaded some Western European nation, the United States might just respond with nuclear weaponry. Dulles, in fact, hinted that even in localized military situations the United States might use nuclear weapons.

Dulles's so-called "massive retaliation" policy was really only one part of a national security policy based upon increased dependence on collective security—that is, defense agreements with other nations—more training and equipping of native troops, and a greater reliance on the U.S. Air Force and Navy to support the armies of those nations.

Quotes from the Cold

The press and the public read it either as the serious intent of the U.S. government to transform every border incident into a nuclear showdown, or else as a glaringly transparent bluff that would (by proving wholly inapplicable to the task of guiding revolutionary change in the fringe areas) serve to weaken the credibility of American policy everywhere.

—Townsend Hoopes, Dulles's biographer, on public reaction to the "New Look" policy from *The Devil and John Foster Dulles*

New Realities

"New Look" was the first major departure from the Truman-Acheson defense policy and was prompted by at least two major factors: The first was Eisenhower's desire to cuts costs. Using the threat of nuclear weapons was much less expensive than training and maintaining large armies around the world—especially considering the Soviets' large advantage in ground forces in Europe.

Second, Eisenhower and Dulles believed that the Soviet Union would soon begin placing more emphasis on nuclear missiles and moved decisively to achieve superiority in this area. By the 1950s, that effort proved very successful. The United States would enjoy a huge lead in nuclear missile development by the late 1950s.

Cold Facts

Driven by a desire for economy as much as by strategic military concerns, Eisenhower's "New Look" military policies ushered the United States into a new era of greater dependence on its nuclear arsenal. From 1953 to 1956, federal spending on national defense declined from $50.4 billion to $40.3 billion. By the end of the decade, annual expenditures for national defense were only $46.6 billion. And during the period 1953 to 1959, the army reduced its forces by 671,000 men and women.

Critics of "New Look" would charge that the new policy did not give the United States enough flexibility to respond to regional conflicts. Clearly, the United States could not threaten to attack with nuclear weapons every time its interests were threatened in some remote part of the world. If so, those threats, if not acted upon, would soon become hollow and the U.S. policy would appear ineffectual. Indeed, as the outbreak of hostilities in Indochina and the Middle East would soon prove, that criticism was sometimes valid.

Cold Facts

Eisenhower and others argued that "New Look" would give the country's defense policies "more bang for the buck." Critics charged, however, that the policy might be met by the Soviet response of more "rubble for the ruble."

McCarthy Crashes

After almost four years of demagoguery, Joseph McCarthy's time was up. It wasn't that the country was tired of the congressional hunt for domestic subversives or that it did not believe McCarthy when he charged that communists had infiltrated the U.S. government. What Americans reacted to were McCarthy's bad manners.

Senators, especially, finally had enough of his recklessness and his antics. In August 1954, the Senate appointed a special committee to consider disciplinary proceedings against McCarthy. Members did not investigate his witch-hunting tactics or his veracity. Only considered were violations of Senate decorum, that is, rules against questioning the integrity or motives of another senator. During the Army-McCarthy hearings, McCarthy had done this with reckless abandon, calling the committee's chairman, Republican Arthur Watkins, "stupid," and labeling the entire committee "handmaidens of the Communist party." By November 1954, the special Senate committee recommended McCarthy's censure and the Senate voted 67 to 22 to censure the Wisconsin Republican.

Cold Facts

At times, during the Senate hearings on his conduct, Senator Joseph McCarthy seemed determined to ensure that the Senate would formally condemn him. He often went out of his way to personally insult committee members. He called J. William Fulbright of Arkansas "half-bright," said that Ralph Flanders of Vermont was "senile," and charged that Robert Hendrickson of New Jersey was the only person who ever lived so long "without brains or guts." He also accused Guy Gillette of Iowa of "dishonesty."

McCarthy never recovered from the unmasking at the hands of his Senate colleagues. Senator Clinton Anderson of New Mexico accompanied a group of oil men to McCarthy's office several months later and recalled that "during the discussion, McCarthy, sallow-faced and haggard, swigged from a bottle of whisky at his side."

For all the damage McCarthyism inflicted on its instigator, the damage to the nation was as severe. The paranoia he, Nixon, and HUAC had fanned contributed to the nation's hard-line Far Eastern policy and prevented future presidents from exploiting the rift between China and the Soviet Union. Partly because of the divisive events of the 1950s, presidents Kennedy and Johnson would feel the need to wage war in Southeast Asia for fear of being labeled soft on communism. But McCarthy would not live to see the damage he had helped to cause. He died of hepatitis in May 1957, a broken and, aptly, discredited man.

The Least You Need to Know

- President Eisenhower's secretary of state, John Foster Dulles, helped persuade Eisenhower to take a hard line toward the Soviet Union in the 1950s.
- Dulles believed that Harry Truman's containment policies had been akin to appeasement of communist regimes.

- Dulles and Eisenhower altered U.S. defense policy in 1953 with a program known as "New Look" that stressed nuclear power over the threat of conventional military forces. Dulles indirectly threatened the Soviets with "massive retaliation" should they seek to extend their reach deeper into Western Europe or elsewhere.
- Eisenhower's reliance on nuclear weapons to deter Soviet aggression was motivated as much by budgetary concerns as by strategic considerations.
- The U.S. Senate in 1954 formally condemned the communist-hunting Wisconsin senator, Joseph McCarthy, for his reckless actions. McCarthy died 1957.

Chapter 14

Ike and the Spread of the Cold War

In This Chapter

- Fighting the Soviets in the Third World
- Ike challenges the Soviets in Egypt
- The Cold War goes into space
- Communism in Cuba; Castro comes to power

President Eisenhower and Secretary of State John Foster Dulles weren't concerned only with the spread of the Soviet Union's influence into Western Europe. They also feared that communism might work its way into the Third World, or developing nations, where the Soviets were befriending colonial states straining under domination by American allies such as Britain, France, Belgium, Portugal, and the Netherlands. And indeed, the Soviets did have designs on these parts of the world—not simply for the sake of pulling them into the Soviet orbit, but to prevent them from becoming allies of the United States.

It was in the Third World that the United States increasingly employed the Central Intelligence Agency (CIA) to wage war against the Soviet Union. While the CIA was not legally permitted to exceed its congressionally mandated role of gathering foreign intelligence, Eisenhower allowed the CIA to do much more. On several occasions, he used CIA operatives to prop up faltering U.S. allies, as well as to overthrow its adversaries.

In this chapter, we look at how the Cold War began to spread around the world during the 1950s.

Cold War Comes to the Third World

Struggling against Soviet influence in the *Third World* wasn't an easy proposition. In the early 1950s, there were simply too many countries and regions that appeared threatened. Eisenhower's "New Look" policy precluded large military deployments to handle each and every hotspot. That's where the CIA entered the picture. Using spies and foreign operatives to influence or overthrow foreign governments was a relative inexpensive way to assert U.S. policy. It had the added benefit of keeping the public, Congress, and much of the world in the dark about what the United States was doing in these countries.

Cold Words

Third World is the term used to describe the underdeveloped nations of Asia, Africa, and Latin America. These are the world's poorest countries and they usually have the world's highest rates of population growth, disease, and illiteracy and often have very unstable forms of government, in many cases dominated by the military.

Iran

In the summer of 1953, the CIA conducted the first covert operation of the Eisenhower presidency in response to growing unrest in Iran. The trouble began in May, when Iranian Prime Minister Mohammed Mossadeq requested Eisenhower's help to resist a boycott of Iranian oil by a group of international oil companies. The oil companies had initiated their boycott after Iran nationalized British oil interests in the country in 1951.

Implicit in Mossadeq's request was this threat: If he did not receive U.S. assistance, he might have no choice but to seek help from the Soviet Union. Unfortunately for Mossadeq, he did not enjoy the best of relations with the National Security Council, which had already advised Eisenhower to seek his overthrow, fearing that the Iranian leader might already be making overtures to Moscow.

In response to Mossadeq's cable, Eisenhower issued a veiled threat of U.S. intervention and urged the Iranian government to solve the problem itself. Mossadeq ignored the warning, dissolved the country's parliament, and opened Iran's doors to a Soviet aid mission.

Cold Facts

The Central Intelligence Agency (CIA) was created in 1947 to gather foreign intelligence for the president and the National Security Council. In 1949, Congress gave the CIA special powers: The director could spend money without public accountability and the size of its workforce could be kept secret. To safeguard the American public, however, the agency was given no domestic police authority.

The CIA grew quickly during the 1950s as the Cold War spread to the Third World. In 1952, it had a budget of $82 million and more than 2,800 full-time employees, not counting another 3,100 "contract" workers overseas. Its foreign stations had grown from an initial 7 to 47 by the early 1950s.

In August 1953, a CIA-backed coup restored the country's pro-Western shah, Muhammed Reza Pahlavi, to power. To ensure his continued support, the United States gave the shah $85 million in economic aid (and much more in subsequent years). In return, Iran gave American oil companies a 40 percent interest in the country's oil operations.

Cold Facts

Soviet leader Joseph Stalin's death in 1953, just after President Eisenhower took office, might have led to improved relations between the Soviet Union and the United States. The new Soviet premier, Georgi Malenkov, actually made attempts to ease tensions between the two countries as he focused more on his country's internal problems.

Eisenhower was initially open to improved diplomatic relations, but cooled to the idea after Secretary of State John Foster Dulles persuaded him a Soviet peace offer was really an attempt to interfere with U.S. efforts to rearm West Germany and admit the country into NATO. Thus, Malenkov's peace initiative—and, with it, any chance to an early end to the Cold War—died shortly after it was born.

Guatemala

Eisenhower's success with the CIA operation in Iran emboldened him to try covert operations in other regions of the Third World that were "threatened" by communism. His next opportunity came in June of 1954 in Guatemala, where the country's extreme poverty made it ripe for Soviet influence.

In 1953, the country's new, popularly elected president, Jacobo Arbenz Guzmán, tried to alleviate his country's poverty when he imposed a land reform program that aimed to more equitably distribute property ownership (70 percent of the land was held by 2 percent of the people). But Arbenz's program quickly ran afoul of the U.S.-owned United Fruit Company, one of the country's largest landowners.

As was often the case, the United States sided with those who were perceived as enemies of the common man—in this case, the nation's wealthy landowners—and against those trying to enact reforms. When the government tried to expropriate 234,000 acres of United Fruit Company's land, the company protested that the government's compensation was insufficient.

When company officials petitioned the Eisenhower administration for assistance, their pleas fell on willing ears. Dulles, who had once performed legal work for the company, urged Eisenhower to intervene out of fears that domestic communist support for Arbenz's programs meant that the Guatemalan leader was sympathetic to the Soviet Union.

Fearing the spread of communism from Guatemala throughout Central America, Eisenhower told his Cabinet, "My God, just think what it would mean to us if Mexico went communist." Eisenhower ordered a CIA plan to overthrow Arbenz. In June 1954 a force led by U.S. ally Carlos Enrique Castillo began marching toward Guatemala City, supported by gunfire from CIA-piloted aircraft. By July, Arbenz was forced to flee Guatemala and control of the country fell to Castillo, who subjected the country to three years of oppressive, brutal rule.

In 1953, President Dwight D. Eisenhower began using the resources of the Central Intelligence Agency to combat Soviet influence in the Third World.

(Courtesy of the Library of Congress)

Indochina

Quotes from the Cold

Step by step, we are moving into this war in Indochina, and I am afraid we will move to a point from which there will be no return.

—Mississippi Senator John Stennis, Senate speech, February 9, 1954

The Korean War was barely over (the armistice was signed in June of 1953) before Eisenhower had another Asian communist threat on his hands. This time, the place was Indochina, the region of Southeast Asia comprised of Vietnam, Cambodia, and Laos. In the spring of 1954, the eight-year war between the communist Vietminh and French colonialist forces came to a head at the French garrison of Dien Bien Phu in northern Vietnam.

For years, the United States had been giving substantial financial support to the French in their fight against the indigenous communist forces. As in Iran and Guatemala, there was little evidence of a direct attempt by the Soviet Union to take over Indochina, but French warnings about the dire communist threat more than earned the American dollars needed to finance the war.

For years, U.S. officials had hoped France would eventually prevail without further U.S. involvement. But when the Vietminh succeeded in pinning down the French forces at Dien Bien Phu, it appeared that U.S. intervention might be the only way the French could hope to prevail.

At first, Eisenhower was agreeable to American involvement. But over time, he came to realize that U.S. air strikes would only postpone the inevitable French defeat. When congressional leaders made it clear that they would not support unilateral U.S. military involvement in Indochina, Dulles went about trying to assemble a U.S.-British-French coalition, but ultimately failed.

In May 1954, the French garrison finally collapsed. It was a disastrous defeat for the French that soon resulted in their full-scale retreat from Indochina. This was not what the U.S. government had wanted. Financing the war was seen as the primary means to keep the United States from being dragged into the fight. Now, it seemed certain that the United States would be required to take up, in some form, at least, where the French had left off.

The Geneva Conference

At the 1954 Geneva Conference, the United States, China, Britain, France, and the Soviets met to discuss the political future of Indochina. At the conference, the Vietminh leader, Ho Chi Minh, demanded a united, independent Vietnam. Pressured by the Soviets and the Chinese, he reluctantly settled for less. Vietnam would be split at the seventeenth parallel, and controlled by two different governments, in anticipation of countrywide elections in 1956.

Cold Facts

When the French left Indochina, the United States took over the war, supporting the U.S.-allied government of South Vietnam. From 1954 to 1959, U.S. government assistance to South Vietnam totaled $1.2 billion. That amounted to about 80 percent of the country's military spending and almost half of its nonmilitary expenditures.

The United States, however, refused to endorse the accords. Dulles, instead of signing the agreement, negotiated the Southeast Asian Treaty Organization (its signatories were the United States, Britain, France, Australia, New Zealand, the Philippines, Pakistan, and Thailand). It was a weak and loosely organized mutual defense treaty that bound the member nations to nothing more than consultation in the event of an armed attack. Years later, however, it would serve as the constitutional basis for much of the American military involvement in Southeast Asia.

Eisenhower and Dulles did not completely reject the Geneva accords. The two years leading up to the national elections (which the United States eventually undermined) would at least give the CIA and other American operatives time to influence the ultimate outcome and prevent a communist takeover.

Cold Facts

Following the French retreat from Indochina in 1954, the CIA entered the picture. Heading up the U.S. effort in Vietnam was Colonel Edward Lansdale. A personable and colorful figure, Lansdale enjoyed a reputation as the wily and resourceful operative who had most recently helped Philippine leader Ramón Magsaysay defeat the communist rebels in his country. In Vietnam, Lansdale, a former advertising executive, would eventually become famous for his war of dirty tricks and sabotage against the Vietminh. (Within a few years, Lansdale's many exploits would be chronicled in two novels loosely based upon his activities—Graham Greene's *The Quiet American* (Viking) in 1956 and *The Ugly American* (W.W. Norton) by William J. Lederer and Eugene Burdick in 1958.)

Ike's Doctrine

It seemed that every time Eisenhower and Dulles turned around, the Soviets were applying their influence to some new part of the world. In the summer of 1956, it was Egypt's turn, when President Gamal Abdel Nasser sought Soviet assistance in his war against Israel. The Soviets were more than happy to help, sending military supplies through their client Czechoslovakia.

Eisenhower and Dulles responded by withdrawing American support for one of Nasser's pet projects, the Aswan High Dam. Nasser quickly retaliated by announcing that he would nationalize the Suez Canal and use the proceeds to finance the dam's construction.

Worried that Nasser might use the dispute as an excuse for greater Soviet influence in the Middle East, Eisenhower went before Congress in January 1957 to request authority to send American troops "to secure and protect" the region from "overt armed aggression from any nation controlled by international communism." He also asked for $200 million a year in economic assistance for countries in the region that might be susceptible to Soviet influence.

"If power-hungry communists should either falsely or correctly estimate that the Middle East is inadequately defended, they might be tempted to use open measures of armed attack," Eisenhower told the Congress. "If so, that would start a chain of circumstances which would almost surely involve the United States in military action." Congress, generally agreeable to Eisenhower's request, approved a resolution stating that the United States was "prepared" to use its armed forces if the president "determines the necessity thereof."

Quotes from the Cold

If the Middle East is to continue its geographic role of uniting rather than separating East and West; if its vast economic resources are to serve the well-being of the peoples there, as well as that of others; and if its cultures and religions and their shrines are to be preserved for the uplifting of the spirits of the peoples, then the United States must make more evident its willingness to support the independence of the freedom-loving nations of the area.

—President Dwight D. Eisenhower, speech to Congress, "The Eisenhower Doctrine," January 5, 1957

While the Eisenhower Doctrine of protecting the Middle East from Soviet influence succeeded to a point, it failed to provide any permanent solution to the disputes between the Arabs and the Israelis. As world events over subsequent decades would prove, it was the regional conflict between Arabs and Israelis—not Soviet influence—that posed the greatest threat to peace in the region.

Sputnik and the Missile Gap

After Stalin's death in 1953, Nikita Khrushchev rose to power as first secretary of the Soviet Communist Party. Khrushchev proved a different leader than Stalin or Malenkov. At the 1956 All-Union Party Congress, he officially began the process of "destalinization," when he denounced Stalin's "megalomania," as well as his foreign policies. "During Stalin's leadership," he said, "our peaceful relations with other nations were often threatened, because one-man decisions could cause, and often did cause, great complications." Khrushchev restored many civil liberties, reined in the Soviet secret police, and closed many concentration and forced labor camps.

In Washington, officials hoped that this meant the dawn of a new era in U.S.-Soviet relations. For a while, it appeared that this might be possible. That was, however, until the Soviet Union launched a beach-ball-size satellite into orbit.

Sputnik

On October 4, 1957, the Soviets put *Sputnik I* into orbit. It weighed 184 pounds, six times as heavy as Vanguard, the satellite the United States was planning to launch. Next came the November 3 launch of *Sputnik II*, this time a 1,120-pound satellite carrying a dog named Laika with medical instruments attached to its body.

Quotes from the Cold

Oh little Sputnik
With made-in-Moscow beep, You
tell the world it's a Commie sky
And Uncle Sam's asleep.

—Poem composed by Democratic Governor G. Mennen Williams of Michigan in 1956

Quotes from the Cold

Never before had so small and so harmless an object created such consternation.

—Daniel J. Boorstin, *The Americans: The Democratic Experience* (Random House, 1973)

In response, the U.S. Navy invited television cameras to broadcast the launch of its Vanguard satellite on December 6. The test was an embarrassing disaster. The rocket sputtered 2 feet off the ground and crashed. Some critics jokingly called it "Flopnik" and "Stay-Putnik." The United States finally succeed in putting the 36-pound Explorer in orbit on February 1, 1958.

The Soviets' success with both Sputniks shocked the American people. They asked how such a seemingly backward, unsophisticated nation could develop something so technologically advanced. But the more important question was: Did *Sputnik* signal that Khrushchev was truthful the previous year when he boasted that his nation had also developed an intercontinental ballistic missile? To many, it was very plausible.

Government-sponsored reports quickly recommended a number of responses. One, commissioned by the National Security Council, called for a large increase in military spending and for development of bomb shelters. Another report more ominously suggested that the Soviet Union had pulled ahead of the United States in the development of nuclear missiles.

Missile Gap?

Out of *Sputnik* developed the notion, nurtured by Democrats and some Republicans, that a dangerous "missile gap" in favor of the Soviet Union had developed. (This issue would become a major feature of the 1960 presidential campaign, with Senator John F. Kennedy leveling just that charge at Vice President Richard Nixon.)

The truth was that while the Soviets did have an advantage when it came to the thrust capacity of their rockets, they were far behind the United States in the development of useable nuclear warheads. Contrary to Khrushchev's assertion, they did not yet possess intercontinental ballistic missiles.

Quotes from the Cold

The military power of the United States is falling behind that of the Soviet Union: We are on the wrong end of the missile gap.
—Columnist Walter Lippmann, 1960

Because of secret surveillance flights by U-2 planes, Eisenhower knew the truth. But he believed that he could not reveal what he knew—and thus absorbed the political attacks—because he feared compromising the nation's intelligence collection methods. (Unbeknownst to Eisenhower, the Soviets knew about the U-2 flights.) As best he could, Eisenhower also resisted the urge to greatly increase defense spending. "Look," he told his Cabinet, "I'd like to know what's on the other side of the moon, but I won't pay to find out this year."

Eisenhower's primary concession to his critics was to accelerate the U.S. missile program, an act that only increased the missile gap in favor of the United States and that, ironically, diminished the value of *Sputnik* to the Soviet Union. Later, some historians would argue that the resulting missile imbalance in favor of the United States would prompt Khrushchev to place ballistic missiles in Cuba in 1962, an act that brought the world to the brink of nuclear war.

Castro Takes Cuba

New Year's Day 1959 brought about cataclysmic change in Cuba. On that day, the longtime revolutionary Fidel Castro succeeded in overthrowing the government of the American-backed dictator Fulgencio Batista. Since 1934, Bastista had ruled Cuba and enjoyed official U.S. government support, primarily because he allowed U.S. business interests wide latitude in his country. Like most Latin American countries, Cuba was poor and the American business had done nothing but exploit the Cuban people and hasten the day of the ultimate revolution.

Like Guatemala's Jacobo Arbenz Guzmán, Castro (unlike Arbenz, he was not elected) immediately set about enacting radical reforms. He instituted land reform, fought against organized crime, increased education spending, and worked to improve housing conditions and medical care for the poor citizens of Cuba.

Communist?

It was the land reform that most troubled American business interests and, therefore, the Eisenhower administration. Of course, Eisenhower was also troubled by the way Castro had executed hundreds of Batista's supporters. Therefore, while the United States initially recognized the Cuban government, Eisenhower refused to meet with Castro when he visited the United States in 1959. And he also refused to give Castro the economic assistance he wanted to fully enact his reforms.

Castro was no communist, but Eisenhower and his advisors feared that he was dangerously close. They were particularly alarmed by the nationalization of private industries and foreign interests, as well as the economic agreement Castro signed with the Soviets in February 1960.

Soviet Alliance

In March 1960, Eisenhower approved a CIA plan to overthrow Castro by training a group of Cuban émigrés to invade the country and lead a revolt against the Cuban leader. When Castro learned of the plan, he moved more decidedly into the Soviet orbit. By May, he had established diplomatic relations with the Soviets. By that summer, the Soviet Union would become Cuba's number-one economic and military sponsor.

The Soviet Union's sphere of influence was now at America's back door, and Eisenhower responded by turning up the heat. As Castro seized American investments on the island, Eisenhower slashed Cuba's sugar quota by 700,000 tons (later he would cut off imports of Cuban sugar entirely for the first three months of 1961). In October 1960, Eisenhower embargoed all U.S. exports to Cuba (except for medical and emergency supplies) and he mined the area around the U.S. naval base at Guantanamo, vowing that the United States would never permit Cuba to take the base (Indeed he didn't. In fact, as recently as 2002, American officials were using the base to house and interrogate terrorists and others suspected of supporting the September 11, 2001 attacks on New York and Washington.)

In early 1961, after Castro delivered a bitter denunciation of the United States during a UN speech, Eisenhower severed all diplomatic ties to Cuba. As Eisenhower left office, the audacious plan to invade Cuba and overthrow Castro was still in the planning stages. One of Ike's final acts in office was to tell the new president about the plan.

Quotes from the Cold

[The United States] never asked us about our problems, not even to express sympathy or because of their responsibility in creating [Cuba's] problems. They never asked us how many died of starvation in our country, how many were suffering from tuberculosis, how many were unemployed. No. Did they ever express solidarity regarding our needs? Never. Every conversation we had with the representatives of the U.S. government centered around the telephone company, the electricity company, and the problem of the land owned by U.S. companies. The question they asked was how we were going to pay. Naturally, the first thing they should have asked was not "How?" but "With what?

—Fidel Castro, speech to United Nations, September 26, 1960.

Like Vietnam and a host of other hot spots around the world, the Cold War and all its problems would soon belong to John F. Kennedy.

The Least You Need to Know

- Beginning in 1953, the Eisenhower administration began to combat perceived or threatened communist gains in Iran, Guatemala, Indochina, and other Third World countries by ordering covert operations carried out by the CIA.
- In 1957, motivated by fear of Soviet influence in Egypt, Eisenhower articulated the "Eisenhower Doctrine," which called for greater U.S. involvement in the region, but it did little to address the real cause for unrest in the Middle East—the Israel-Arab conflict.
- The successful launch of the Soviet satellite *Sputnik* in October 1957 caused great alarm among the American people and sparked fears of a "missile gap" favoring the USSR.
- As Eisenhower left office, the Soviet Union had extended its reach deep into the Western Hemisphere when it established strong military and economic ties with Cuba and its revolutionary leader, Fidel Castro.

Chapter 15

Charisma and Camelot

In This Chapter

- The Kennedys come to power
- JFK grapples with Cuba, Laos, and Berlin
- Kennedy and Khruschev meet in Vienna
- To the brink of nuclear war over missiles in Cuba
- The U.S. presence in Vietnam increases
- Diem is assassinated in Vietnam

A new president and a new approach to governing. That's what Americans believed the young, charismatic John F. Kennedy would bring to the White House in January 1961. After eight years of the grandfatherly Eisenhower, many Americans were excited about the possibilities of an administration led by the youngest man ever elected president.

What they didn't know, however, was that Kennedy's view of the world wasn't all that different from Eisenhower's. While his style of governing might have been more relaxed, Kennedy was—like the president before him—a fervent anticommunist Cold Warrior with a deep distrust of the Soviet Union. Those who hoped the new administration might open up possibilities for greater cooperation with the Soviets would soon be disappointed. From Berlin to Cuba to Vietnam, relations with the Soviets would grow only colder and more dangerous.

Jack, Bobby, and Teddy

They were charmed and tragic all at once. The story of the Kennedys has more tragedy, glamour, heroism, and scandal than that of any other American family. For all their foibles, the Kennedys are still regarded by most Americans as the closest thing to royalty that the country has ever produced. And considering the travails of the British royal family in recent years, the comparison may be apt.

JFK

John F. Kennedy was born May 29,1917, into one of Boston's most prominent families. His father, Joseph, had transformed the family's lucrative liquor trade into a business dynasty that included banking, movies, and real estate. His mother, Rose, was the daughter of two-time Boston mayor John "Honey Fitz" Fitzgerald.

Kennedy was a sickly but popular child (he was one of nine Kennedy children) who went to Harvard University and managed to turn his senior honors thesis into a best-selling book, *Why England Slept*, a study of Britain's refusal to take seriously the threat of Nazism in the 1930s.

During World War II, Kennedy volunteered for the U.S. Navy and, as commander of a patrol boat, PT-109, became a war hero. In May 1943, Kennedy's craft was struck and sunk by a Japanese destroyer in the Pacific. The young commander's heroic actions resulted in his crew's rescue.

To his father, John Kennedy was not the son destined for politics. Those hopes had originally been invested in older brother, Joseph. But when Joseph died in World War II, the hopes and dreams of the father fell to the second son, John.

In 1946, John Kennedy was well on his way to making history when he was elected to Congress from one of Boston's poorest districts. A Democrat, Kennedy championed low-cost housing for war veterans and opposed efforts to restrain organized labor. But he was not always a loyal Democrat. In the early 1950s, he joined Republicans in their attacks on President Harry Truman for the "loss" of China to communism.

Quotes from the Cold

[Kennedy] had little ideology beyond anti-Communism and faith in active, pragmatic government. And he had less emotion. What he had was an attitude, a way of taking on the world, substituting intelligence for ideas or idealism, questions for answers. What convictions he did have, on nuclear proliferation or civil rights or the use of military power, he was often willing to suspend, particularly if that avoided confrontation with Congress or the risk of being called soft.

—Richard Reeves, *President Kennedy: Profile of Power*

Elected to the Senate in 1953, Kennedy never distinguished himself as one of the Senate's harder working members. But he was usually well-informed on the issues and, during the early 1950s, paid considerable attention to the U.S. effort to assist the French in their war against the communist Vietminh in Indochina.

President John F. Kennedy became president just as tensions between the United States and the Soviet Union were heating up in Cuba, Berlin, Laos, and Vietnam.

(Courtesy of the Library of Congress)

Owing to his less-than-inspiring Senate record, Kennedy's bid for the Democratic vice presidential nomination in 1956 was unsuccessful. That effort, however, whetted his appetite for the White House. In 1960, aided by his father's considerable personal wealth, he waged a spirited, successful campaign for his party's presidential nomination, beating fellow senators Lyndon B. Johnson of Texas and Hubert H. Humphrey of Minnesota. Kennedy chose Johnson as his running mate and the pair defeated the Republican nominee, Vice President Richard Nixon, in the closest presidential election of the twentieth century.

RFK

Kennedy's younger brother Robert had been one of his closest advisors since 1953 when he had managed John's successful Senate campaign. A lawyer, Robert was counsel to the Senate subcommittee, chaired by Joseph McCarthy, that had investigated alleged communist infiltration of the U.S. government. Later, in 1957, he achieved some notoriety when he became chief counsel to a Senate subcommittee investigating labor rackets.

When John F. Kennedy ran for president in 1960, Robert was again his brother's campaign manager and his closest political advisor. Over the objections of some who cried nepotism, President Kennedy appointed Robert U.S. attorney general. In that position, Kennedy eventually distinguished himself as an outspoken advocate of civil rights.

To many, Robert Kennedy was as charismatic as his more famous brother, and to some, perhaps more so. He was passionate, emotional and combative—in many ways the polar opposite of his brother. And it was these qualities that would eventually attract so many voters to him when he later entered the U.S. Senate, representing New York.

Quotes from the Cold

Because he wanted to get things done, because he was often impatient and combative, because he felt simply and cared deeply, he made his share of mistakes, and enemies. He was a romantic and an idealist, and he was also prudent, expedient, demanding and ambitious. Yet the insights he brought to politics—insights earned in a labor of self-education that only death could stop—led him to see power not as an end in itself but as the means of redeeming the powerless.

—Arthur M. Schlesinger, Jr., *Robert Kennedy and His Times* (Houghton Mifflin, 1978)

At first, a strong supporter of his brother's foreign policies—he was, perhaps, a more fierce anticommunist than JFK—he would later distinguish himself as one of the most vociferous opponents of U.S. policy in Vietnam.

Teddy

The youngest Kennedy son was Edward Moore "Teddy" Kennedy. Like his older brother Robert, Teddy studied law, and he worked as an assistant district attorney in Massachusetts before being elected to the U.S. Senate in 1962, the year after his brother's election as president. All at once, the Kennedys were the most prominent political family in America. One brother was president, another attorney general, and another a U.S. senator. The possibilities for the Kennedy family appeared bright and limitless. But all that was before events in Cuba, Berlin, Vietnam, and Dallas intervened.

Crisis Management

President Kennedy didn't have much time to enjoy the trappings of his new office before world events began to close in around him. Suddenly, the Cold War threatened to get much hotter. Americans realized that their rivalry with the Soviets might soon turn into nuclear war.

Cuba

Kennedy inherited the Cuban problem from Dwight Eisenhower, upon whose authority plans for an American-backed, CIA-sponsored invasion had been planned. Later, Kennedy would admit that he had not asked enough questions and had put too much blind faith in the skill and judgment of the CIA and the Joint Chiefs of Staff.

On April 17, 1961, barely three months into office, Kennedy gave the go-ahead. But the invasion was a disaster. Castro's forces promptly routed the 1,400 CIA-trained Cuban exiles as they landed at the Bay of Pigs. Sensing the mission's inevitable failure, Kennedy did not order the U.S. military to intervene on behalf of the Cuban invaders and the invasion collapsed after only three days of fighting.

The Bay of Pigs was a humiliating defeat for the new president. Far from driving Castro from power, Kennedy had helped strengthen the ties between Cuba and the Soviet Union and, thus, made the Cuban leader all the more powerful at home and abroad.

Cold Facts

Unlike so many political leaders in times of crisis, President Kennedy did not publicly blame the CIA or the Pentagon for the Bay of Pigs debacle. "There's an old saying that victory has a hundred fathers and defeat is an orphan," he told reporters. "I am the responsible officer of the government." Privately, however, he was outraged at how the CIA and the military had let him down. "All my life I've known better than to depend on the experts," he said to an aide. "How could I have been so stupid, to let them go ahead?"

In the invasion, 114 men had died and 1,189 had been captured by Castro's forces. In December 1962, Kennedy bought their release with $53 million in food and medical supplies.

Laos

Barely over the humiliation of the Bay of Pigs, Kennedy's attention was diverted to another communist hotspot—this one in Laos, halfway around the world in Southeast Asia. Although supposedly neutral under terms of the 1954 Geneva Accords, the government of Prince Souvanna Phouma had for years received covert military assistance from the United States, about $300 million funneled mostly through the CIA. An outbreak of civil war in 1959 attracted the attention of U.S. and Soviet officials, who saw the conflict as an opportunity to achieve dominance in the region.

Quotes from the Cold

The **Southeast Asia Treaty Organization** (SEATO) was the collective security organization formed in 1954 by Australia, France, Great Britain, New Zealand, Pakistan, the Philippines, Thailand, and the United States. Its primary objective was to protect Southeast Asia from communist aggression. SEATO, however, proved to be an ineffectual association and was disbanded in 1974.

By the time Kennedy took office, both countries had taken sides and were supplying the opposing factions with military assistance, although the Viet Cong–backed Pathet Lao were gaining ground. In a meeting with Eisenhower and his advisors before taking office, Kennedy was told by outgoing Secretary of State Christian Herter that the United States was duty bound to intervene if Laos requested assistance under terms of the *Southeast Asia Treaty Organization* (SEATO) treaty. Eisenhower agreed.

In late March 1961, after Pathet Lao troops appeared to be sweeping the country, Kennedy ordered the Seventh Fleet on alert for possible deployment to the waters off Thailand. And on March 23, he went before a national television audience to threaten American military action in pursuit of a "neutral," as opposed to a "free," Laos.

If Kennedy's rhetoric was resolute, his true intentions were less so. While it was not entirely clear exactly what he intended in defense of Laotian neutrality—and Kennedy wanted it that way—his message was designed to intimidate the Kremlin and the Viet Cong, while also sending a strong political message to the Congress and the American people.

Events early in his administration might have drawn Kennedy toward military intervention in Laos; that is, until the Bay of Pigs made him far more skeptical of the military advice he received from the Pentagon. It was the Bay of Pigs disaster in mid-April—enthusiastically advocated and its success virtually guaranteed by Kennedy's military advisors—that badly shook Kennedy's faith in the Joint Chiefs of Staff. "Based on the Bay of Pigs," Robert Kennedy recalled, the president "started asking questions that were not asked at the Bay of Pigs." And he was not happy with the answers he received. After consulting congressional leaders, Kennedy was persuaded that a foray into Laos would be ill-advised at best, and a calamity at worst.

By May of 1961, U.S. and Soviet representatives agreed to support a cease-fire in Laos and began work in Geneva on a negotiated settlement. By the fall, the negotiations produced a neutrality agreement for Laos. By early 1962, the agreement would still not be implemented and the fighting would continue. In May of 1962, after the Pathet Lao appeared ready to thrust across the Thai border, Kennedy raised the stakes in an attempt to force compliance with the neutrality accord.

Prodded by U.S. officials, Thailand requested assistance under terms of SEATO. Kennedy then moved naval and air forces into the area and dispatched more than five thousand marines and army personnel toward the Thai-Laotian border, joined by troops from Britain, Australia, and New Zealand. The bold move had its desired affect. The Pathet Lao backed down and by June 1962, an uneasy truce guaranteeing a coalition government dedicated to the country's neutrality emerged from the Geneva talks.

Berlin

Nothing symbolized Cold War tensions between the United States and the USSR more than Berlin. In 1961, passions over the German city flared again. It seemed that this stubborn, unresolved dispute between the Allies and the Soviets over Germany, in general, and Berlin, in particular, just wouldn't go away.

The Vienna Summit

At their first and only *summit meeting*, Kennedy and Soviet Chairman Khrushchev met in early June 1961 in Vienna, Austria. The meeting went badly and only increased tensions between the two nations. Kennedy arrived for the summit hoping to find some common ground with the Soviet leader, despite Khrushchev's promise that the Soviets would support "wars of national liberation" in the Third World. From the beginning, however, Khrushchev bullied his younger counterpart and left the new president, in the words of his advisors "shattered" and "tongue-tied." Kennedy complained to his aides: "He treated me like a little boy."

Cold Words

A **summit meeting** is a formal gathering of heads of state and/or heads of government to discuss issues of mutual concern to their respective nations.

The next day, the two men got down to specifics. It was Berlin—all of it—that the Soviets wanted. For years, the Allied-controlled half of Berlin, surrounded on all sides by Soviet-dominated East Germany, had served, Khrushchev complained, as "the bone in my throat." And now, Khrushchev boldly told Kennedy that he was prepared to sign a peace treaty with East Germany that would close off Berlin to the West. This time, Kennedy did not flinch. Such an arrangement was, he told Khrushchev, "out of the question."

The Soviet leader slammed his fist on the table and barked, "I want peace. But if you want war that is your problem." Kennedy responded, "If that is true, then, Mr. Chairman, there will be war. It will be a cold winter."

By the following month, Kennedy was actively preparing the nation for war. Congress responded by authorizing the calling up of reserve forces and gave Kennedy additional military appropriations. All across America, citizens began building bomb shelters.

Quotes from the Cold

West Berlin … has many roles. It is more than a showcase of liberty, a symbol, an island of freedom in a Communist sea. It is even more than a link with the Free World, a beacon of hope behind the Iron Curtain, an escape hatch for refugees.

West Berlin is all of that. But above all it has now become—as never before—the great testing place of Western courage and will, a focal point where our solemn commitments stretching back over the years since 1945, and Soviet ambitions now meet in basic confrontation.

—President John F. Kennedy, speech to the nation, July 25, 1961

The Wall

In Berlin, in August, tensions reached a peak when East Germany shut down the Berlin border and began erecting a wall of concrete and barbed wire that soon separated West Berlin from the Russian-dominated East Berlin. Khrushchev ordered construction of the Berlin Wall primarily to halt the flow of refugees who were fleeing into West Berlin to escape communist rule.

Kennedy responded to Berlin's isolation with a measure Harry Truman had considered but rejected during the previous Berlin crisis in the late 1940s: He sent a battle force of 1,500 U.S. troops to West Berlin by way of the German autobahn. He made it clear to his aides that he was prepared to go to war with the Soviets over Berlin, even as he hoped for a peaceful solution to the dispute.

Rejecting advice to tear down the wall, Kennedy encouraged Khrushchev to believe that negotiations over Berlin were still possible. While serious talks between the two countries never took place, the promise of such talks gave Khrushchev the excuse he needed to postpone his treaty with East Germany.

Quotes from the Cold

To Germans, the Wall's greatest mischief is its aim of permanently dismembering a divided nation whose people yearn to be reunified.

—*Time*, August 31, 1962

Cold Facts

Contrary to popular belief, John F. Kennedy wasn't entirely opposed to construction of the Berlin Wall. Kennedy saw the wall as a means for Chairman Khrushchev to ease the crisis. "East Germany is hemorrhaging to death [with refugees fleeing to the West]," Kennedy told an aide. "The entire East bloc is in danger. He has to do something to stop this. Perhaps a wall." Later, Kennedy observed: "A wall is a hell of a lot better than a war."

In a matter of weeks, the crisis waned. But the wall remained and the Soviets sought to cover their tactical retreat by breaking a 34-month moratorium on nuclear weapons testing. In two month's time, the Soviets tested more than 50 nuclear weapons in atmospheric explosions. Kennedy believed he had no choice but to respond in kind, and ordered resumption of U.S. nuclear tests.

The Cuban Missile Crisis

Relations with the Soviets got only worse. The world next came to the brink of war in October 1962 after the United States learned that the Soviet Union was in the process of deploying, in Cuba, 36 medium-range ballistic missiles (they had a 1,000-mile range) and 24 intermediate-range ballistic missiles (these could travel up to 2,200 miles).

For years, the United States had stationed its Jupiter intermediate range ballistic missiles (IRBMs) in Turkey, next door to the Soviet Union. And so Khrushchev thought that basing nuclear missiles just 90 miles from Florida was only fair play. "It was high time," he later wrote, "America learned what it feels like to have her own land and her own people threatened."

Perhaps Khrushchev also saw the basing of missiles in Cuba as a way to force a permanent resolution of the Berlin problem. In any event, Kennedy and his advisors reacted with extreme alarm when they received the news on October 16 that an Air Force U-2 had located the Soviet missiles in place on Cuban soil. And it also appeared that the Soviets were busily constructing launch pads for those missiles.

CIA photos of Soviet missile sites in Cuba taken by an American U-2 spy plane in October 1962. The standoff with the Soviets over the nuclear missiles brought the world to the brink of war.

(Courtesy of the John F. Kennedy Library)

Kennedy reacted quickly and firmly, rejecting a purely diplomatic or military course to solve the crisis. Instead, he opted for an approach that mixed strong language and obvious preparations for a military response—including nuclear attack—with quiet but determined diplomatic effort to diffuse the crisis and head off a war.

Overruling his Joint Chiefs of Staff, who wanted to take out the missile sites with air strikes, Kennedy imposed a naval blockade, or "quarantine" of Cuba that prevented Soviet ships from entering Cuban waters. On October 22, in a speech to the nation, Kennedy alerted the American people to the crisis and demanded that the Soviets "halt and eliminate this clandestine, reckless and provocative threat to world peace."

Quotes from the Cold

I call upon Chairman Khrushchev to halt and eliminate this clandestine, reckless and provocative threat to world peace and to stable relations between our two nations. I call upon him further to abandon this course of world domination, and to join in an historic effort to end the perilous arms race and to transform the history of man.

He has an opportunity now to move the world back from the abyss of destruction—by returning to his government's own words that it had no need to station missiles outside its own territory, and withdrawing these weapons from Cuba—by refraining from any action which will widen or deepen the present crisis—and then by participating in a search for peaceful and permanent solutions.

—John F. Kennedy, speech to the American people, October 22, 1962

Kennedy was prepared to attack, but he didn't have to. Two weeks into the crisis, he had in hand two conflicting letters from Khrushchev and, upon the advice of Robert Kennedy, replied to the more conciliatory one. In that letter, the Soviets had agreed to remove all offensive weapons from Cuba as long as the United States promised not to invade Cuba.

Publicly, Kennedy agreed to those terms. And it appeared that the United States had not made any real concessions. But, secretly, Kennedy had informed Khrushchev that, in return for removal of the missiles from Cuba, the United States would remove its Jupiter missiles from Turkey within six months.

Kennedy won almost-universal praise for his calm handling of the crisis and for the way he forced the Soviets to back down. However, the crisis eventually cost Khrushchev his job in October 1964. And the new Soviet leader, Leonid Brezhnev—determined never to be humiliated by the United States—initiated a nuclear weapons production program that would, by the decade's end, put the USSR's nuclear stockpile on par with the United States.

The Vietnam Challenge

The adverse political fallout from Kennedy's failure at the Bay of Pigs and his decision to seek compromise in Laos made it all the more essential early in his term to take a strong stand elsewhere against communist aggression. "Vietnam is the place," advisor Walt Rostow told the president on April 21, 1961, "where … we must prove that we are not a paper tiger."

President John F. Kennedy and Defense Secretary Robert McNamara took the nation deeper into the war in Vietnam in the early 1960s.

(Courtesy of the John F. Kennedy Library)

Rostow believed that, other than Cuba, no country provided a better example of the Soviets' appetite for supporting "wars of national liberation." Here, Kennedy and his advisors believed, the resolve of the United States was being tested.

Diem

It is ironic that during his Senate years, Kennedy was very critical of U.S. involvement in Indochina. He was especially annoyed by the attitude of the French, who persisted in their efforts to recolonize Indochina instead of granting the people of Vietnam, Cambodia, and Laos their independence. By the time Kennedy became president, however,

> **Quotes from the Cold**
>
> The [Kennedy] administration was impregnated with the belief that Communism worldwide … was on the offensive, that this offensive had been allowed to gain dangerous momentum in the last two years of the Eisenhower Administration, and that it must now be met solidly.
>
> —William Bundy, Kennedy's deputy assistant secretary of defense, quoted by William C. Gibbons in *The U.S. Government and the Vietnam War,* Vol. II, (Princeton, 1986)

> **Cold Words**
>
> The **Domino Theory** was the term coined by President Eisenhower in 1954 to describe the cascade of events that would occur in Southeast Asia if South Vietnam fell to the communists. "You have a row of dominoes set up, you knock over the first one, and what will happen to the last one is the certainty that it will go over very quickly," Eisenhower told reporters during a press conference.

the French were gone and the United States had been funding and advising the South Vietnamese for almost seven years. And for most of those seven years, the U.S. policy had appeared to be working.

Throughout the mid and late 1950s, the struggle against the communist rebel fighters known as the Vietminh (later called Vietcong) appeared to be succeeding. Most American leaders, including Kennedy, strongly supported South Vietnam's leader, Ngo Dinh Diem. To much of the world, Diem was hailed as a charismatic leader valiantly struggling to maintain a democracy in the face of Soviet-backed communist aggression. The truth was, however, that Diem, especially in the early 1960s, was becoming increasingly autocratic. He imprisoned his political opponents, cracked down on the press, resisted economic and political reforms, and rigged elections to remain in power.

At first, Kennedy believed he had no choice but to back Diem in his fight against the Vietcong. As a committed Cold Warrior, the new president was a true believer in the *Domino Theory*, as first articulated by President Eisenhower. Vietnam, he believed, had to be saved from communism.

Kennedy had the misfortune of inheriting the problem of Vietnam just at the time when the failure of Eisenhower's policies was becoming evident. Eisenhower had been unwilling to demand serious reforms from Diem in return for continued U.S. assistance. And his "New Look" and the threat of nuclear attack had no currency in Vietnam, where the conflict was a guerrilla war like nothing the United States had ever seen.

Guerrilla War

The Kennedy's administration's solution to Vietnam was to create a new counterinsurgency force, which the president dubbed the "Green Berets." This was a recognition by Kennedy that conventional tactics of warfare would not apply to Vietnam. And yet, Kennedy was not prepared to assume all the responsibility for the fighting in Vietnam, even if Diem had wanted a large contingent of U.S. troops.

The best that he and Diem could do was work out an arrangement under which the United States would supply increasing numbers of military "advisors" to train the South Vietnamese forces in the ways of counterinsurgency. By the time of Kennedy's death in November 1963, the numbers of U.S. military "advisors" in Vietnam had risen from 700 to 16,000. But the advisors offered more than advice. Unknown to the American people, these U.S. troops often joined South Vietnamese troops in combat missions against the Vietcong.

Quotes from the Cold

I don't think that unless a greater effort is made by the [South Vietnamese] Government to win popular support that the war can be won out there. In the final analysis, it is their war. They are the ones who have to win it or lose it. We can help them, we can give them equipment, we can send our men out there as advisers, but they have to win it—the people of Viet-Nam—against the Communists.

We are prepared to continue to assist them, but I don't think that the war can be won unless the people support the effort, and, in my opinion, in the last two months the Government has gotten out of touch with the people.

—John F. Kennedy, interview on CBS television network, September 2, 1963

Losing the War

Despite all this help from the United States, the situation in Vietnam continued to deteriorate. Despite years of U.S. assistance and training, the South Vietnamese forces were just not up to the task of fighting the Vietcong. At the heart of the problem was Diem's penchant for appointing military commanders based on their loyalty, rather than on their military skills.

Had Diem's deficiencies been limited to the military aspect of the war, that would have been distressing enough. But on top of his military ineptitude was his increasing political repression. Not only were the Vietcong winning the war, but Diem was undermining civilian support for his government by his brutal handling of Buddhists and other government critics.

The Coup

By the summer of 1963, Kennedy and his men had decided that Diem had to go and gave their support to a coup being planned by his opponents in the South Vietnamese military. Kennedy later tried to withdraw his support from the coup, but it was too late. On November 1, the opposing generals gave the order and the coup began. Diem and his brother, Nhu, were murdered and the government of South Vietnam switched hands in the first of many coups that Saigon would endure throughout the 1960s.

Cold Facts

While he opposed Diem's murder, Undersecretary of State George Ball believed that South Vietnamese leader Ngo Dinh Diem still had to go, not because he was inept, but because he was a corrupt tyrant. "The Nhus were poisonous connivers," Ball wrote in his memoirs, "and America could not, with any shadow of honor, have continued to support a regime that was destroying Vietnamese society by its murderous repression of the Buddhists."

When he learned about Diem's death, Kennedy was horrified. But the essence of the events of early November were exactly what Kennedy had wanted: a new government to deal with and the hopes of closer cooperation between the United States and South Vietnam in the war against the Vietcong. But Diem's death, as it would soon be evident, had solved nothing. The South Vietnamese government remained unstable and corrupt and the South Vietnamese military never mustered the desire or the ability to fight effectively against the Vietcong.

Kennedy, of course, would not live to see the results of his fateful actions. On November 22, 1963, just three weeks after Diem's assassination, Kennedy himself was dead at the hands of an assassin's bullet.

The Least You Need to Know

- Although he was the youngest person ever elected president, John F. Kennedy was no less a Cold Warrior than his predecessors.
- Shortly after taking office, Kennedy faced his first international crisis when a U.S.-backed invasion of Cuba turned into a debacle.
- Kennedy had better success in dealing with crises in Berlin, where the Soviets erected a wall to isolate West Berlin, and in Laos, where he successfully negotiated the country's neutrality in the growing war in Southeast Asia.
- In October 1962, the world went to the brink of nuclear war over Soviet offensive missiles based in Cuba.
- Under Kennedy's leadership, the United States became more deeply involved in Vietnam with little success to show for the effort.

Chapter 16

Death in Vietnam

In This Chapter

- John F. Kennedy's assassination
- Lyndon Johnson takes the nation deeper into Vietnam
- The United States struggles to gain ground in Vietnam
- The Vietnam War drives Johnson from office

Ask almost anyone who grew up during the era and they will tell you that their most enduring images of the 1960s are the assassinations of John and Robert Kennedy, Martin Luther King Jr., and the Vietnam War. For the United States, the 1960s was the greatest period of social upheaval during the twentieth century. What began with the hope and promise of John F. Kennedy ended with tens of thousands of U.S. casualties in the cruel jungles of Vietnam.

To some historians, the decade marked the end of America's innocence and the beginning of greater public cynicism and distrust of all institutions, particularly the government. By any standard, it was a trying time for most Americans and permanently altered Americans' view of their country and its relationship to the world.

Nothing characterized the Cold War of the 1960s more than our nation's disastrous experience in Vietnam. The Vietnam War represented America's first loss in war, and right or wrong, it served as the standard against which subsequent U.S. military actions would be judged.

A Casualty in Dallas

In the 1960 election, President John F. Kennedy had barely carried Texas, a state that proved crucial to his narrow victory over Richard Nixon. In the fall of 1963, with the next presidential election less than a year away, Kennedy knew that Texas would again be important to his reelection chances. This time around, Kennedy's advisors knew that relying on the popularity of Vice President Lyndon Johnson, who had served as senator from Texas from 1949 to 1961, might not be enough.

On November 22, 1963, the president and First Lady Jacqueline Kennedy, along with Johnson and a host of Texas political leaders, converged on Dallas for a series of public events aimed at bolstering public support for the administration. Tragically, Kennedy did not leave Dallas alive. At 12:30 P.M., as his motorcade weaved through downtown, three shots rang out in quick succession, fired from a sixth-floor window in the Texas School Book Depository Building. Kennedy was mortally wounded and Texas Governor John Connally, sitting in front of Kennedy in the black convertible, was seriously injured. Thirty minutes later, doctors pronounced the president dead at a nearby hospital.

President John F. Kennedy died from an assassin's bullet in Dallas, Texas, on November 22, 1963. He had served as president less than three years.

(Courtesy of John F. Kennedy Library)

Less than two hours after the shooting, Kennedy's body was placed on Air Force One for a woeful last flight to Washington. Before the plane took off, however, a Dallas judge climbed aboard to administer the oath of office to the country's new president, Lyndon Baines Johnson.

Quotes from the Cold

All I have I would have given gladly not to be standing here today. The greatest leader of our time has been struck down by the foulest deed of our time. Today John Fitzgerald Kennedy lives on in the immortal words and works that he left behind. He lives on in the mind and memories of mankind. He lives on in the hearts of his countrymen.

—Lyndon Johnson, speech to joint session of Congress, November 27, 1963

Oswald

Within hours of the shooting, Dallas police had a suspect. Lee Harvey Oswald, an employee of the book depository who had a shady past that included brief residence in the Soviet Union, was arrested and charged with the murder. Two days later, as police officers transferred Oswald to a different jail facility, a Dallas nightclub owner, Jack Ruby, sprang forward and shot Oswald in the stomach with a .35-caliber revolver. Millions of horrified Americans watched the entire scene on television.

Mourning

Perhaps as many as one million people lined the streets of Washington on November 24, the day of Kennedy's funeral, standing in solemn tribute to the slain president as his body was carried to Arlington National Cemetery by horse-drawn carriage.

The Warren Commission

The Kennedy assassination spawned an entire industry of conspiracy theories about who was behind the murder. Some believed, and still do, that Cuban leader Fidel Castro was behind the crime (retribution for Kennedy's role in trying to have Castro killed). Other attributed the Mafia or the CIA.

President Johnson immediately recognized the need to qualm public doubts about the assassination and appointed a commission chaired by Chief Justice Earl Warren to evaluate and report on all evidence regarding Kennedy's death. After more than a year of hearings—the commission interviewed 552 witnesses—the Warren Commission concluded that Oswald had acted alone, without accomplices. Nonetheless, a significant percentage of the public greeted the commission report with skepticism. Almost 40 years later, in 2001, a nationwide survey by the Gallup polling organization revealed that 81 percent of Americans doubted that Oswald acted alone.

Quotes from the Cold

Scientific acoustical evidence establishes a high probability that two gunmen fired at President John F. Kennedy. Other scientific evidence does not preclude the possibility of two gunmen firing at the president. Scientific evidence negates some specific conspiracy allegations. The committee believes, on the basis of the evidence available to it, that President John F. Kennedy was probably assassinated as a result of a conspiracy.

—Conclusion of the U.S. House committee investigating the Kennedy assassination, 1979

Lyndon Johnson and Victory

By the terms of the twenty-second Amendment, Johnson could finish out Kennedy's term and still run for the office two times, and on Election Day in 1964, Johnson and Humphrey won in a landslide, achieving the largest popular-vote margin in modern U.S. history—61 percent of the vote. During the presidential campaign, Johnson's opponent, Republican Barry Goldwater, was ridiculed for his desire to use "low-yield atomic weapons" to defoliate the forests of Vietnam.

From Tonkin to Tet

Like John Kennedy before him, Johnson inherited the nation's struggle in Vietnam—a war that would eventually be Johnson's undoing. Since the early days of Harry Truman's White House years, the United States had been involved in one way or another in Indochina. We had supported the French who, after being run out of the region by the Japanese during World War II, wanted to reestablish their colonial empire. Under the guise of fighting communism, the French enlisted U.S. assistance in the fight.

It was a war in which we were happy to help. If denying the communists another large piece of the world's territory was the aim, then the United States was all for it. While the French fought Ho Chi Minh and his Vietminh fighters, the Americans helped pay for the guns and ammunition to beat them.

President Lyndon B. Johnson (center) and his Vietnam War advisors: Secretary of State Dean Rusk (left) and Defense Secretary Robert McNamara (right).

(Courtesy of Lyndon B. Johnson Library)

When the French began leaving the country in 1954 (after their debacle at Dien Bien Phu), we helped establish and support the government of South Vietnam—and the fight against Ho Chi Minh raged on. But Ho and his determined troops proved to be very formidable. American guns, ammunition, equipment, and the like did not do the trick. The Vietcong progressively claimed more and more of the South Vietnamese countryside.

By the early 1960s, it was clear that South Vietnam needed more U.S. assistance and military know-how. Kennedy gave them 16,000 U.S. military advisors, many of whom tried to train the South Vietnamese military in guerilla warfare. That effort proved a failure. For various reasons, the South Vietnamese army proved a lackluster fighting force commanded by inept, but politically astute, commanders.

Trust Me

While he was running for president in 1964, Johnson did not want the war in Vietnam to intrude into his campaign. When he did speak of Vietnam, it was usually to reassure voters that he would seek "no wider war" and that "we don't want our American boys to do the fighting for Asian boys." But the attacks on the American destroyers, the USS *Maddox* and USS *C. Turner Joy*, in the Gulf of Tonkin in August 1964 drastically changed American policy toward Vietnam. At the time, the attacks appeared to be unprovoked (it later became evident that the Americans had provoked the incident). Johnson promptly went to Congress and won broad authority to respond to the attacks and to use the U.S. military in a broad fight against communist aggression in the region.

Quotes from the Cold

… Congress approves and supports the determination of the President, as Commander in Chief, to take all necessary measures to repel any armed attack against the forces of the United States and to prevent further aggression. … [T]he United States is, therefore, prepared, as the President determines, to take all necessary steps, including the use of armed force, to assist any member or protocol state of the Southeast Asia Collective Defense Treaty requesting assistance in defense of its freedom.

—From the Gulf of Tonkin Resolution, August 1964

Cold Facts

Only two members of Congress—both of them senators—voted against the Gulf of Tonkin Resolution in August 1964: Democrat Ernest Gruening of Alaska and Republican Wayne Morse of Oregon. Both were later defeated when they sought reelection.

Johnson's poll numbers shot up and the crisis only helped to solidify his lead over Republican challenger Barry Goldwater. Later, it became evident that Johnson and his aides had lied to Congress about the specifics of the attacks in order to gain the broad war-making authority Johnson wanted.

Johnson did not want a war in Vietnam. But, like Kennedy before him, he believed that he had little choice but to fight. He believed that America's reputation among nations was on the line. Furthermore, Johnson embraced the domino theory and feared that he and his party could not withstand the partisan political attacks that would result if South Vietnam fell to the communists on his watch.

Rolling Thunder

By 1965, the United States was well on its way to taking control of the war in Vietnam. In February 1965, after a Vietcong attack on a U.S. air base at Plieku killed eight Americans and wounded another 126, Johnson began to steadily escalate the U.S. role in Vietnam. That month, U.S. war planes began a bombing campaign aimed at North Vietnam, called Rolling Thunder by the Pentagon. It would last until the spring of 1968.

Cold Facts

The average U.S. infantryman in Vietnam saw 240 days of combat, due to mobility afforded by helicopters. By contrast, the average U.S. infantryman in World War II saw 40 days of combat.

In March 1965, the first wave of U.S. combat troops landed on the beaches at Da Nang. Before the year was out, 80,000 American troops would be deployed in Vietnam.

The original mission of the Marines who landed at Da Nang was to protect the U.S. air base. That quickly changed. Under the command of General William Westmoreland, head of the Military Assistance Command in Vietnam (MACV), the mission of U.S. ground troops went from defensive to offensive.

Search and Destroy

With Johnson's approval, Westmoreland had a plan to bring about a quick end to the war. He would stage large numbers of U.S. forces and then send them fanning out across the countryside on "search and destroy" missions to root out and kill the Vietcong. His strategy was one of "attrition," that is, he hoped to inflict such heavy casualties on the enemy that it would impair their will and ability to fight.

The first big "search and destroy" mission came in October 1965 when the Army's First Cavalry Division engaged the North Vietnamese in a major battle in the Ia Drang Valley. Both sides sustained heavy casualties in the battle, but the damage to the North Vietnamese was greater, and Westmoreland was persuaded of the wisdom on his "attrition" strategy.

What he didn't realize at the time was that the North Vietnamese learned more than the Americans from their battle experience. The battle of Ia Drang left Ho Chi Minh and his advisors "serenely confident," according to retired Lieutenant General Harold G. Moore, then an army colonel who commanded men of the First Battalion, Seventh Cavalry, in the first ground engagement at Ia Drang.

"Their peasant soldiers had withstood the terrible high-tech fire storm delivered against them by a superpower and had at least fought the Americans to a draw," Moore wrote in his classic account of the battle, *We Were Soldiers Once … and Young* (Random House, 1992). "By their yardstick, a draw against such a powerful opponent was the equivalent of a victory. In time, they were certain, the patience and perseverance that had worn down the French colonialists would also wear down the Americans."

In other words, the North Vietnamese also saw the war as one of attrition in which they were willing to commit more men and resources than were the Americans. Time would prove Ho Chi Minh correct. The intensification of the war—the increased bombing, the massive defoliation of forests and fields, and the aggressive search-and-destroy missions—wreaked havoc throughout the countryside and won many converts to the communist cause.

Quotes from the Cold

You will kill 10 of our men, and we will kill one of yours, and in the end it will be you who tire of it.

—Ho Chi Minh to an American official, recalled upon his death in September 1969

Quotes from the Cold

The cause of our difficulties in Southeast Asia is not a deficiency of power but an excess of the wrong kind of power, which results in a feeling of impotence when it fails to achieve its desired ends. We are still acting like Boy Scouts dragging reluctant old ladies across streets they do not want to cross. We are trying to remake Vietnamese society, a task which certainly cannot be accomplished by force and which probably cannot be accomplished by any means available to outsiders. The objective may be desirable, but it is not feasible.

—Senator J. William Fulbright of Arkansas, April 1966

Stalemate

From Ia Drang on, the North Vietnamese learned to fight on their terms. They would attack quickly, often by surprise, and then retreat to avoid direct contact with U.S. forces. The result was a stalemate on the battlefield. By 1967, President Johnson, Defense Secretary Robert McNamara, and other U.S. officials reluctantly concluded that the war effort was stalled. Despite all the bombing and the presence of 525,000 U.S. troops, the massive infusion of U.S. military resources had not turned the tide of battle.

LBJ in Vietnam. President Lyndon Johnson awards the Distinguished Service Cross to First Lieutenant Marty A. Hammer at Cam Rahn Bay, South Vietnam, in October 1966.

(Courtesy of Lyndon B. Johnson Library)

Hoping to reverse U.S. fortunes in Vietnam, Johnson ordered still more bombing. But even this did not work. By August 1967, McNamara acknowledged the futility of the bombing in testimony to a Senate committee. "We have no reason to believe," he said, "[that more bombing] would break the will of the North Vietnamese people or sway the purpose of their leaders."

But the bombing did continue and as the fighting raged on, antiwar protests throughout the country grew larger and more impassioned. A series of antiwar rallies around the country culminated in October 1967 with a huge protest at the Lincoln Memorial, in which more than 100,000 marchers demanded an end to the bombing, withdrawal of American forces from Vietnam, and immediate peace talks with the North Vietnamese.

Quotes from the Cold

The [Vietnam] war did not bring about the decline of American power, as some have suggested, but was rather symptomatic of the limits of national power in an age of international diversity and nuclear weaponry.

—George C. Herring, *America's Longest War: The United States and Vietnam, 1950–1975*

For Johnson, Vietnam had become a quagmire that threatened his political future. Much of the president's problems resulted from the deceptive ways he had treated the Congress and the American people. First, he had not told the complete truth about the Gulf of Tonkin incidents. Then, he covered up the real costs of the war in an effort to maintain congressional support for his Great Society programs. Finally, he and his military advisors destroyed their credibility by continually depicting the flagging U.S. war effort in the most rosy and inaccurate terms.

Tet

Despite the stalemate in Vietnam, most Americans still labored under the impression, given them by the White House and the Pentagon, that the U.S. Army had all but crippled the Vietcong fighters in South Vietnam. "We are making steady progress without any question," General Westmoreland declared unequivocally at a White House briefing for members of Congress in November 1967.

The events of January through February 1968 proved how wrong Westmoreland was. In the early morning hours of January 30—during the traditional cease-fire period of Tet, the Vietnamese New Year—a squad of Viet Cong commandos laid siege to the U.S. embassy in Saigon and killed a young U.S. Army guard who vainly attempted to stop the raid. Before their assault was over six hours later, the commandos would kill five U.S. soldiers in fierce fighting that was amply covered by American network television crews.

Elsewhere in the city, the Viet Cong attacked Westmoreland's headquarters, as well as the South Vietnamese general staff offices. That evening in the United States, millions of Americans who watched the network news broadcasts were shocked to learn that, despite the presence of half a million American troops in South Vietnam, the Viet Cong appeared as strong and viable as ever.

By the time officials in Washington learned of the attack, more than 84,000 Viet Cong and North Vietnamese troops were staging well-coordinated attacks on 44 provincial capitols, 64 district capitols, and five of the six major cities in South Vietnam.

Taken by surprise, the American and South Vietnamese forces performed well. In Saigon, American troops inflicted heavy causalities, took hundreds of prisoners, and quickly regained control of the city. The same was true in a number of other cities and towns where the Viet Cong made early tactical mistakes. Within two weeks, American and South Vietnamese troops had gained the upper hand.

While Viet Cong attacks were quickly quashed in almost every city and town, the Tet offensive had a devastating impact on American public opinion. For months, Johnson and Westmoreland had promised that within months the U.S. military could begin gradually turning over the fighting to the South Vietnamese.

Many Americans, including many in the Congress, now realized that Johnson had deceived them about the strength of the Viet Cong. Despite three years of difficult fighting and bombing and the presence of more than 500,000 American troops on the ground, the Viet Cong were still viable enough to stage simultaneous attacks on more than a hundred cities and towns throughout the country.

Quotes from the Cold

To say that we are closer to victory today is to believe, in the face of the evidence, the optimists who have been wrong in the past. To suggest we are on the edge of defeat is to yield to unreasonable pessimism. To say that we are mired in stalemate seems the only realistic, yet unsatisfactory, conclusion .... But it is increasingly clear to this reporter that the only rational way out [of Vietnam] will be to negotiate, not as victors, but as an honorable people who lived up to their pledge to defend *democracy,* and did the best they could.

—CBS news anchor Walter Cronkite's commentary of February 27, 1968, following his visit to Vietnam

The Master Retires

By early 1968, more than 15,000 American soldiers had died in Vietnam. Another 110,000 had been wounded. In Washington, the war claimed another casualty: President Lyndon B. Johnson.

As antiwar protests escalated, Americans increasingly concluded that the war in Vietnam was not winnable. Events in March 1968 persuaded many that Johnson's reelection prospects were just as bleak. That month, Minnesota Senator Eugene McCarthy, a vocal opponent of the Vietnam War, opposed Johnson in the New Hampshire Democratic presidential primary and finished a strong second. On the heels of McCarthy's strong showing, Senator Robert Kennedy of New York entered the race for the Democratic nomination.

Meanwhile, Johnson had reluctantly acknowledged to himself and aides the dim prospects for victory in Vietnam. Now, he was forced to face his own dim reelection chances. On March 31, Johnson shocked the nation with his decision. At the end of a nationally televised speech to declare a partial bombing halt over North Vietnam, Johnson announced that he would not seek reelection.

Quotes from the Cold

With America's sons in the fields far away, with America's future under challenge right here at home, with our hopes and the world's hopes for peace in the balance every day, I do not believe that I should devote an hour or a day of my time to any personal partisan causes or to any duties other than the awesome duties of this office—the Presidency of your country.

Accordingly, I shall not seek, and I will not accept, the nomination of my party for another term as your President.

—Lyndon Johnson, March 31, 1968

One of the most skilled politicians of the twentieth century had been brought down by a war he not wanted, but one he had fought because he believed he had no other choice.

The Least You Need to Know

- President John F. Kennedy was assassinated on November 22, 1963 in Dallas by Lee Harvey Oswald.
- Upon Kennedy's death, Vice President Lyndon Johnson became president and appointed the Warren Commission to dispel public fears about a conspiracy to kill Kennedy.
- Johnson had hoped that the war in Vietnam would not intrude on his domestic initiatives, but he escalated the U.S. military presence in Vietnam beginning in early 1965.
- Despite hopes for an early victory, U.S. forces fought the Vietcong and the North Vietnamese to a stalemate; domestic support for the war, and Johnson, waned and Johnson was forced to retire at the end of his term in January 1969.

Part 4 Doubting the Commitment

Was the Cold War worth it all? Tens of thousands of dead American soldiers in Vietnam, streets and colleges campuses aflame, political leaders assassinated and discredited. On top of all that, America was losing the Vietnam war.

Richard Nixon vowed to end the war quickly, but he didn't. In the end, the "peace with honor" that he promised proved illusory, and the United States looked ineffectual and defeated. Nixon would try to undo that perception with bold diplomatic endeavors in China and the Soviet Union, but Watergate cut short his presidency. The next two presidents failed to live up to the public's expectations.

Then, along came Ronald Reagan.

Chapter 17

The Vietnam Divide

In This Chapter

- Vietnam is the backdrop for the 1968 Democratic presidential campaign
- Richard Nixon's Vietnam strategy
- Robert Kennedy assassination
- Vietnam and the 1968 Nixon-Humphrey race

Nothing so much characterized the 1968 presidential campaign as the Vietnam War and the political fallout over Lyndon Johnson's policies in Southeast Asia. On the Democratic side, Hubert Humphrey, Robert Kennedy, and Eugene McCarthy all waged war for a Democratic nomination that some believed wasn't worth having, especially considering that two successive Democratic presidents had taken the country into the quagmire of Vietnam.

The Republicans would nominate former Vice President Richard Nixon, a wily politician who had remade himself in the years since his 1960 defeat at JFK's hands. Once a militant, anticommunist conservative, Nixon's new image would be that of a pragmatic statesman whose new approach to the world's problems would quickly end the fighting in Southeast Asia. Of course, Nixon's willingness to undermine the peace talks in 1968 didn't hurt his chances, either.

Humphrey, Kennedy, and McCarthy

Lyndon Johnson's surprise retirement announcement in March 1968 only intensified the struggle for the Democratic nomination. Within days of Johnson's speech, Vice President Hubert Humphrey jumped into the race. By then, however, it was too late to organize a primary campaign to effectively compete against Robert Kennedy and Eugene McCarthy. Instead, the vice president chose to avoid most direct electoral confrontations with his Democratic rivals and focused, instead, on the delegate-rich nonprimary states.

Backed by the money and organization of the Democratic Party's establishment, Humphrey quickly assembled an impressive, well-funded coalition that included labor, business, civil rights and Jewish leaders, party regulars, and even some pro-war southern segregationists.

But no matter how hard he tried, Humphrey could not remove the stains of his intimate association with Lyndon Johnson. Since 1966, the vice president had been among the most vocal and unequivocal supporters of Johnson's Vietnam policies. In the public's mind, Humphrey was intimately associated with a very unpopular war—a war that he had publicly and enthusiastically championed at home and abroad.

Cold Facts

The turbulent election year of 1968 was further roiled on April 4, 1968, with the assassination of the Reverend Martin Luther King Jr., in Memphis. The winner of the 1964 Noble Peace Prize, King had won international acclaim for his leadership of the American civil rights movement. By 1968, however, he had turned his attention to the problem of persistent poverty and his growing vocal opposition to the Vietnam War.

The Kennedy juggernaut, meanwhile, rolled effortlessly through the primaries. On May 7, Kennedy won in Indiana with 42 percent of the vote to McCarthy's 27 percent. Determined to remain in the race, McCarthy blithely dismissed the results by telling reporters that it did not matter who finished first. "That's not what my father told me," Kennedy replied.

One week later, Kennedy rolled up another victory, this time in Nebraska where he won 51.5 percent of the vote. McCarthy finished at 31 percent. Kennedy saw his vote, combined with McCarthy's, as a resounding repudiation of the Johnson-Humphrey administration. "The people want to move in a different direction," he said. "We can't have the politics of happiness and joy [an indirect slap at Humphrey's 'politics of joy' campaign theme] when we have so many problems in our own country."

New York Senator Robert F. Kennedy (left) entered the race for the 1968 Democratic presidential nomination after President Lyndon Johnson (right) announced his retirement from politics. One of Kennedy's major themes was his opposition to U.S. policy in Vietnam.

(Courtesy of Cecil Stoughton, Lyndon B. Johnson Library)

During the primaries, Kennedy's only disappointing showing would come in Oregon, where McCarthy beat him, 45 to 39 percent. The morning after Oregon, Kennedy headed to California where he hoped a strong victory there would propel him, victorious, toward the Democratic nomination in August.

The "New" Nixon

Richard Nixon, meanwhile, was virtually assured of the Republican president nomination. And he had long assumed that Lyndon Johnson would be his general election rival. Weakened by an unpopular war, a sagging economy, and the growing, often-violent domestic unrest that had spilled into the nation's streets, Johnson was just the kind of opponent Nixon wanted.

Now, with LBJ's sudden retirement, Nixon faced the possibility that he would confront not a weakened, unpopular president, but a strong, charismatic antiwar Democrat like Kennedy. Nixon had already lost to one Kennedy in 1960. He did not relish the prospect of running against another.

Nixon's Plan

For Nixon, Vietnam was also a problem. For years, he had portrayed himself as someone who favored intensifying the war. He had steadfastly opposed most efforts aimed at a diplomatic solution in Vietnam. However, by late 1967, planning another run for the White House and pragmatic enough to know that a military victory in Vietnam was unlikely, Nixon began to relax his hard-line opposition to peace talks.

Quotes from the Cold

It is not news that [Nixon] was devious, manipulative, driven by unseen and unknowable forces, quick as a summer storm to blame and slow as a glacier melt to forgive, passionate in his hatreds, self-centered, untruthful, untrusting, and at times so despicable that one wants to avert one's eyes in shame and embarrassment.

—Stephen E. Ambrose, *Nixon: The Triumph of a Politician, 1962–1972*

The nation was tired of war and Nixon knew that while a strong, pro-military stance might have won him votes in 1966, that position would not play well with a growing segment of the public. While he cryptically suggested that he had a peace plan (he pledged to "end the war and win the peace"), Nixon knew that he needed a new strategy for the changing times.

Former Vice President Richard Nixon confers with President Lyndon Johnson in the Oval Office. Nixon campaigned for president in 1968 suggesting that he would seek a quick end to the Vietnam War.

(Courtesy of Yoichi R. Okamoto, Lyndon B. Johnson Library)

In early March 1968, he unveiled his new approach when he told a radio audience that Johnson had "frittered away the nation's military power in a misguided policy of gradualism." Had Johnson employed "our power quickly, we could have ended it with far less than we are now using," Nixon asserted, without offering specifics.

At the same time, Nixon insisted that military power alone would not be decisive. Better and more determined diplomacy was needed. Instead of questioning the need for a diplomatic solution as he had done for more than two years, Nixon would now claim that stronger diplomatic efforts were needed because the war was harming U.S.-Soviet relations.

The solution to Vietnam, Nixon said, could lie in Moscow, where Soviet officials, hoping for better relations with the United States, might be persuaded to urge their North Vietnamese allies to accept a negotiated settlement.

Hawk or Dove?

Nixon's new strategy was imaginative, politically canny, and very cynical. His stance on the war had something for everyone. He portrayed himself as a *hawk* who faulted Johnson for not using massive military force soon enough. Then he cast himself as a *dove* who advocated a negotiated settlement, believing that the opportunity for a military victory had passed. Finally, he was a clever moderate who advocated an imaginative effort to involve the Soviets in a peace plan, while opposing a hasty withdrawal of American troops and warning against an overly flexible bargaining position at the Paris peace talks.

Nixon's political strategy also reflected his desire for maximum diplomatic and military latitude should he win the election. "I've come to the conclusion that there's no way to win the war," Nixon confessed to his aides in March, after learning from his sources that Johnson's advisors had urged him to abandon a military solution. "But we can't say that, of course. In fact, we have to seem to say the opposite, just to keep some degree of bargaining leverage."

For Nixon, Johnson's retirement changed everything. With Johnson fading from the scene, and Kennedy's star rising, Nixon feared that public frustration over the war might not have its former political potency. But Johnson's decision to remove himself from politics also devalued Vietnam as an issue for Kennedy and McCarthy. Now Nixon could claim that he was merely following Johnson's lead by declaring a temporary "moratorium" on statements about Vietnam.

> **Cold Words**
>
> **Hawk** was the term used to characterize those who not only favored the war in Vietnam, but who wanted to fight it with utmost intensity. By the same token, a **dove** (an ancient symbol of peace) became the term used to describe those who called for a quick end to the war, either by withdrawal of U.S. troops or by negotiations.

Death in California

Meanwhile, running behind Humphrey in the delegate hunt, Robert Kennedy gained momentum and his campaign now enjoyed a certain air of inevitability. "If the New York Senator is going to be stopped," *U.S. News & World Report* said, "Hubert Humphrey will have to do the stopping."

Indeed, Kennedy's primary victories in South Dakota and California on June 4, 1968, put him in a strong position to make a powerful case for his candidacy in the two and a half months before the Democratic National Convention in Chicago. Kennedy, after all, had

Cold Facts

In all of American history, only two U.S. senators have been assassinated: New York Senator Robert Kennedy, shot in Los Angeles in June 1968, and Louisiana Senator Huey P. Long, shot in Baton Rouge in September 1935.

won most of his delegates not in the backrooms as Humphrey did but in primary contests across the nation.

Despite Humphrey's lead in the delegate count, Kennedy was closing in fast. "What I think is clear," a victorious Kennedy told a rally in Los Angeles after the June 4 California returns were in, "is that we can work together in the last analysis."

Moments later, Kennedy left the stage and walked with his entourage through the kitchen of the Los Angeles Ambassador Hotel. There, he encountered Sirhan Bishara Sirhan, a 24-year-old Jordanian immigrant who worked as a busboy in the hotel. Believing that Kennedy was a symbol of Zionism, Sirhan shot Kennedy three times. Kennedy died the next day.

Humphrey Versus Nixon

The crisis of Humphrey's ill-fated association with Lyndon Johnson only deepened in early July 1968 when Johnson ordered more B-52 bombing raids along the infiltration routes north of the demilitarized zone. Everywhere Humphrey went, protesters heckled him, chanting "Dump the Hump!"

Meanwhile, there was little for Humphrey to cheer about in the polling data. One national survey in mid-July showed him only narrowly ahead of Nixon, while McCarthy enjoyed an eight-point lead over the presumptive Republican nominee.

That Johnson appeared to be again escalating the war in Vietnam just weeks before Humphrey's nomination was bad enough; worse, was that despite having pledged to stay out of politics for the remainder of the year, Johnson and his aides refused to allow Humphrey to control his own convention.

Quotes from the Cold

… [T]he year 1968 had been one of incredible, even unprecedented disappointment and heartache. Courtiers of hope like Martin Luther King Jr., and Robert Kennedy were gunned down, Eugene McCarthy, carrying the dreams of a generation to end a hated war and recapture a government and a country gone wrong, had faltered and failed; Lyndon Johnson, had been broken. … Racial division wracked the nation and American cities, and campuses were aflame with protests against the war.

—Jules Witcover, *The Year the Dream Died,* Warner Books, 1997

Vice President Hubert Humphrey won the 1968 Democratic presidential nomination, but was saddled with negative public perceptions associated with President Lyndon Johnson's Vietnam War policies.

(Courtesy of Yoichi R. Okamoto, Lyndon B. Johnson Library)

Debacle in Chicago

Down to the smallest detail, the Chicago convention held during the last week in August was a Lyndon Johnson affair including the drafting and approval of the pro-war, Vietnam platform plank. Humphrey tried his best to influence the platform, but only as a supplicant. The convention was deeply divided over Vietnam. When antiwar forces proposed a platform plank that demanded a quick withdrawal of U.S. forces, 40 percent of delegates voted for it.

> **Quotes from the Cold**
>
> The convention presented to the vast nation-wide audience a picture of division, of old-fashioned city bossism, of clashes between the young and old, of events out of control and of a party unable even to govern itself or maintain order. … [There is] little Humphrey can do to heal his party.
>
> —James Reston, writing in the *New York Times,* August 1968

Outside the Chicago convention hall there was mayhem. As many as 15,000 antiwar demonstrators violently clashed with members of Mayor Richard Daley's police force. When the young demonstrators, some of them waving Viet Cong flags, tried to march on the convention hall, Daley's police force staged a ferocious attack, assaulting them with clubs, rifle butts, and tear gas. The angry demonstrators responded by hurling rocks and bottles. More than 100 protesters were injured; another 175 were arrested.

Unfortunately for Humphrey, the street violence received more attention than the substance of the convention. As journalist Stanley Karnow later wrote, the televised scenes "alienated many Americans sympathetic to the antiwar movement."

The disarray among Democrats was a boon for Nixon, to whom Republican delegates had awarded their nomination at a peaceful, largely unified national convention earlier that month in Miami. When compared to Humphrey, who was tied inextricably to Johnson and his policies, the recently bellicose Nixon was now a dove. At the convention, Nixon explained that his failure to offer specific recommendations to end the war was a patriotic impulse, an expression of his sincere desire to give Johnson a completely free hand in the Paris peace talks.

Cold Facts

During the 1968 presidential election, Richard Nixon promised a quick end to the Vietnam War. He argued that if the war was not over by January of 1969 (the month the next president would take office), then it "can best be ended by a new administration that has given no hostages to the mistakes of the past."

If elected, Nixon promised to "conduct a thorough reappraisal of every aspect of the prosecution of the war and the search for peace." And, ironically, he promised to "do what the present administration has so signally failed to do: … arm the American people with the truth." Within months of becoming president, Nixon would launch a secret bombing campaign over Cambodia.

"The war must be ended," Nixon said. "It must be ended honorably, consistent with America's limited aims and with the long-term requirements of peace in Asia." He favored "a negotiated settlement" to the war. However, he offered few specifics, other than to suggest that the United States "keep the pressure on" North Vietnam militarily, while engaging in more aggressive diplomatic, economic, and political initiatives in South Vietnam.

Humphrey's Gambit

Nixon's artful dodges on Vietnam were maddening to Humphrey. Finally, in frustration, Humphrey agreed to take the plunge. Instead of supporting Johnson's position of waiting for North Vietnamese concessions before stopping the bombing, Humphrey suggested that he would "stop the bombing of North Vietnam as an acceptable risk for peace." If the North Vietnamese failed to respond, then Humphrey reserved "the right to resume the bombing."

The statement turned Humphrey's campaign around. Antiwar liberals returned to the fold and Humphrey, now invigorated, began to energize Democratic voters, dissuading many of them from voting for third-party candidate George Wallace, the segregationist former governor of Alabama.

Nixon's Ploy

Nixon was worried. Not only had Humphrey's promise to end the bombing revived the flagging Democratic campaign placing the two major candidates neck and neck in public opinion polls, now there was word of a potential breakthrough in the Paris peace talks. Through his sources, Nixon not only knew about the potential deal, he saw it as a direct threat to his campaign. So he actively began working to sabotage the peace talks by turning the South Vietnamese government against any preelection peace agreement.

Nixon quietly sent word to the South Vietnamese that they should hold out for a better deal under a Nixon administration. Unlike Humphrey, who would end the bombing, Nixon pledged that he would negotiate with the North Vietnam only from a position of strength.

Meanwhile, in public, Nixon reaffirmed his commitment to the success of the Paris talks at the very time his representatives were actively working to undermine them. "As long as there is a chance for an honorable peace through the Paris talks, candidates should offer nothing in the political arena that would risk undercutting our negotiators," Nixon said. "I hope President Johnson can honorably end this war."

In the fall of 1968, President Lyndon Johnson tried in vain to persuade South Vietnamese President Nguyen van Thieu (left) to accept a peace deal with North Vietnam. Republican presidential candidate Richard Nixon had persuaded Thieu to reject the agreement. Johnson meets here with Thieu at a conference in July 1968.

(Courtesy of Yoichi R. Okamoto, Lyndon B. Johnson Library)

Humphrey was furious when he learned about Nixon's stunning duplicity. But he was persuaded to do nothing because, as one of his advisors later explained, "It would be considered by the American people as a last-minute, last-ditch charge leveled by Humphrey out of desperation."

Johnson did his best to salvage the talks, announcing an end to all air, naval, and artillery bombardment of North Vietnam in hopes of striking a deal. Encouraged by Nixon, however, South Vietnam's president finally balked at the peace agreement, clearly expecting more favorable treatment from a Republican administration.

On November 5, 1968, in one of the closest presidential elections in American history—thanks to Wallace's strong third-party challenge—Nixon beat Humphrey by fewer than 500,000 votes out of more than 62 million cast.

Cold Facts

Third-party candidate George Wallace, the former segregationist governor of Alabama, won five states in the 1968 election: Arkansas, Louisiana, Mississippi, Alabama, and Georgia. He received more than 13 percent of the vote. He waged a spirited campaign against Nixon and Humphrey, charging that there was not "a dime's worth of difference" between the two.

While other issues had played a role in the Republican victory, the Vietnam War was paramount. Nixon had campaigned skillfully and encouraged voters to believe he had a plan to end the conflict, although he never discussed its specifics. When an agreement appeared imminent, Nixon slowed it down by persuading the South Vietnamese to object, assuring them that he would be tougher on North Vietnam than Humphrey. Even after Johnson announced the bombing halt, Thieu played into Nixon's hands by rejecting the deal.

Now Nixon was the new president and Americans rightly expected from him a quick end to the war. But, as they would eventually learn, much more fighting and bombing and dying was ahead.

The Least You Need to Know

- Lyndon Johnson's surprise retirement announcement in March 1968 sparked a vigorous fight for the Democratic nomination between Robert Kennedy, Hubert Humphrey, and Eugene McCarthy.
- The leading candidates, Humphrey and Kennedy, pursued different paths to the nomination: Humphrey relied on the support of party bosses and union representatives, while Kennedy campaigned vigorously, and successfully, against McCarthy in the party primaries.
- Just as Kennedy appeared to have the momentum to overtake Humphrey's lead, he was assassinated in Los Angeles in June 1968.
- Republican Richard Nixon's campaign rhetoric led many to believe that he had a concrete plan to end the Vietnam War.
- Nixon secured his narrow victory in 1968 by secretly undermining the Johnson administration's efforts to secure a negotiated settlement of the war.

Chapter 18

Cooling the Cold War

In This Chapter

- Nixon's policy of détente toward the Soviet Union
- The war goes to Cambodia
- Nixon goes to China
- Nixon accelerates the U.S. withdrawal from Vietnam
- Nixon, Kissinger and the bid for a Vietnam peace deal

Throughout the 1960s, tensions between the United States and the Soviets improved. After coming to the brink of war during the 1962 Cuban missile crisis, both sides knew that they could not afford a repeat performance. In the nuclear age, the margin for error was simply too small—and the consequences cataclysmic.

While Presidents Kennedy and Johnson laid the groundwork of improved U.S.-Soviet relations, it fell to President Richard Nixon to consummate the relationship. With his unquestioned strong anticommunist credentials, Nixon was one of the few American leaders who could embrace the leaders of the Soviet Union and China and not pay a steep political price. With skill, and more than a little deceit, Nixon and his top foreign policy advisor, Henry Kissinger, initiated bold changes in the way the United States viewed the world.

It was a period during which the United States began to extract itself from the quagmire of Vietnam. Instead of a quick withdrawal of forces, however, Nixon would engage in a painfully slow retreat that would cost the lives of another 20,000 American soldiers and would spread the war beyond the borders of Vietnam.

Nixon, Kissinger, and Détente

Relations with the Soviets had been warming ever since 1963, the last year of John Kennedy's presidency. Following the Cuban missile crisis, Khrushchev and Kennedy moved decisively to improve relations between their two countries. This began a period that would come to be known as *détente* under President Nixon.

1960s Détente

In August 1963, Kennedy and Khrushchev signed the "Treaty Banning Nuclear Weapons Tests in the Atmosphere, in Outer Space and Under Water," otherwise known as the Nuclear Test Ban Treaty. They also took other steps to reduce tensions. Both sides installed a hot line between the White House and the Kremlin to improve communications during crisis periods. In October 1963, Kennedy approved the sale of $250 million in surplus American wheat to Russia.

Cold Words

Détente is a French word meaning a relaxation of tensions or strained relations.

Johnson supported this trend of warmer U.S.–Soviet relations. He reduced export controls on trade with the Soviets and their allies, allowed the Export-Import Bank to extend credits to the USSR and their satellites, and negotiated a U.S.-Soviet civil air agreement. He also proposed mutual reductions in NATO and Warsaw Pact troop strength.

In 1967, the two nations signed the Outer Space Treaty, in which they agreed to refrain from using space for basing or testing of weapons of war. That year, they also agreed to the Treaty of Tlateloco—signed by every Latin American nation but Cuba and Guyana—in which they pledged respect for the denuclearization of the region.

Quotes from the Cold

Let us reexamine our attitude toward the Soviet Union. … Let us not be blind to our differences—but let us also direct attention to our common interests and to the means by which those differences can be resolved. And if we cannot end now our differences, at least we can help make the world safe for diversity.

—President John F. Kennedy, June 19, 1963, Commencement Address at American University

The two countries signed another important document in 1968: the Nuclear Nonproliferation Treaty, banning the sale of nuclear weapons to countries without nuclear weapons programs. Hoping for a dramatic strategic arms limitations treaty (SALT) agreement to crown his presidency, Johnson looked forward to negotiations with Soviet Premier Alexi Kosygin at their September 1968 summit. But Johnson would never be able to boast of a SALT breakthrough. After the Soviets invaded Czechoslovakia in August, he reluctantly cancelled the September summit.

Cold Facts

Nikita Khrushchev fell from power in October 1964, but not as a result of his foreign policies. His critics in the Kremlin instead cited his "harebrained schemes" to reorganize the Communist Party and the Soviet state structure, as well as his ambitious plans for economic and agricultural reforms. He was deposed while on vacation in the Crimea.

Détente Nixon Style

President Richard Nixon said that his presidency would bring about "an era of negotiation" with the Soviet Union and other communist nations. It wasn't that Nixon, the old Cold Warrior and Redbaiter, had gone soft. Nixon and his national security advisor, Henry Kissinger, believed that they brought to the White House an outlook of realistic pragmatism, or realpolitik, regarding world affairs.

Among the reasons Nixon wanted to reduce tensions between the United States and the Soviets was his belief that better relations with the Soviet Union and China might help the United States end its involvement in Vietnam by isolating the North Vietnamese. And like Johnson before him, Nixon also wanted to count a SALT treaty among his foreign policy successes.

SALT was especially important in the late 1960s because of the alarming increase in the numbers of nuclear intercontinental ballistic missiles (ICBMs). From 1967 to 1969, the number of Soviet ICBMs went from 570 to 1,050 and the Soviet stockpile now equaled the U.S. nuclear arsenal.

While the Soviets eagerly agreed to resume the SALT talks, both sides clearly had their own agendas. Nixon saw SALT as a way to slow down the Soviets' nuclear arms buildup and to prevent them from constructing a national antiballistic missile (ABM) defense system that U.S. officials regarded as destabilizing.

Quotes from the Cold

We had never claimed détente would result in friendship; for us, too, détente was a method for conducting the Cold War.

—Henry Kissinger, *Years of Upheaval* (Little, Brown, 1982)

The Soviets, meanwhile, saw SALT as a way to preserve their nuclear parity with the United

States, while slowing down American deployment of new multiple-warhead missiles (MIRVs). Economic factors also motivated the Soviets, who believed that relaxed diplomatic relations with the West would bring them badly needed economic and technical assistance from the United States and its allies.

Cold Facts

Shortly after Richard Nixon became president, his national security advisor, Henry Kissinger, proposed a bold strategy for dealing with the Soviet Union. He called it linkage, meaning that different areas of U.S.-Soviet relations—trade, arms control, Vietnam—would be linked.

Kissinger hoped that if the Soviets desired progress in areas such as trade and arms control, they would force North Vietnam to accept a negotiated end to the Vietnam War. "The Soviet leaders should be brought to understand," Nixon told American diplomats, "that they cannot expect to reap the benefits of cooperation in one area while seeking to take advantage of tension or confrontation elsewhere."

Henry Kissinger served as President Richard Nixon's national security advisor and later as secretary of state. He was a principal architect of U.S. foreign policy during the late 1960s and early 1970s.

(Courtesy of the National Archives)

The Nixon Doctrine

Ever since President Truman had articulated the Truman Doctrine in 1947, the United States had pledged itself to challenge communism wherever it posed a threat. In John F. Kennedy's famous words from his 1961 inaugural address, the country would "pay any price, bear any burden, meet any hardship, support any friend, oppose any foe to assure the survival and the success of liberty." In 1969, however, Nixon replaced the Truman Doctrine with one of his own.

The country's failure in Vietnam had proved the weaknesses of the Truman Doctrine. In Southeast Asia, the U.S. military had not checked the spread of communism. The new Nixon Doctrine was a crafty acknowledgement of this failure and a bold new strategy for creating what one historian termed "a triangular balance with the Soviet Union and China."

In other words, Nixon did not want the process of withdrawing U.S. troops from Vietnam to be cast as the retreat that it was; instead, he would portray it as a shrewd move in his geopolitical chess game to isolate North Vietnam from its allies while playing the USSR and China against one another.

During a trip to Guam in July 1969, Nixon told reporters that "as far as the problems of internal security are concerned, the U.S. is going to encourage and has a right to expect that this problem will increasingly be handled by … the Asian nations themselves." In other words, Nixon was saying that the United States no longer considered China to be a military threat and that the United States, while helping to fight communism in Asia, would no longer commit its ground troops to that fight.

Replacing direct U.S. involvement was Vietnamization, a policy in which responsibility for fighting the Vietcong and the North Vietnamese would be gradually turned over to the South Vietnamese military. Nixon announced that by August 1969, 25,000 American troops stationed in Vietnam would be heading home (there were roughly half a million American troops in Vietnam at the time). By year's end, he would accelerate the withdrawal of troops by calling home another 65,000.

Cold Facts

Nixon's Vietnamization policy gave the false impression that the United States was gradually ending its military involvement in Southeast Asia. But far from ending the war, Nixon expanded it during this period by escalating the bombing, including a secret campaign over Cambodia. By one estimate, the U.S. military dropped one ton of bombs for every minute Nixon was president.

More SALT

Nixon and Kissinger hoped for a quick SALT agreement. But soon after the talks began in Helsinki, Finland, they bogged down in dispute over whether to include both offensive and defensive weapons in the agreement. The Soviets wanted to limit only defensive weapons (to prevent a U.S. ABM system, while they developed their own MIRV program). The United States, meanwhile, wanted to limit both types of weapons, primarily hoping to block the Soviet MIRV program.

The SALT talks lagged for 18 months, until May 1971, when Soviet negotiators finally agreed to discuss limitations on offensive and defensive nuclear weapons. In the end, the Soviets agreed to overlook U.S. missiles based in Europe and the United States let stand the Soviets' three-to-two advantage in ICBMs. Nixon and Soviet President Leonid Brezhnev signed the historic SALT treaty in May 1972 during Nixon's historic visit to Moscow.

The Cambodian Stumble

The American people could be forgiven if they wrongly concluded that the Nixon Doctrine and the country's new Vietnamization policy meant that the war in Vietnam was winding down. Actually, it was intensifying.

In March 1969, Nixon had secretly ordered intense U.S. bombing raids over Cambodia, aimed at destroying North Vietnamese and Vietcong base camps just across South Vietnam's border. Nixon believed the raids were a vital component of his Vietnamization policy that would give South Vietnam's military time to train, fortify, and reinforce.

Bombing

Nixon also believed that the bombing was the best way to force the North Vietnamese to negotiate an end to the war. During the 14-month bombing campaign, the United States dropped 100,000 tons of bombs on Cambodia. The massive raids killed as many as 100,000 Cambodian peasants and drove at least two million others from their homes. But the operation's affects on the North Vietnamese were negligible.

President Richard Nixon ordered the secret bombing of Cambodia shortly after taking office in 1969.

(Courtesy of the National Archives)

Invasion

The following year, Nixon intensified the war in Cambodia again when he dispatched U.S. troops into the country, ostensibly to increase security for U.S. forces that were withdrawing from Vietnam. In reality, the incursion was designed to buy more time for the South Vietnamese military and Nixon's own Vietnamization policy.

In announcing the invasion, Nixon was defiant and went directly at his detractors who were attacking him for not moving quickly enough to withdraw U.S. forces from Vietnam, saying …

> If when the chips are down, the world's most powerful nation, the United States of America, acts like a pitiful, helpless giant, the forces of totalitarianism and anarchy will threaten free nations and free institutions throughout the world.

Cold Facts

By expanding the Vietnam War into Cambodia beginning in 1969, Richard Nixon helped destabilize the country and radically disrupted Cambodian life. The bombing and subsequent invasion, supported by the country's right-wing government, brought thousands of new recruits into the country's communist opposition force, the Khmer Rouge. After a ferocious and gruesome war, the Khmer Rouge overthrew the government in 1975 and imposed a brutal, dictatorial regime that resulted in the deaths of more than two million Cambodians. The brutal regime would hold power into the late 1970s.

Domestic Unrest

News of the Cambodian invasion sparked violent protests on college campuses around the country. One third of U.S. colleges shut down temporarily because of student walkouts. At Kent State University in Ohio, the unrest turned deadly when National Guard troops killed four protesting students. Two days later, at Jackson State College in Mississippi, two more protesting students were killed.

The Cambodian invasion roused Congress to action. In June 1970, the Senate voted overwhelmingly to repeal the 1964 Gulf of Tonkin Resolution, the basis for Lyndon Johnson's initial escalation of the war. Later, senators also approved a measure cutting off all funding for the war in Cambodia after June 30.

While the House did not approve the Senate measure, it was clear that the Cambodian incursion had increased Nixon's domestic woes. The resulting outcry and Nixon's falling poll numbers intensified the pressure for faster troop withdrawals.

"Within the iron gates of the White House, quite unknowingly, a siege mentality was setting in," a Nixon aide later wrote. "Gradually, as we drew the circle closer around us, the ranks of 'them' began to swell."

Playing the China Card

Returning from Guam in July 1969, where Nixon had just announced his "Nixon Doctrine," Kissinger learned from White House Chief of Staff H.R. Haldeman that the president intended to visit China by the end of his second term. "Fat chance," was Kissinger's initial response.

But the chances of establishing a U.S.-China relationship were far better than Kissinger first imagined. As early as October 1967, Nixon had written in an article for the periodical *Foreign Affairs* that "any American policy must come urgently to grips with the reality of China. There is no place on this small planet for a billion of its potentially most able people to live in angry isolation." By the time he became president, Nixon also saw improved relations with China as a way to get the United States out of Vietnam with "honor" and as a means to force Soviet concessions in the SALT negotiations.

In October 1969, after several months of hostile encounters between Soviet and Chinese troops at the Ussuri River near the Siberian-Manchurian border, Nixon placed the U.S. Strategic Air Command on high alert to defend against a possible Soviet nuclear attack on China. That bold move got the Soviets' attention, forced a resolution to the Ussuri River dispute, and signaled strongly that U.S.-Chinese relations had changed dramatically.

Kissinger's Secret Mission

In the fall of 1970, Nixon took another bold step to improve relations with China when he opened secret diplomatic channels with Chinese leaders who, in turn, invited Nixon to send an envoy to Beijing. In July 1971, Kissinger traveled to the Chinese capitol to begin secret talks about Vietnam and other issues. During this meeting, the Chinese proposed that Nixon visit China, an invitation the president immediately accepted.

Nixon Goes to China

Nixon shocked the world on July 15, 1971, when he announced that he would travel to China before May 1972. While announcing the trip, the president also signaled his desire to remove the dispute over Taiwan as an impediment to U.S.-Chinese relations. He cut the number of U.S. troops on the breakaway island by 9,000.

In February 1972, Nixon made his historic visit to China, and by the trip's conclusion had completed agreements on travel, tourism, trade, and the ultimate, but gradual, withdrawal of all U.S. troops from Taiwan. Before he left China, Nixon declared that the visit had been "a week that changed the world."

Cold Facts

From 1974 to 1975, the U.S. envoy to China was the future, forty-first U.S. president, George Bush.

Aftermath

Nixon's mission to China had changed the world. Much to the chagrin of the North Vietnamese, the Chinese were now pledged to help the United States find its way out of Vietnam. The Soviets, meanwhile, reacted to Nixon's China trip with disdain. Instead of decreasing military assistance to North Vietnam, they accelerated their help to the communist regime in hopes of keeping the U.S. military tied down in Southeast Asia for as long as possible. But the objectives of Nixon's trip had largely been achieved. The United States had driven a wedge between the Soviets and the Chinese, and the North Vietnamese were being gradually isolated from their Chinese allies.

Vietnamization

Nixon was turning up the military and diplomatic heat on the North Vietnamese, with little immediate success. In Washington, however, he was also feeling the heat of public opinion and congressional unrest. Increasingly, the nation was eager to get out of Vietnam and wanted the troop withdrawals speeded up.

President Richard Nixon visits U.S. troops in South Vietnam in July 1969.

(Courtesy of the National Archives)

"After two years of continued heavy fighting, intensive secret diplomacy, and political maneuver, Nixon's position was worse than when he had taken office," observed historian George C. Herring. By the summer of 1971, Nixon's approval ratings had dropped to 31 percent. Polls showed that 71 percent of Americans believed that U.S. involvement in the war had been a mistake.

Instead of revamping his policy, Nixon simply pushed for more of the same. He ordered the withdrawal of 100,000 American troops from Vietnam by the end of 1971, leaving 175,000 troops in the country—75,000 of them combat forces.

Nixon's policy was a retreat disguised as an offensive. As he was withdrawing ground troops, the president was actually intensifying the fighting. Nixon approved a major invasion of Laos in February 1971 and later increased the number of air strikes against communist supply lines and bases in Cambodia and Laos.

The Easter Offensive

By the spring of 1972, with only 95,000 American troops (6,000 combat) in South Vietnam, the North Vietnamese took the offensive. On March 30, 30,000 communist troops, backed by 150,000 Vietcong fighters, attacked and routed the South Vietnamese military in a northern province of South Vietnam.

Cold Facts

Richard Nixon reacted angrily to North Vietnam's 1972 Easter Offensive. "The bastards have never been bombed like they're going to be bombed this time," he vowed. True to his word, Nixon unleashed a furious series of attacks. U.S. planes dropped 112,000 tons of bombs on North Vietnam.

Advised against a strong military response for fear it would imperil his upcoming summit with Soviet leader Brezhnev, Nixon nonetheless ordered a drastic escalation of the war. On May 8, he told the nation that he had ordered massive, sustained bombing of North Vietnam, the mining of Haiphong Harbor, and a naval blockade of the country.

In the end, the worst fears of Nixon's advisors were not realized. By then, the Soviets and the Chinese did not consider winning in Vietnam as a goal more important than improved relations with the United States. As a consequence, both nations began pressuring North Vietnam to negotiate an end to the conflict.

Peace Is at Hand

1972 was an election year and Richard Nixon wanted a peace deal before November. In Hanoi, the North Vietnamese leaders were just as eager to end the war. Pressured by China and the Soviets, battered by the bombing, and hopeful of a good, preelection deal from the United States, the communist leaders in North Vietnam finally signaled their willingness to talk.

Tentative Deal

By late summer, negotiations between the United States and North Vietnam were underway in Paris. Especially eager for a deal before the November election, Kissinger made concessions that would prove loathsome to South Vietnam's leader, Nguyen van Thieu. In return for U.S. prisoners of war and other concessions, Kissinger agreed to a total U.S. withdrawal and recognition of the political legitimacy of the Vietcong. He also signaled that the United States would allow North Vietnamese troops to remain in South Vietnam after the war.

Kissinger hoped that Nixon would go ahead with the agreement, despite Thieu's strong objections. On October 27, shortly before the election, Kissinger announced that "peace is at hand." Nixon, however, did not believe he needed a peace deal in order to win reelection. He would not, at least for now, force an agreement on South Vietnam.

Talks Stall

Nixon's steadfast support for Thieu undermined Kissinger's peace deal. By mid-December 1972, the talks broke off. Making the most of what time he had left to strengthen Thieu's military, Nixon began shipping more than $1 billion in military equipment to South Vietnam.

After informing Thieu that the United States would eventually be forced to negotiate a separate peace deal with North Vietnam, Nixon promised the South Vietnamese president that he would employ the U.S. military to guarantee Hanoi's compliance with the agreement. In other words, Thieu was being told that his choice was to accept the best deal possible or lose U.S. backing altogether.

Jugular Diplomacy

Next, Nixon employed what Kissinger later described as "jugular diplomacy." During the 1972 Christmas holidays, the United States waged another massive bombing operation, inflicting heavy damage on strategic and civilian areas in and around Hanoi and Haiphong. While the Christmas bombing sparked furious cries of protest in the United States and around the world, the North Vietnamese did return to the bargaining table on January 8.

Agreement

This time, the two sides—with almost no input from the South Vietnamese government—struck a deal. With Congress threatening to cut off all funding for the war, Nixon agreed to remove all U.S. troops from Vietnam, allow North Vietnamese troops to remain in

Cold Facts

Of the 58,000 Americans soldiers who died in Vietnam, more than 20,000 of them lost their lives during Richard Nixon's presidency.

South Vietnam, and to give the Vietcong's political representatives a role in any new government that emerged in a unified Vietnam. In return, the North Vietnamese would return all American POWs and allow Thieu to temporarily remain in power. Thieu had no choice but to endorse the plan.

For years, Nixon had preached the need for "peace with honor." Few then and now regarded the plan as peaceful or honorable. Ink on the agreement was barely dry before the South Vietnamese began to violate its terms. And as historian George C. Herring noted in *America's Longest War*, the agreements did not end the war. They "merely established a new framework for continuing the struggle without direct American participation."

The war in Vietnam had destroyed Lyndon Johnson's presidency. And now, in a more profound way, it would claim Richard Nixon's. Not only did the protracted, deadly fighting destroy Nixon's popularity; it would lead directly to the worst presidential scandal in American history—Watergate.

The Least You Need to Know

- During the 1960s and early 1970s, relations between the United States and the Soviet Union improved considerably, and several arms control agreements were signed.
- While he began withdrawing American troops from Vietnam beginning in 1969, Richard Nixon escalated and expanded the war by bombing and invading Cambodia.
- Nixon used improved relations with the Soviet Union and China to pressure North Vietnam into negotiating an end to the Vietnam War.
- During his presidency, Nixon made dramatic, groundbreaking visits to the Soviet Union and China, moving the United States toward better relations with both nations.
- Nixon's policy in Vietnam was called Vietnamization, a process by which he gradually withdrew American troops while beefing up the South Vietnamese military.
- The United States and North Vietnam finally reached a peace accord in January 1973, and all U.S. troops were withdrawn from the country shortly thereafter.

Chapter 19

A Ford Not a Lincoln

In This Chapter

- Tougher times for U.S.-Soviet relations
- Congress asserts its war-making authority
- Nixon and the Watergate scandal
- The American phase of the Vietnam War ends
- Gerald Ford succeeds Nixon

Ending American involvement in Vietnam didn't do much for U.S.-Soviet relations. Just as soon as Vietnam was behind us, renewed conflict in the Middle East threatened the relationship, as did a nasty dispute over Soviet immigration policy. That, in turn, would undermine a U.S.-Soviet trade agreement. After more than 10 years of increased cooperation between Washington and Moscow, our budding friendship with the Soviets was cooling again.

Richard Nixon, of course, wouldn't get to finish his second term in office. The Watergate scandal removed him from the scene in August 1974. And after more than a decade of war and domestic turmoil, the country was ready for the calming influence of a president like Gerald Ford.

Détente Wanes

At first, it appeared the end of the Vietnam War meant even better U.S.-Soviet relations. In June 1973, President Nixon and Soviet leader Leonid Brezhnev met in Washington and signed the Agreement on the Prevention of Nuclear War. The pact obligated the two nations to act "in such a manner as to prevent the development of situations capable of causing a dangerous exacerbation of their relations." If a situation ever threatened to spin out of control, the treaty required "urgent consultation" to ease tensions.

The Yom Kippur War

By October, tensions in the Middle East put the treaty to a severe test. Egypt and other nations in the Arab world were furious over the impending sale of U.S. jet fighters to Israel. On October 6, the Jewish holy day of Yom Kippur, Soviet-allied Egypt staged a preemptive strike. Its army attacked Israeli-held military positions on the Sinai Peninsula, while Syria simultaneously attacked Israeli positions on the Golan Heights.

What most upset U.S. officials was that Soviet leaders obviously knew of the attacks beforehand and, in fact, had consulted with Egypt and its allies during the planning stages—a direction violation of the Agreement on the Prevention of Nuclear War. Believing that he had no choice but to assist the besieged Israelis, Nixon ordered a massive airlift of U.S. military equipment. That assistance not only enabled Israel to repel the attack, but allowed them to take the offensive. In a matter of days, the Israeli army had the Syrians on the run and completely surrounded the Egyptian forces.

> **Cold Facts**
>
> Richard Nixon was more than a little distracted during the Yom Kippur War in October 1973. During the war's two-week duration he struggled with issues relating to the Watergate investigation; received the resignation of Vice President Spiro Agnew, who resigned in a bribery scandal; selected Gerald Ford as the new vice president; and fired his Attorney General Elliot Richardson and the Watergate special prosecutor, Archibald Cox.

The Middle East conflict almost became a superpower conflict when the Soviet Union threatened to rescue the Egyptian army by introducing its army into the region. In response, the United States put its forces on high alert and the situation threatened to spiral out of control. Brezhnev eventually backed down and supported a UN cease-fire resolution that eased tensions in the region.

The incident, however, harmed U.S.-Soviet relations. Both sides had violated the Agreement on the Prevention on Nuclear War by failing to engage in the urgent consultation mandated by the treaty.

Trade Failure

Tensions between the two nations further deteriorated the following year when the Senate, led by Democratic Senator Henry Jackson of Washington, attached an explosive amendment to a U.S.-Soviet trade agreement. Jackson's amendment denied most-favored-nation status to any "nonmarket economy country" that limited the right of its citizens to immigrate. That language, of course, was a thinly disguised attack on the Soviet Union, which prevented the immigration of Soviet Jews to Israel by charging exorbitant immigration taxes.

When Congress finally passed the Jackson-amended trade bill in January 1975, the Soviets responded by refusing to implement the agreement. Once again, relations between the United States and the Soviets grew icy.

The War Powers Act

The Vietnam War not only took its toll on Richard Nixon's popularity, it also gave Congress reason to restrain, in theory at least, the war powers of all future presidents. By the fall of 1973, the spreading Watergate scandal (more on that later) had so weakened Nixon that he was powerless to withstand a congressional assault on his war-making prerogatives. On November 6, Congress overrode his veto of the War Powers Act and enacted legislation strictly limiting the ability of presidents to send U.S. troops into combat for more than 60 days without congressional assent.

The bill was an effort to restore the balance of power that had tilted toward the White House since World War II. Congress now decreed that presidents could no longer send U.S. troops into battle without congressional approval, except in the most extraordinary situations. Even so, presidents would be required to explain their actions to the leaders of both houses within 48 hours and would be forced to terminate the military action within 60 days unless Congress declared war or specifically authorized the commitment of forces. And adding to the indignity of the War Powers Act, Congress also refused to go along with Nixon's requests to increase military assistance to the government of South Vietnam.

Quotes from the Cold

The President in every possible instance shall consult with Congress before introducing United States Armed Forces into hostilities or into situations where imminent involvement in hostilities is clearly indicated by the circumstances, and after every such introduction shall consult regularly with the Congress until United States Armed Forces are no longer engaged in hostilities or have been removed from such situations.

—Section 3 of the 1973 War Powers Act

Watergate

The Watergate scandal that forced Nixon to resign in August 1974 had its genesis in the Cold War. The lies, deception, burglary, and other criminal activities that occurred grew out of Nixon's worries about communist infiltration of the antiwar movement.

Nixon believed that the protesters "were being aided and abetted, if not actually inspired, by Communist countries." He wanted the evidence as well as the identities of those officials who were leaking sensitive information about the war to reporters. Thus, Nixon pushed the FBI to plug the leaks and investigate the antiwar groups. To do so, he ordered illegal wiretaps and surveillance of White House and State Department officials, as well as reporters. But it was the Kent State killings that, in H.R. Haldeman's words, "marked a turning point for Nixon; a beginning of his downhill slide toward Watergate."

Angrier and more defiant than ever, Nixon was persuaded that the FBI was not equal to the task of ferreting out the sources of administration leaks. He pushed for even more aggressive surveillance. On June 5, 1970, the president summoned the heads of the CIA, FBI, the Defense Intelligence Agency, and the National Security Agency. He demanded a special task force and a plan to better investigate the sources of the domestic unrest.

Cold Facts

Richard Nixon's vice president, Spiro Agnew, became the first U.S. vice president to resign his office because of criminal allegations. In October 1973, the U.S. Justice Department charged him with accepting more than $100,000 in bribes while he was a Maryland county executive, governor of Maryland, and vice president of the United States. Agnew denied the allegations, but pled no contest to tax evasion charges and resigned his office in a deal that permitted him to avoid a prison sentence. Nixon nominated the House Republican leader, Gerald Ford of Michigan, as Agnew's successor.

Pentagon Papers

Nixon's concern about leaks were only exacerbated by the publication of the Pentagon Papers in the summer of 1971. In June, *The New York Times* began to publish the classified history of decision making in Vietnam that had been compiled by the U.S. Defense Department in the late 1960s. The documents were leaked to the *Times* by Daniel Ellsberg, a former Defense Department official who had turned against the war.

More obsessed with leaks than ever, Nixon ordered the Justice Department to obtain a court injunction against the *Times* to prevent further publication of the documents. When the Supreme Court finally overturned the injunction, permitting continued publication, Nixon created a secret group of "plumbers" to plug administration leaks. Another part of their job was to discredit Ellsberg. And that involved burglarizing the office of his psychiatrist in a search for damaging information.

Cold Facts

Richard Nixon was goaded into fighting publication of the Pentagon Papers by Henry Kissinger, who forcefully argued that it would "destroy our ability to conduct foreign policy in confidence." Many historians believe that this was an overreaction, especially because the papers had nothing in them about Nixon's conduct of the war. "Without Henry's stimulus," one Nixon's aide later observed, "the president and the rest of us might have concluded that the papers were Lyndon Johnson's problem, not ours."

The Burglary

By 1972, in the midst of the presidential campaign, the clandestine unit that had originally focused on the antiwar movement was now aimed at the Democratic National Committee. On June 17, burglars under the direction of Nixon's campaign were arrested inside the Democratic National Committee's suite at the Watergate office building.

By the following spring, a number of Nixon's aides would be caught up in the unfolding scandal. Eventually, the scandal and subsequent cover-up would entangle U.S. Attorney General John Mitchell, White House Counsel John Dean, White House Chief of Staff H.R. Haldeman, White House Special Assistant on Domestic Affairs John Ehrlichman, and others.

By August 1974, it was clear that Nixon had participated in an extensive effort to obstruct justice by covering up the White House connection to the Watergate burglary and other clandestine activities. On August 9, with the House about to impeach him, Nixon quit in disgrace. He remains the only American president to have resigned.

Quotes from the Cold

People have got to know whether or not their President is a crook. Well, I'm not a crook. I've earned everything I've got.

—Richard Nixon at a November 1973 press conference

Bye, Bye, Vietnam

Only the day before Nixon left Washington, in the fiercest fighting since before the 1973 peace accords, communist troops in South Vietnam—in violation of the cease-fire agreement—seized a strategic outpost 330 miles north of Saigon, near Da Nang. While the new president, Gerald Ford, assured Thieu that he supported the government of

Quotes from the Cold

My fellow Americans, our long national nightmare is over. Our Constitution works; our great Republic is a government of laws and not of men. Here the people rule.

—President Gerald Ford, Swearing-in Speech, August 9, 1974

Cold Words

Amnesty is exemption from criminal prosecution sometimes conferred upon draft dodgers or deserters. It is derived from the word amnesia, and literally means to forget a wrongdoing or crime.

South Vietnam, he had little more than words to back up his promises. In late August, Ford reluctantly accepted a drastically scaled-back assistance plan for Vietnam passed by Congress.

Ford was a decent man, eager to heal the festering wounds of the 1960s and the early 1970s. The new president acted quickly to begin the nation's recovery. He pardoned Nixon in early September and then, a week later, began the process of reconciliation by announcing a program of "earned" *amnesty* for the 50,000 draft evaders and deserters from the Vietnam War.

The mood of forgiveness and healing that Ford hoped to bring to the national debate over Vietnam was what most Americans wanted in general, but not in particular. Ford's pardon of Nixon angered Democrats, while his amnesty program found little support among Republicans and other conservatives. By late September, the new president's public approval ratings dropped significantly.

Beginning of the End

In South Vietnam, the drastic reduction in American military and economic assistance had taken its toll on the government's ability to withstand the encroaching communist forces. President Thieu didn't help matters when he cracked down on domestic dissent by closing newspapers and outlawing public demonstrations. Nothing, however, could contain the unrest for long. Rising inflation combined with falling wages decimated South Vietnam's army. In 1974 alone, 200,000 men deserted.

By January 1975, the North Vietnamese captured the province of Phuoc Long, 50 miles north of Saigon on the Cambodian border, including its provincial capitol, Phuoc Binh. As March passed, the communists enjoyed control over 13 provinces, most of them taken after South Vietnamese forces offered little or no defense. Thieu frantically adopted a last-minute enclave strategy, pulling back his country's forces to defend the Mekong Delta area around Saigon.

Ford was eager to help, but his options were limited. On April 10, he made an impassioned appeal for more military assistance, asking Congress to spend a billion dollars for military and economic assistance. But Congress, tired of the war, refused.

Saigon Falls

On April 19, the battle for control of Saigon began when communist forces laid siege to the city. The next day, Thieu resigned and six days later fled the country for Thailand. In Washington, Ford knew the end was near and ordered the evacuation of the 6,000 American personnel still in Vietnam.

In Saigon, pandemonium reigned, as thousands of South Vietnamese citizens flocked to the airport, hoping for a ride on departing U.S. military aircraft. Frantic refugees streamed onto the runway and prevented planes from landing. "The only option left," Ford explained, "was to remove the remaining Americans, and as many South Vietnamese as possible, by helicopter from the roof of the U.S. embassy in Saigon." With the helicopters standing by on the decks of navy ships off the coast, Ford finally ordered the commencement of the final, desperate evacuation in the early morning hours of April 29. For 16 grueling hours, U.S. Navy helicopters ferried 6,500 American and South Vietnamese citizens to safety.

Thus ended America's 25-year effort to defeat communism in Southeast Asia. The United States, for the first time in its 199-year history, had lost a war. Less than a year before the country would begin to celebrate its Bicentennial, American citizens were forced to consider, for the first time during the twentieth century, the limitations of their country's awesome power.

Quotes from the Cold

The high hopes and wishful idealism with which the American nation had been born had not been destroyed, but they had been chastened by the failure of America to work its will in Indochina. Now, the world and the ability of the United States to influence it have changed.

—*Newsweek*, April 1975

A Time for Healing

At first, Americans were charmed by the middle-class informality of their new president, Gerald Ford. After more than 10 years of humorless and brooding chief executives, Ford's openness and accessibility was a refreshing change. "I am acutely aware that you have not elected me as your President by your ballots," he told the American people, "and so I ask you to confirm me as your President with your prayers."

Soon, however, Ford would have need of those prayers. His unconditional pardon of Richard

Cold Facts

When Gerald Ford went before the House Judiciary Committee in October 1975 to testify about the Nixon pardon, he was only the second sitting president in history to appear before a congressional committee. The first had been Abraham Lincoln, during the Civil War.

Nixon sparked an outcry in Congress. The president was accused of having cut a deal with Nixon before the disgraced president left the White House. "There was no deal, period," Ford told a congressional committee during an extraordinary committee session.

Troubles Galore

By the end of 1974, Ford faced a multitude of problems. The U.S. economy, battered by government spending on the war and social programs during the 1960s, was beset with high inflation.

Adding to the inflationary pressures were escalating world energy prices, brought about by an oil embargo imposed by the Organization of Petroleum Exporting Countries (OPEC). The Arab OPEC nations, angry over Western support for Israel in its war with Egypt and Syria in 1973, cut off oil shipments to Israel's allies.

Gerald Ford became the thirty-eighth president in August 1974 when Richard Nixon, facing impeachment over the Watergate scandal, resigned office.

(Courtesy of the Gerald R. Ford Library)

In the United States, oil prices jumped 350 percent. Spurred by the embargo, inflation rose dramatically—from 3.3 percent in 1972 to 6.2 percent the following year and to 11 percent in 1974. As gas consumption fell, so did the demand for new cars. That sparked a recession in the automotive industry and a dramatic rise in unemployment. Soon the recession spread to other industries.

Ford's domestic problems were serious enough. But it was his foreign policies—particularly his posture toward the Soviet Union—that caused him serious troubles within the Republican Party.

> **Cold Facts**
>
> President Gerald Ford's efforts to combat inflation were widely ridiculed by the news media and by his political opponents. In October 1974, he unveiled the Whip Inflation Now (WIN) program. Among its most prominent features was the WIN button. As the recession worsened, however, Ford was forced to abandon his program in favor of stimulative economic measures that threatened to increase inflation. Later, Ford observed that the WIN effort, especially the button, was "probably too gimmicky."

Vladivostok

Ford made his own attempts to repair the tattered U.S.-Soviet relationship. In November 1974, he and Brezhnev met in Vladivostok, where they signed an agreement to limit their respective arsenals of strategic offensive nuclear weapons and delivery vehicles. The two leaders also worked out a framework to salvage the stalled SALT talks that included a ceiling on delivery vehicles and MIRVs for both sides. Although Kissinger, then secretary of state, called the agreement a "breakthrough" that would halt the arms race "for ten years," some Republicans were less than thrilled.

Conservatives, especially, complained that Ford had made a bad deal. The treaty, they argued, made no provision for controlling actual warhead numbers, nor did it address *throw weight*, a category in which the Soviets possessed a three-to-one advantage over the United States.

Liberals, meanwhile, complained that Ford and Kissinger had agreed to arms limitation numbers that were too high. The treaty would not actually reduce the number of nuclear missiles, but merely slow their *proliferation*.

> **Cold Words**
>
> **Throw weight** is the weight of a missile's payload. It is the missile's warhead and guidance system, but does not include the rocket that propels it.
>
> Nuclear **proliferation** is the rapid increase in the production of nuclear weapons by a nation or group of nations.

Helsinki Accord

Ford's support of the Helsinki accords was another sore spot for conservative Republicans and further undermined his standing within his party. On August 15, 1975, in Helsinki, Finland, the United States joined representatives of Canada and 35 European nations in signing the Final Act of the Conference on Security and Cooperation in Europe.

The agreement called for greater cooperation between East and West in economics, science, technology, and the environment. It established principles for the free movement of people and ideas, including more cultural and educational exchanges. The nations also affirmed their resolve to settle disputes peacefully.

What most outraged conservatives, however, was wording in the Final Act that recognized Soviet domination of Eastern Europe in return for assurances that the Soviets would respect the human rights of its citizens. Few expected the Soviets to honor their promises (and they didn't). And the conservatives were further outraged by comments from one State Department officials who encouraged the Eastern European nations to develop "a more natural and organic" relationship with the Soviet. Like Roosevelt at Yalta, Ford was now accused by some of having again delivered Eastern Europe into communist domination.

Quotes from the Cold

Where the age-old antagonism between freedom and tyranny is concerned, we are not neutral. But other imperatives impose limits on our ability to produce internal changes in foreign countries. Consciousness of our limits is recognition of the necessity of peace—not moral callousness. The preservation of human life and human society are moral values, too.

—Henry Kissinger, congressional testimony, September 1974

Helsinki, however, wasn't the sellout that the conservatives alleged. The accord didn't give them one square inch of new territory. And, as Cold War historian Ronald E. Powaski observed in his book, *The Cold War: The United States and the Soviet Union, 1917–1991:* "While the Soviets and their satellites did not implement the human rights provisions of the Helsinki accord, the fact that they had signed a document recognizing them established another standard by which communism could be judged, and ultimately undermined."

Ford's Defeat

Weakened by his pardon of Richard Nixon, the country's deep recession, and the collapse of conservative support over his foreign policies, Ford ran for election in his own right in 1976. But the nomination wasn't his for the asking. Former California Governor Ronald Reagan, a vocal opponent of the Helsinki Accord, mounted a fierce challenge that almost succeeded. Ford narrowly won his party's nomination and limped into the general election season with lukewarm support from many in his own party.

Running as the Democratic Party's nominee was former Georgia Governor Jimmy Carter, an engaging moderate who promised that he would never lie to the American people. With memories of Watergate still fresh in the public consciousness, it was a promise that had currency. What may have hurt Ford the most in the campaign's latter stage was his assertion, during a debate with Carter, that Poland was not dominated by the Soviet Union. That raised questions about whether Ford was up to the job of president. On Election Day, Carter won by a narrow margin.

Cold Facts

While challenging Gerald Ford for the Republican presidential nomination in 1976, former California Governor Ronald Reagan charged that Ford's pursuit of détente with the Soviet Union had jeopardized U.S. security. The United States, he said, "has become Number Two in a world where it is dangerous—if not fatal—to be second."

The Least You Need to Know

- U.S.-Soviet relations turned sour in 1973 when the two countries came to the brink of direct conflict over the conflict in the Middle East; a dispute with the Soviets over immigration policy in 1975 further damaged relations between the two nations.
- Over President Nixon's veto, Congress enacted the War Powers Act in 1973, limiting the president's ability to wage war without congressional approval and consultation.
- The Watergate scandal, which had its roots in Richard Nixon's distrust of the antiwar movement, culminated in August 1974 with his resignation.
- As communist troops approached the South Vietnamese capital in April 1975, President Gerald Ford ordered the evacuation of all remaining American personnel from Saigon, after which South Vietnam fell to the communists.
- While Ford struggled to deal with the country's dire economic woes, conservatives attacked him for his posture toward the Soviet Union; in 1976, Ford survived a tough primary challenge and narrowly lost to Jimmy Carter in the general election.

Chapter 20

Cynicism on Film

In This Chapter

- Vietnam's impact on the American psyche
- How Hollywood portrayed the Vietnam War
- Television treats Vietnam with kid gloves
- *M*A*S*H* takes on the Vietnam War

The 1970s were a time of dramatic social change. The Vietnam War not only transformed the way Americans viewed themselves and their country, it sparked profound changes in popular culture that are still being felt today.

Movie producers finally turned to Vietnam as a subject and gave us some of the best films of the decade. From *Apocalypse Now* to *The Deer Hunter*, movie producers explored the carnage of combat, the futility of war and the physical and emotional wounds suffered by returning Vietnam War veterans. But television, less an art form than movies, largely shied away from war programs. In this chapter, we will examine Vietnam's impact on American popular culture.

The Vietnam Impact

The Vietnam War left many Americans deeply disenchanted about their nation and its place in the world. Just as our success in World War II had spawned decades of unbridled optimism, Vietnam dragged the country into a morass of despair and self-doubt.

After Vietnam and Watergate, Americans came to realize that their leaders had regularly lied to them about the nation's affairs. The trust and admiration that leaders like Roosevelt and Eisenhower had enjoyed was gone. Even honest men like Gerald Ford and Jimmy Carter were viewed more skeptically and cynically by Americans, especially the news media.

Young people were especially disillusioned by the country's disastrous involvement in Vietnam. And that disillusionment was not confined merely to the government or the U.S. military. National polls during 1970 and 1971 revealed that one third of college-age Americans regarded marriage as obsolete. Fifty percent of them said they regarded no living American as heroic. Nearly half reported the feeling that America was "a sick society."

This didn't simply mean that young people were wearing their hair longer and questioning the value of voting. Stronger social gales were blowing through America. Because of their disillusionment with the previous generation, many young people no longer saw the value in honoring their parents' views on drug use, sex, music, clothing, living arrangements, and authority itself. More than anything, however, it was the ugly, deadly war in Vietnam—its tragedy compounded by the crimes of Watergate—that caused so many Americans to ask if their country had lost its way.

Quotes from the Cold

Many Americans sensed that the nation had entered a period of decline. No longer able to lead the world, the United States could no longer even find its own way at home. These intimations of decline were everywhere to be heard and seen in the 1970s—as the war ground toward defeat, as the Watergate cover-up unraveled, as the Arab oil embargo humiliated a seemingly impotent nation, as the economy worsened.

—Bruce J. Schulman, *The Seventies: The Great Shift in American Culture, Society, and Politics* (Free Press, 2001)

Hollywood Complains

If the war in Vietnam had been so wrong and without redeeming value, then why would American filmmakers possibly believe that moviegoers would be interested in seeing films about it? Undoubtedly, many were asking themselves the same question.

Vietnam had, indeed, been a different kind of war. Unlike World War II, when Washington recruited Hollywood to build and maintain public support for the war effort, Vietnam inspired no similar outpouring of patriot movie making. There were a few pro-Vietnam War movies, most notably the super-patriotic, one-dimensional 1968 John Wayne movie, *The Green Berets.*

For the most part, however, Washington didn't need Hollywood's help in recruiting. The draft took care of that. As for public opinion, Lyndon Johnson purposefully played down the Vietnam War for fear that it would detract from his Great Society agenda. And by the time Richard Nixon came along, U.S. leaders were mostly looking for ways to get the U.S. military out of, not deeper into, Southeast Asia.

Simply put, Vietnam was unlike World War II in almost every respect. Too many Americans, especially by the late 1960s, did not regard our role in Vietnam as honorable or proper. In other words, a very unpopular war did not seem like the best material from which to make popular movies.

The Vietnam Movie

The 1970s was a time of great creativity in the movie business. Power was more decentralized than ever and a new crop of young, university-trained filmmakers began to burst onto the scene: Martin Scorsese (*Taxi Driver* and *Raging Bull*), Steven Spielberg (*Jaws* and *Close Encounters of the Third Kind*), George Lucas (*American Graffiti* and *Star Wars*), and Francis Ford Coppola (*The Godfather* and *Apocolypse Now*).

It was a decade that produced the first of the big summer blockbusters. Movies like *Star Wars*, *Jaws*, *Close Encounters of the Third Kind*, and *The Godfather* dominated movie houses during the decade. While most directors and film producers shied away from Vietnam as a subject for their movies, some did not—and they produced memorable films that explored the postwar travails of Vietnam veterans or helped explain the brutal senselessness of the war.

Cold Facts

The ten most successful films of the 1970s:

1. Star Wars (1977)
2. Jaws (1975)
3. Grease (1978)
4. The Exorcist (1973)
5. The Sting (1973)
6. Close Encounters of the Third Kind (1977)
7. National Lampoon's Animal House (1977)
8. Saturday Night Fever (1977)
9. The Rocky Horror Picture Show (1975)
10. The Godfather (1972)

The best Vietnam War movies did not appear until the late 1970s. But for many moviegoers, it was worth the wait. A spate of memorable films about the American experience in Southeast Asia was brought forth during 1978 and 1979:

- *The Deer Hunter*, a 1978 movie produced and directed by Michael Cimino and starring Robert De Niro and Meryl Streep, was a powerful and disturbing look at the lives of three blue-collar friends before, during, and after their shattering experience in Vietnam. The film received nine Academy Award nominations and won five.
- *Apocalypse Now*, the 1979 masterpiece produced and directed by Francis Ford Coppola, starred Marlon Brando, Robert Duvall, and Martin Sheen. Called by some "the greatest war movie ever made," it is the story of a U.S. army mission to assassinate a lawless warlord who has established his own fiefdom deep in the Southeast Asian jungles. The movie was nominated for eight Academy Awards and won two.
- *Coming Home*, the Academy Award-winning 1978 film starring Jane Fonda and Jon Voight, told the story of the lingering wounds of the Vietnam War. The movie examined the relationship between an embittered paraplegic veteran and the woman who volunteered to care for him.
- *The Boys in Company C*, was a brash, realistic 1978 film about a squadron of five young Marines in Vietnam, all whose lives were drastically altered by the war.
- *Go Tell the Spartans*, a 1978 film starring Burt Lancaster, is one of the least known, but one of the most highly regarded by film critics. It is the story of a tough U.S. military advisor assigned to an abandoned French outpost in 1964. As the Lancaster character tries to assemble a platoon out of inexperienced American soldiers, he begins to question the U.S. role in Vietnam.

Cold Facts

The epic 1979 film *Apocalypse Now*, filmed on location in the Philippines, was originally budgeted at $12 million, an extravagant amount at the time. But delays and various catastrophes plagued the film (actor Martin Sheen suffered a heart attack during filming) and it ultimately cost more than $30 million.

Quotes from the Cold

A true war story is never moral. It does not instruct, nor encourage virtue, nor suggest models of proper human behavior. … If a story seems moral do not believe it. If at the end of a war story you feel uplifted, or if you feel that some small bit of rectitude has been salvaged from the larger waste, then you have been made the victim of a very old and terrible lie. There is no rectitude whatsoever. There is no virtue.

—Tim O'Brien, *The Things They Carried* (Houghton Mifflin, 1990)

Cautious Television

In the 1960s and early 1970s, television news had brought the Vietnam War and its violence into the living rooms of most Americans. But when it came to television's entertainment side, Vietnam was hardly a story at all.

While a few moviemakers tackled the war, television producers largely shied away from Vietnam in the 1970s. When they did address the war, it was indirectly, as in the case of *M*A*S*H*, the popular CBS program that ran from 1972 to 1983.

Based on the 1970 Robert Altman movie by the same name, *M*A*S*H* is remembered as one of the television's most popular and successful programs. Ostensibly about the struggle of a field medical unit during the Korean War, *M*A*S*H*'s obvious targets were U.S. policy in Vietnam, the blind patriotism of some of its supporters, and the pretensions of American popular culture.

When the show's main characters, particularly Hawkeye Pierce (played by Alan Alda), railed against the madness and mindlessness of the war, they could just as well be talking about Vietnam as Korea. When the show poked fun or ridiculed the U.S. military culture—its rules, rank, bureaucracy, and patriotism—it was a broadside, not against the military of the Korean War era, but of Vietnam.

In the movie version, Altman had purposely omitted references to Korea. "If you look at that film," the filmmaker told a reporter in 2001, "there's no mention of what war it is." Even though the movie studio forced Altman to put a disclaimer at the beginning of the movie, identifying it as a Korean War story, most viewers got the point. "If you ask people now what *M*A*S*H* was about, 75 to 80 percent would say it was Vietnam."

But the movie and the popular TV series were about more than a military war. As one cultural commentator has observed, the program "reenacts the 'culture war' that was going on in America when the show started." At the time, liberalism, the counterculture, and the antiwar movement were in a battle against popular American culture, government, and the U.S. military. "*M*A*S*H* takes these two cultures and turns each into a kind of society," pitting them against each other in ways that were symbolic of the cultural battles being waged in the United States.

Cold Facts

After the success of the movie *The Deer Hunter* in 1978, the television networks commissioned scripts for several Vietnam dramas. NBC put one pilot on the air, *6:00 Follies*, but the show never attracted a large audience. "I don't think people want to hear about Vietnam," one network executive said at the time. "I think it was destined for failure simply because I don't think it's a funny war."

The Least You Need to Know

- In the aftermath of the Vietnam War, many Americans, especially young people, were disenchanted about the nation, its culture, and its role in the world.
- While most film producers shied away from the Vietnam War as a theme during the 1970s, some did not. Successful films about the war or its aftermath included *The Deer Hunter*, *Apocalypse Now*, and *Coming Home*.
- With the exception of news reporting, television shied away almost completely from Vietnam as a theme for its other programming.
- The hit 1970s television series *M*A*S*H*—ostensibly about the Korean War—dealt with themes that could be construed as criticism of the Vietnam War and the U.S. military.

Chapter 21

Jimmy's Good Intentions

In This Chapter

- Jimmy Carter's foreign policy
- Human rights takes center stage
- Carter normalizes relations with China
- Agreement on a SALT II treaty
- The Soviet invasion of Afghanistan; U.S.–Soviet relations on the rocks
- Carter and the faltering U.S. economy

Jimmy Carter was a different kind of president. A former Democratic governor of Georgia, Carter was a liberal by southern standards. He was an avowed outsider, following a long line of post-World War II presidents who had risen to power on the basis of their considerable Washington experience.

In the aftermath of Watergate, Carter's apparent openness and honesty and his unabashed religious fervor appealed to many Americans hungry for a strong leader they could admire. In so many ways, Carter was what Americans wanted in a president in the immediate post-Vietnam, post-Watergate era.

What they wanted and what they got, however, were two different things. Carter failed to deliver many of the reforms he had promised. And when it came to managing U.S.-Soviet relations, he proved a disaster. In the end,

Carter's foreign policy record would be a mixed one. He courageously championed human rights and normalized relations with the People's Republic of China. But those and other actions only infuriated the Soviets. By the end of his term, the détente of the Nixon-Ford years was a thing of the past.

Jimmy Takes On the World

Jimmy Carter was no foreign policy expert. As a governor with no real foreign affairs experience, the new president—at the beginning of his term, at least—relied heavily on his two top foreign policy advisors, Secretary of State Cyrus Vance, and National Security Advisor Zbigniew Brzezinski. Unfortunately for Carter, his advisors' approaches to world affairs, and especially U.S. relations with the Soviet Union, could not have been more different from each other.

A Polish-born political science professor, Brzezinski first met Carter at meetings of the Trilateral Commission—an organization dedicated to increasing cooperation among Western Europe, North America, and Pacific Asia. Brzezinski was an anti-Soviet hard-liner who believed the Soviets were primarily *hegemonic*—that is, they wanted to expand their empire and spread communism throughout the world. The only way to counter Soviet *hegemony*, Brzezinski believed, was with military might. When it came to unrest in the Third World, Brzezinski suspected that the Soviets were almost always involved.

Cold Facts

Jimmy Carter was a southern politician noted for his liberal views on civil rights. In the 1950s, he was the only white man in his hometown of Plains, Georgia, to decline membership in the White Citizens Council, an organization dedicated to preserving racial segregation. In the mid-1960s, the Carters and another family were the only members of the Plains Baptist Church who supported admitting blacks to the congregation.

Vance saw the world differently. Like Henry Kissinger before him, he believed in the power and usefulness of diplomacy. While he was realistic about the Soviet Union's avarice, Vance believed that a patient, diplomatic approach to addressing U.S.-Soviet disputes would maintain the progress of détente and lead to mutually advantageous agreements, particularly an arms control treaty.

Cold Words

Hegemony is the power that one nation exercises over another. **Hegemonic nations** are those that seek to influence or dominate other nations.

Brzezinski, on the other hand, believed that SALT II, the potential strategic arms limitation treaty, was simply another way to limit Soviet hegemony and that progress in negotiations should be linked to Soviet behavior in other areas. Vance, however, maintained that arms control was too important to world peace to link to any other issue.

Vance Predominant

Despite his inexperience, Carter planned to take control of the country's foreign policy. He would not leave that part of his administration to others. In the early months of his presidency, however, Carter basically shared Vance's view of the world: The United States should work vigorously for peace within the community of nations.

In his heart, Carter embraced the idealism of Woodrow Wilson's foreign policy, professing in his inaugural address that he wanted to "help shape a just and peaceful world that is truly humane." Those fundamental American principles, he believed, had been jettisoned during the Nixon years of *realpolitik*.

Carter disdained the secret diplomacy and covert support for repressive regimes of previous administrations. His view of U.S. foreign policy also included an active, aggressive promotion of human rights. "Human rights is the soul of our foreign policy," he said in 1978, "because human rights is the very soul of our sense of nationhood."

Cold Facts

Jimmy Carter was the first president elected from the Deep South since Andrew Jackson in 1828.

Cold Words

Realpolitik is an approach to foreign policy and politics based primarily on pragmatism and practical calculation, not idealism.

Carter was idealistic, but not naive. Like Vance, he understood the basic expansionist desires of the Soviets. But he also believed that by downplaying the two nations' ideological differences and focusing, instead, on their mutual desire for peace and security, he could achieve an advance of détente. If this were to happen, Carter knew that it would be in the form of revived SALT II talks.

SALT: Stop and Start

Both the Soviets and the United States were eager to revive the stalled SALT II talks. But the going wasn't easy. Conservatives in Congress, led by Democratic Senator Henry Jackson of Washington, insisted on deep cuts in the Soviet arsenals of ICBMs and IRBMs. If based on the Vladivostok Accord, negotiated under President Ford, the conservatives believed that the limits established for Soviet missiles were unacceptably high and were a threat to U.S. security.

Carter could not afford to ignore these concerns if he ever wanted Senate ratification of SALT II. But when he tried to move the Soviets away from the Vladivostok framework, Leonid Brezhnev balked. He would not negotiate the sizable reductions in nuclear forces that Senate conservatives demanded. If the United States continued pressing for substantial cuts, then Brezhnev warned that he might insist, among other things, on the removal of U.S. military bases in Western Europe.

President Jimmy Carter. U.S.-Soviet relations suffered serious setbacks during his troubled presidency.

(Courtesy of the Library of Congress)

Finally, in May 1977, the two nations agreed on a three-tier framework for negotiations. They would first negotiate a treaty based on the Vladivostok Accord that would expire in 1985. Next would come a separate, three-year protocol to the treaty limiting specific weapons systems, like cruise missiles, mobile ICBMs, and other new missiles. Finally, the two sides agreed on a joint declaration of principles for future negotiations that would lead to a SALT III agreement.

Negotiations on a new SALT accord would begin. But Carter's vigorous human-rights campaign wouldn't make it any easier.

The Human-Rights Campaign

The civil rights struggle in his native Georgia had opened Jimmy Carter's eyes to the larger, worldwide struggle for human rights. "To me," he said later, "the political and social transformation of the Southland was a powerful demonstration of how moral principles should and could be applied effectively to the legal structure of our society."

In his inaugural address on January 20, 1977, Carter declared that the world's "passion for freedom is on the rise." There could be "no nobler nor more ambitious task," he said, "than for America to undertake on this day of a new beginning than to help shape a just and peaceful world that is truly humane."

The new president meant what he said. More than almost anything else, his presidency would be characterized by his crusade for human rights in the Soviet Union and Latin America. While his policies were noble, they were not always pragmatic, especially when squared against his stated desire to reach agreement on SALT II.

Soviet Abuses

Shortly after he entered the White House in 1977, Carter began highlighting Soviet human-rights abuses by offering well-publicized support for Soviet dissidents, including Andrei Sakharov. Simultaneously, Carter asked Congress for large budget increases for U.S. propaganda aimed at the Soviets and their allies via Radio Free Europe, Radio Liberty, and the Voice of America.

Carter somehow did not believe that these actions would impede progress on the SALT II talks. But Brezhnev did. In a letter to Carter in February 1977, the Soviet leader attacked the American president's support of Sakharov, a man he denounced as "a renegade who proclaimed himself an enemy of the Soviet state." He told Carter that he would not "allow interference in our internal affairs, whatever pseudo-humanitarian slogans are used to present it."

Carter didn't back off. He continued pressing his case against the Soviets for the rest of his term, despite the damage it did to overall U.S.-Soviet relations.

Cold Facts

Jimmy Carter's strong criticism of Soviet human-rights abuses did have some impact on Soviet behavior, particularly in the area of Jewish immigration. The number of Jews permitted to leave the Soviet Union increased from 14,000 in 1976 to more than 50,000 in 1979.

Cold Facts

At their only summit during the Carter presidency, Jimmy Carter and Soviet leader Leonid Brezhnev sparred over the issue of human rights. "Human rights is a sensitive subject for us and is not a legitimate ground for discussion between you and me," Brezhnev told Carter. Refusing to back down, Carter replied: "The subject of human rights is very important to us in shaping our attitude toward your country. You voluntarily signed the Helsinki Accords, which made this issue a proper item of state-to-state relations."

Human Rights Elsewhere

Carter also expended considerable energy on improving human rights in Latin America, particularly in Argentina, Brazil, and Chile. Deploring past U.S. policy in Latin America, where the country had often supported repressive, autocratic regimes, Carter sought to make amends and wanted to make the region, as one historian put it, "a showcase for the human-rights policy."

He focused the most attention on Argentina, where he cut U.S. economic assistance to the country, ended the sale of conventional weapons, blocked Inter-American Development Bank loans, and delayed an Export-Import Bank credit for the purchase of generator turbines.

Quotes from the Cold

Even if our human-rights policy had been a much more serious point of contention in Soviet-American relations, I would not have been inclined to accommodate Soviet objections. We have a fundamental difference in philosophy concerning human freedoms, and it does not benefit us to cover it up.

—Jimmy Carter, *Keeping Faith: Memoirs of a President,* (Bantam, 1982)

Panama Canal

Another aspect of Carter's new approach to Latin America was his drive to return the Panama Canal to the people of Panama. In 1903, the United States had supported Panama's succession from Colombia and had virtually seized the land for the canal and appropriated access to it in perpetuity.

Carter renegotiated the 1903 treaty between the two countries and, in 1978, persuaded the U.S. Senate to ratify the new agreement. By the end of the century, the canal would revert to Panamanian control, although the United States would retain its rights to defend it militarily.

Whenever Carter met with a foreign leader whose government stood accused of human right abuses, he raised the issue. While the United States sometimes paid a price for his dogged human-rights crusade, his campaign did result in the release of thousands of political prisoners around the world and again established the United States as the world's leading champion of human rights.

Cold Facts

Future president Ronald Reagan emerged as one of the most vocal opponents of the Panama Canal Treaty negotiated by President Jimmy Carter. In 1976, when the issue came up in the Republican presidential primaries, Reagan declared: "We bought it, we paid for it, it's ours and we're going to keep it." California Senator S.I. Hayakawa wryly summarized Reagan's position: "We stole it fair and square."

Relations with China

Slowly but surely Secretary of State Vance was being edged out of foreign policy decision-making by Brzezinski, Carter's national security advisor who favored a hard-line approach.

One example of the evolution of Carter's thinking about U.S.-Soviet relations was found in U.S. efforts to normalize relations with China—a decision guaranteed to aggravate the Soviets.

In the spring of 1978, realizing that the Chinese were eager for better relations with the United States, Brzezinski urged Carter to explore the possibility of normalizing relations with the former adversary. But the subject of Taiwan was a sticking point. If China were to establish full diplomatic relations with the United States, then Carter would first have to sever diplomatic relations with Taiwan, terminate a mutual defense treaty it had with the country, and withdraw all American troops from the island.

Vance was hesitant, knowing that the move, especially if taken precipitously, would alarm the Soviets and imperil the SALT II negotiations. But Carter overruled Vance and dispatched his national security advisor to Beijing in May 1978 to begin negotiations with Chinese leaders.

By the end of 1978, the two countries had struck a deal: The United States agreed to recognize the People's Republic of China as the only government of China. That meant that the United States would end diplomatic relations with Taiwan and would terminate its mutual defense treaty. (The United States did reserve the right to sell Taiwan defensive weapons and to maintain cultural and trade ties to the country.)

Cold Facts

One of President Jimmy Carter's great foreign policy triumphs was the Camp David Accords. In September 1978, Carter brought Egyptian President Anwar al-Sadat and Israeli Prime Minister Menachem Begin together at the presidential retreat in the Maryland mountains. After a series of difficult negotiations, the two men, prodded by Carter, reached a framework for peace between their two countries. The resulting peace treaty between the two countries was signed in Washington on March 26, 1979.

Predictably, the decision infuriated the Soviets. Before the announcement, Soviet Foreign Minister Gromyko insinuated that normalized relations between the two nations was a "dirty game" designed to pit China against the Soviet Union. After the announcement, the Soviets responded by putting the brakes on negotiations to complete SALT II.

And the Soviets also tried to turn up the heat on China by signing a friendship treaty with former Chinese ally Vietnam. With the backing of their new ally, the Soviet Union, an emboldened Vietnam staged a massive invasion of Cambodia in December 1978 and installed a puppet government. The Cambodian invasion prompted China to respond, with Carter's tacit blessing, by invading Vietnam.

The furor over normalization of U.S.-Chinese relations undermined another Carter administration effort—improved relations with Vietnam. Because Carter and Brzezinski chose to play the "China card," normal relations with the former U.S. enemy would not occur until the administration of President Bill Clinton in the 1990s.

An End to SALT

March 1979 finally brought about a breakthrough in the SALT II talks. In announcing the agreement, both sides agreed that Carter and Brezhnev would sign the treaty at a summit to be held in Vienna in June 1979.

Agreement

The treaty limited each side's nuclear arsenals and restricted the amount and kind of weapons development and modernization. Not a part of the SALT II agreement was the Soviet deployment of the SS-20, a new, medium-range nuclear missile, targeted at American allies in Western Europe. Both sides had previously agreed that the United States would develop its own new generation of medium-range missiles. Moscow would have three years to negotiate limits on medium-range missiles or the United States would be free to station Cruise and Pershing nuclear missiles in Europe.

Carter made a determined effort to sell the treaty in the United States. Hoping to gain Republican support for the agreement, he reversed his previous opposition to the deployment of 200 U.S. mobile MX ICBMs. And he appealed to skeptical liberals by arguing that the treaty, if ratified, would make relations between the two nations "safer and more predictable."

Cold Facts

Nothing bedeviled Jimmy Carter's turbulent presidency more than the Iranian hostage crisis. In January 1979, followers of Ayatollah Ruhollah Khomeini, a radical Muslim clergyman, overthrew the Shah of Iran, Mohammad Reza Pahlavi, a long-time U.S. ally.

In November of 1979, anti-U.S. sentiment reached the boiling point and a mob attacked the American embassy in Tehran and seized 66 hostages. While the Iranian militants subsequently released 13 of the hostages, the remaining 53 endured 444 days of imprisonment before they were released on January 20, 1980, minutes after Carter's term of office ended.

The 14-month saga captivated the American public and much of the world and became a symbol of American impotence that, more than anything, cost Carter a second term.

In November 1979, the Senate Foreign Affairs Committee approved SALT II, but by a narrow margin that portended tough times once the document reached the full Senate. A month later the Soviet invasion of Afghanistan ended all hopes that SALT II would become a realty on Carter's watch.

Afghanistan

Any chance that Carter could push SALT II through the Senate collapsed on December 27, 1979, when the Soviet Union invaded Afghanistan to prop up a beleaguered Marxist government struggling against the Mujahedeen, an indigenous Islamic resistance movement. The Soviets claimed that the Afghan government had asked them to intervene. But the Afghan leader was a Soviet puppet and it was clear to much of the world that the operation was entirely the Soviets' idea.

Carter was shocked by the invasion, calling it "the greatest threat to peace since the Second World War." Brzezinski's hard-line approach to the Soviets had fully matured. Carter abruptly altered his Soviet policy. Détente was dead. He asked the Senate to postpone consideration of SALT II, slashed high technology transfers to the USSR, imposed a grain embargo, and cancelled U.S. participation in the upcoming 1980 Olympic games in Moscow.

Quotes from the Cold

Let our position be absolutely clear: An attempt by any outsider force to gain control of the Persian Gulf region will be regarded as an assault on the vital interests of the United States of America, and such an assault will be repelled by any means necessary, including military force.

—President Jimmy Carter, annunciating the "Carter Doctrine" in his 1980 State of the Union Address

The Carter Doctrine

In his 1980 State of the Union Address, Carter unveiled the "Carter Doctrine," vowing to defend the Persian Gulf region, producer of much of the U.S. foreign oil supply, from Soviet aggression. His defense department, he said, would assemble a military force capable of moving quickly to the Gulf region in a crisis. And he asked Congress to give him more money for overall defense programs and for authority to require all men between 18 and 26 to register for a potential draft.

Another China Card

Brzezinski was on a roll. With détente now officially dead, he persuaded the president to exert more pressure on the Soviets by way of China. The first step in that process was to improve the U.S.-Chinese defense relationship by allowing China to buy military hardware and high technology items withheld from the Soviets. The United States also granted China another privilege denied the Soviets—most-favored-nation trade status.

But the Soviets didn't budge. They continued pumping more men and supplies into the morass of Afghanistan—about 120,000 soldiers by 1986—to the point that the country became for the Soviets in the 1980s what Vietnam had been to the United States in the 1960s. The war in Afghanistan devastated that nation. Fully half of the country's population was killed, wounded, or forced to migrate to other areas of the country or flee Afghanistan altogether. As many as 1.3 million people died in the war and the nation's economy was destroyed.

By the mid-1980s, the Soviet leadership recognized the futility of the conflict and began withdrawing its forces, a process finally completed in early 1989.

Falling Apart

Jimmy Carter had entered the White House pledging to ease tension between America and the Soviets. By the end of his term, U.S.-Soviet relations were in shambles. But it wasn't entirely Carter's fault. Despite the hurdles of the human-rights campaign and Carter's decision to establish full diplomatic relations with China, the two nations still managed to produce a SALT II agreement. But the 1979 invasion of Afghanistan ended all hopes of better relations.

The Economy

At home, the U.S. economy was in shambles, as well. A severe recession, the worst since the Great Depression, had hit the country in 1976. Inflation was worsening and unemployment rising. At first, Carter responded with a series of voluntary programs to persuade labor and business to cooperate in order to limit the damage. But the effort failed as both sides could not overcome their historic differences.

In November 1978, after failing to extract assurances of voluntary wage and price controls from business and labor leaders, Carter and Federal Reserve Chairman G. William Miller announced plans to raise interest rates to put a reign on inflation. The federal discount rate—the rate the government charges for loans to banks—rose to a record 9.5 percent.

But Carter's effort to strangle inflation with higher interest rates didn't work. In 1979, the national inflation rate climbed to 11.3 percent. In 1980, it rose to 13.5 percent.

Energy

In the wake of the 1973 Arab oil embargo, Carter tried to persuade Congress to adopt a national energy policy that would make the country more independent of foreign oil. But his program of conservation, oil and gas deregulation, and incentives for development of alternative fuels largely failed to achieve congressional approval.

The 1979 revolution in Iran precipitated another embargo of oil from the Middle East. Fuel prices soared again, by as much as 50 percent, and by October 1979 the inflation rate had climbed to 12.2 percent. Long gas lines began forming, a bitter reminder of the 1973 embargo. Interest rates briefly hit 20 percent.

Cold Facts

Demonstrating his personal commitment to solving the nation's energy problems, President Jimmy Carter practiced conservation by ordering White House thermostats turned down to 55 degrees during winter nights. During the day, they were kept at 65 degrees.

Malaise

Carter's popularity plunged in public opinion polls. Distraught, the president retreated to Camp David for 10 days, inviting dozens of experts and advisors to help him reassess his administration and its goals and policies. When he finally returned to Washington, Carter delivered a dramatic televised address in which he blamed the country's problems on "a crisis of confidence." It became known as the "malaise" speech (he never actually used the word in the speech) and his opponents accused him of blaming the American people for his own political problems.

Quotes from the Cold

It is a crisis of confidence. It is a crisis that strikes at the very heart and soul and spirit of our national will. We can see this in the growing doubt about the meaning of our own lives and in the loss of a unity of purpose for our nation. The erosion of our confidence in the future is threatening to destroy the social and the political fabric of America.

—President Jimmy Carter from his speech to the nation, July 1979

Next, he demanded letters of resignation from his cabinet members, and accepted five of them. That and other feckless actions only reinforced the popular perception that Carter had no real plan to reverse the country's deep economic woes.

The recession deepened and Carter's presidency, doomed by the Iranian hostage crises, was in dire straits. Republican presidential nominee Ronald Reagan would sound the death knell for Carter's presidency in 1980 when he asked the American people a simple, but powerful question: "Are you better off today than you were four years ago"? Their answer would be a resounding no.

The Least You Need to Know

- President Jimmy Carter entered the White House in 1977 hopeful that he could achieve improved U.S.-Soviet relations through diplomatic means.
- While hoping for better relations with the Soviets, Carter aggravated the relationship with a determined human-rights campaign aimed primarily at the USSR and Latin American nations.
- Carter further isolated the Soviets in 1978 when his administration established full diplomatic relations with the People's Republic of China.
- Despite the difficult success in negotiating an arms limitation treaty (SALT II), the agreement never stood much of a chance in the U.S. Senate; the 1979 Soviet invasion of Afghanistan ended all hopes for the treaty's ratification and spelled a temporary end to détente.
- Carter was plagued by a series of economic crises that undermined popular support for his administration. He entered the 1980 president election a battered and unpopular president.

Chapter 22

The Role of a Lifetime

In This Chapter

- The rise of Ronald Reagan
- Reagan's foreign and military policies
- U.S.–Soviet relations stay sour; Reagan's "Evil Empire" speech
- Arms control talks founder

Jimmy Carter scrapped détente because the 1979 Soviet invasion of Afghanistan dashed his hopes for peaceful coexistence. Ronald Reagan, Carter's White House successor, came to Washington with no such romantic notions about getting along with the Kremlin. Reagan had long distrusted all communists, particularly the Russian variety. These were leaders, he believed, who could not be trusted.

From the beginning, Reagan rejected calls to revive détente. Not long into his presidency, he labeled the Soviets an "evil empire." Instead of discussing ways to reduce nuclear weapons on both sides, Reagan worked to bankrupt the Soviets by calling for massive military spending increases and new weapons programs.

Some called it the "Reagan Revolution," and it was in some respects. Reagan did revolutionize U.S.-Soviet relations in ways that, for a few years at least, made the world a more dangerous place. He also revolutionized domestic policy by slowing down federal expenditures for social programs in favor of large military spending increases. And he drastically slashed federal income taxes—so much so that the federal budget ballooned, leading to record budget deficits and a tripling of the federal debt.

A skilled communicator, Reagan first came to prominence in the 1940s as a star of "B" movies. And despite some critics who regarded him as an intellectual lightweight who was fundamentally unsuited for the presidency, Reagan proved himself an adept and charismatic leader whose popularity with the public earned him respect, and sometimes even fear, among many in Congress.

Hollywood Marries Washington, D.C.

Ronald Reagan was a wonderful performer. As few presidents have done before or since, he could communicate with the American people on a fundamental level. While he had been a successful movie actor and had lived a privileged life in California for much of his life, Reagan connected with middle-class Americans. They trusted him, liked him, and sensed that he shared their values.

He talked about the importance of traditional family values, even though he was twice married and was sometimes estranged from his own children. He preached the importance of religious faith, even though he rarely went to church. Like many Americans, he detested government. "Government isn't the solution," he often said. "It's the problem." And yet he now headed that very government and was helping to make it even larger.

He was a host of contradictions. But many Americans didn't seem to mind because they shared his core beliefs: Government was too big, taxes were too high, and communism was too evil. In Reagan, the American people, weary of the turmoil of the 1960s and 1970s, invested their hopes for restoration of the America of the 1950s. They were hungry for a president like Eisenhower—optimistic, successful, and grandfatherly. Ever the actor, Reagan usually played the role flawlessly.

Quotes from the Cold

[Reagan] proved to be a man less of ideas than of stances, shibboleths, stereotypes. He was a strategist rather than a tactician, a hedgehog who knew one big thing, in Herodotus' famous phrase, rather than a fox who knew many little things.

—James MacGregor Burns, *The Crosswinds of Freedom,* (Knopf, 1989)

Hollywood, California

Born in Illinois in 1911, Reagan went to Hollywood in 1937 and began an acting career that lasted for more than 25 years. He had roles in 50 films and ultimately became an active member of the actors' union, the Screen Actors Guild. He served six terms as union president.

The Guild gave Reagan his first political experience, as he fought against communist influence in Hollywood during the 1940s and 1950s. In 1947, he even testified before the House Un-American Affairs Committee on alleged communist infiltration of the film industry.

But in the 1950s and early 1960s his acting career waned and Reagan became more interested in politics. His first partisan political role was delivering an electrifying speech at the 1964 Republican National Convention on behalf of nominee Barry Goldwater. In 1966, Reagan ran successfully for governor of California and soon established himself as a leading national spokesman for conservative causes.

Cold Facts

Ronald Reagan appeared in 54 films during his 27-year movie career. His most noted role was in *Knute Rockne—All American* (1940), in which he played a Notre Dame University tailback, George Gipp. In one of the movie's dramatic scenes, the Rockne character challenges his team to win a decisive game and dedicate it to the dying Gipp. "Let's win one for the Gipper," he tells the team. Later in life, Reagan adopted the character as his own and became known to many as "The Gipper."

After he left the governor's office, Reagan challenged President Gerald Ford for the Republican nomination in 1976. He lost, but returned to win the nomination and the presidency in 1980.

The Economy

In 1981, President Reagan inherited an economy badly weakened by years of spiraling inflation and high unemployment. The primary medicine prescribed by Reagan and his conservative congressional supporters was known as "supply-side" economics or "Reaganomics."

Supply side adherents believed that government revenues would ultimately increase if taxes were slashed. By giving taxpayers, particularly the wealthy, more money, government could spur significant investment in new and expanded businesses and create more jobs. The result would be a stronger economy and, therefore, more government revenue.

Quotes from the Cold

I have always thought of government as a kind of organism with an insatiable appetite for money, whose natural state is to grow forever unless you do something to starve it.

—Ronald Reagan, *An American Life,* (Simon and Schuster, 1990)

Reagan persuaded Congress to go along with his plans. In 1981, both houses passed the Economic

Recovery Tax Act, a bill that cut income taxes by 25 percent over three years. Most of the savings, however, went to the wealthiest taxpayers and large corporations. In fact, between 1977 and 1988, most individual taxpayers actually saw their income tax rates increase slightly. Actually, the poorest taxpayers suffered the largest tax increase—1.6 percent—while the wealthiest one percent of Americans saw their tax rates decline by six percent over the same period.

Spending Cuts

While he slashed taxes for the wealthy, Reagan proposed spending cuts for many government social programs, particularly job training, college loans, food and medical programs, day care centers, and centers for the elderly.

Deregulation

Another aspect of Reagan's economic program was elimination of many regulations that applied to American businesses. Reagan believed that these regulations discouraged free enterprise, and part of his program relaxed environmental and safety standards for many industries.

Although the economy plunged into another deep recession in 1982, conditions improved considerably by 1983. Economists still debate what sparked the robust recovery of the mid-to-late 1980s—Reagan's tax cuts, Federal Reserve intervention, the natural business cycle, or all the above. Whatever the reason, what ensued was a period of robust economic growth and a five-year expansion of the stock market.

Deficits

But Reaganomics had a downside. Because Reagan cut taxes so sharply and increased military spending so dramatically, the federal budget exploded. The federal government's debt ballooned from $908 billion in 1980 to $2.6 trillion in 1988.

Cold Facts

As a popular new president, Ronald Reagan persuaded Congress to enact a series of dramatic tax cuts, including slashing income-tax rates, reducing the top tax rate from 70 percent to 50 percent, and cutting the maximum capital-gains tax rate from 50 percent to 28 percent. Reagan also lowered gift and estate taxes and cut corporate taxes. However, many individuals on the lower end of the income-tax scale actually saw their tax rates increase slightly during his presidency.

Reagan Versus the World

Ronald Reagan had no use for détente. To him, it was a "one-way street" going the Soviets' way. In the White House, Reagan surrounded himself with like-minded advisors who believed that U.S. defenses had been progressively weakened since the 1960s. They believed that the arms control agreements of the past had left the United States only more vulnerable to Soviet attack.

Military Spending

Reagan argued that the United States needed a crash program of military spending to bring it up to par with the Soviets. America, he argued, could keep the peace only with a massive display of military might.

With the support of Congress, Reagan began pouring money into military programs. In the greatest peacetime military buildup ever, Reagan increased the Pentagon's budget from $171 billion in 1981 to $376 billion by 1986. Off the shelf came military projects Jimmy Carter had once rejected: the B-1 bomber, the Trident submarine, and deployment of the MX ICBM. Reagan also initiated research into a new ballistic missile defense system (later dubbed "Star Wars") and an antisatellite weapons system (ASAT). But the money didn't just go to buying more fancy military weaponry. Most of it was used to beef up the military's conventional forces and to increasing the Navy's fleet of vessels from 454 to 600.

Reagan's plan was not just to strengthen the U.S. military. He knew the U.S. spending increases would be matched or exceeded by the Soviet Union, a nation with an unraveling economic system that could ill afford increased spending in this area. "I intended," Reagan wrote in his memoirs, "to let the Soviets know that we were going to spend what it took to stay ahead of them in the arms race."

Quotes from the Cold

I wanted a balanced budget. But I also wanted peace through strength. My faith was in those tax reforms, and I believed we could have a balanced budget within two or three years—by 1984 at the latest.

—Ronald Reagan, *An American Life*, (Simon and Schuster, 1990)

Lebanon

Reagan waded into the Middle East conflict in late 1982 after Christian fanatics began massacring Palestinian refugees in camps near Beirut, Lebanon. American soldiers joined a United Nations' force of troops from France, Italy, and Britain to maintain peace. But the American role in Lebanon was clearly more proactive, aimed at supporting the regime of Lebanon's pro-U.S. president, Amin Gemayel.

In October 1983, after U.S. forces engaged Gemayel's opponents—the Syrian-backed Druze militia—the United States itself came under attack. On October 23, a truck bomb driven by a terrorist plowed into the U.S. Marine barracks near Beirut. When the dust from the enormous blast settled, 241 Marines were dead.

Reagan had hoped to prove that America could effectively use troops in the Middle East, as well as demonstrate that the Vietnam experience would not deter the United States from using its troops elsewhere in the world. But the Lebanon mission was judged by most analysts as a bitter failure and an American military debacle. By February of the next year, Reagan withdrew the troops.

A somber President Ronald Reagan and First Lady Nancy Reagan review the flag-draped coffins of the 241 U.S. Marines who died in October 1983 after a terrorist bomb destroyed a U.S. installation in Beirut.

(Courtesy of the Ronald Reagan Library)

Grenada

Like most hard-liners, Reagan believed the Soviets were to blame for most of the Third World's problems. In Reagan's view, the problem wasn't abject poverty and despair, some of it exacerbated by years of American support for despotic and corrupt regimes. Instead, he believed it was the covert, subversive support of the Soviet Union that spawned communist revolutions in Latin America. Reagan argued that it wasn't American economic assistance that these countries needed, but military backing for the friendly governments that resisted Marxist influence.

In October 1983—only two days after the tragic bombing of the Marine barracks in Beirut—the most famous application of the Reagan Doctrine toward Latin America came in the Caribbean, on the small island of Grenada. When the Marxist government of Maurice Bishop was overthrown by another Marxist regime, Reagan thought it was time to act. He sent in 6,000 Marines and Army troops to liberate the country from what he called a "brutal gang of leftist thugs." The brief "war" was successful, even if Reagan did endure harsh criticism from those who accused him of having recklessly invaded a sovereign nation. To many it did seem that, once again, Uncle Sam was throwing his weight around in Latin America.

Nicaragua

Those disappointed by Reagan's actions in Grenada would be horrified by his record in Nicaragua. In 1979, the left-wing Sandinista organization overthrew the corrupt Nicaraguan government of Anastasio Somoza. Soon, the U.S. government charged that the Sandinistas were supporting Marxist rebels in neighboring El Salvador. In 1981, Reagan cut off all aid to the country and began backing a rival anti-Marxist movement known as the Contras.

When the Sandinista government signed an aid agreement with the Soviet Union in 1982, Reagan accelerated his effort to overthrow the Nicaraguan government. He sent weapons and money to the Contras—as well as to the El Salvadoran military—and provided U.S. military personnel to train the Conta fighters.

Congress, however, didn't share Reagan's obsession with the Sandinistas. Both houses approved legislation capping CIA aid to the Contras and specified that no federal money could be used to overthrow the Nicaraguan government. Later, in 1984, Congress passed even stronger legislation after if was revealed that American CIA operatives had mined Nicaraguan harbors and ports. This time, Congress prohibited the CIA and other intelligence organizations from aiding the Contras.

Cold Facts

A would-be assassin almost killed Ronald Reagan shortly after he became president. On March 30, 1981, a mentally unbalanced young man named John W. Hinkley shot Reagan as he emerged from the Washington Hilton following a speech. Reagan recovered fully from his injuries.

The Iran-Contra Scandal

After the Iran hostage crisis, the United States branded the Middle Eastern nation a terrorist regime. Congress prohibited the sale of arms to the Iranian government. But Reagan and his national security advisors needed a way to continue funding the Contras without spending federal money. And the solution they hatched to solve their problem almost brought down Reagan's presidency.

In order to circumvent the congressional prohibitions on direct U.S. aid to the Contras, Reagan's National Security Council, led by Robert McFarland and Admiral John Poindexter, devised and carried out a bold and illegal plan. During the first half of 1986, they sold arms to Iran as part of a scheme to win the release of U.S. hostages held by pro-Iranian terrorists in Lebanon. Profits from the arms sales were given to the Contras.

The operation finally came to light in October 1986, when the Sandinistas shot down a U.S. transport plane carrying military supplies bought with money from the arms sales. Although Reagan denied that he had direct knowledge of the plan, some of his aides said that he, Vice President George Bush, and other high administration officials were fully informed. Reagan also denied that he had attempted to trade arms for hostages, arguing that he had merely been trying to improve relations with moderate elements in Iran.

The Iran-Contra scandal severely damaged Reagan's standing with the American people. Several members of his national security staff were indicted by a federal grand jury. And extensive congressional hearings solidified the public impression of a president who was either complicit in illegal activities or dangerously out of touch.

The "Evil Empire"

When it came to the Cold War, Ronald Reagan talked a good game. He called the Soviet Union an "evil empire." In March 1982, he signed a national security decision directive (NSDD-32) that established a policy to "neutralize" Soviet control over Eastern Europe. In reality, however, Reagan's actions proved far more moderate than his rhetoric.

As historian H.W. Brands noted in his Cold War history, *The Devil We Knew*, Reagan's Cold War was actually more symbolic than real. "His rhetoric suggested war," Brands wrote, "but his actions stayed well away from everything that carried a real danger of war."

Poland

The Reagan administration had helped and emboldened the Polish Solidarity labor movement in 1981 with covert economic assistance. But when things began to get out of hand in December 1981, Poland's military cracked down on the Solidarity movement, banned it from further organizing, and imprisoned its leaders. The new Soviet-backed military government led by General Wojciech Jaruzelski imposed martial law on Poland, primarily to forestall a Soviet invasion.

Reagan expressed outrage, but in reality did little. He imposed severe economic sanctions on Poland and lighter ones on the Soviets. In a speech to the British House of Commons in June 1982, Reagan's language was strident. "Must freedom wither in a quiet, deadening accommodation with totalitarian evil?" he asked rhetorically.

Quotes from the Cold

The rhetoric of Reagan's first term marked the formal end of the period of détente. America's goal was no longer a relaxation of tensions but crusade and conversion. Reagan had been elected on the promise of militant anticommunism, and he was true to his word.

—Henry A. Kissinger, *Diplomacy*, (Simon and Schuster, 1994)

But despite his strong words, Reagan and his foreign policy advisors did not break ties with the Soviets over their repressive policies in Poland. He continued shipping grain to the USSR, maintained arms control and human rights negotiations, and allowed Secretary of State Alexander Haig to meet with Soviet Foreign Minister Andrei Gromyko. In time, Reagan even cancelled the mild economic sanctions imposed on the USSR after the crackdown in Poland.

The KAL Incident

Another incident that tested Reagan's foreign policy came in August 1983, when a Soviet fighter pilot shot down a Korean Air Lines (KAL) passenger jet after it strayed into Soviet airspace and neared a secret missile test site. All 269 people on board the flight, including a member of the U.S. Congress, died in the crash.

The Soviets explained that they had believed the plane was a U.S. spy craft. Later, evidence suggested that the incident was the result of a tragic misunderstanding. Although he strongly condemned the Soviet action as an "act of barbarism," Reagan's only concrete response to the incident was to suspend Soviet Aeroflot landing privileges in the United States.

But the tragedy did nothing to improve relations between the two nations. Soviet leader Yuri Andropov angrily responded that Reagan was more interested in confrontation than cooperation and he accused the president of following a "militarist course that represents a serious threat to peace."

Reagan, however, never threatened a military response, although one tangible consequence of the disaster was a renewed resolve in Congress to give Reagan the increased military spending he had requested.

The KAL incident also contributed to the collapse, in November 1983, of the talks on intermediate-range nuclear forces and strategic arms reduction.

Quotes from the Cold

Make no mistake about it, this attack was not just against ourselves or the Republic of Korea. This was the Soviet Union against the world and the moral precepts which guide human relations among people everywhere. It was an act of barbarism, born of a society which wantonly disregards individual rights and the value of human life and seeks constantly to expand and dominate other nations.

—Ronald Reagan's televised speech after the KAL tragedy, September 1983

The Arms Control Dance

Reagan and like-mind conservatives were not warm to the idea of arms control agreements. For one thing, they didn't believe the Soviets would keep their promises. But public and congressional pressure forced Reagan to enter into negotiations with the USSR during his first year in office.

Although President Ronald Reagan called the Soviet Union an "evil empire," his anticommunist rhetoric was actually much tougher than his actions. During his presidency, the United States and the Soviet Union never came close to armed conflict.

(Courtesy of the Ronald Reagan Library)

INF Talks

At first, the Reagan administration offered the Soviets a somewhat one-sided INF (intermediate-range nuclear forces) proposal: It would not deploy its Pershing 2 and Tomahawk cruise missiles if the Soviets would dismantle all their intermediate-range missiles. U.S. officials never really thought that the Soviets would take the deal. The treaty would have left in place a significant number of U.S. nuclear weapons deployed in Western Europe. Soviet negotiators responded with their own proposal, but the United States, promptly rejected it, too.

The two sides, however, continued talking, even during the crisis in Poland. Back and forth they negotiated for all of 1982 and much of 1983. And gradually they moved closer to agreement. In October 1983, the Soviets proposed reducing the deployments of SS-20 missiles to Eastern Europe and suspending SS-20 deployments in the Far East. In return, the USSR wanted the United States to halt its Pershing 2 and Tomahawk deployments and freeze the size of the British and French nuclear arsenals.

Reagan, however, was determined to put the U.S. cruise missiles in Europe, and rejected the Soviet proposal. On November 23, after the German parliament voted to support the U.S. cruise missile deployment, the Soviets abandoned the INF talks.

START Talks

The Strategic Arms Limitation Talks (SALT) were renamed the Strategic Arms Reduction Talks (START). But the name change didn't improve the chances that the United States and the Soviet Union would agree on limiting long-range strategic nuclear weapons.

Like the INF discussions, Reagan's first START plan in 1982 was a one-sided proposal that actually would have imposed deeper cuts on the Soviet nuclear arsenal than those suggested in 1977 by President Jimmy Carter. Many observers believed that the proposal was intended to be rejected.

When the Soviets responded in the summer of 1982, their offer was no more appealing. It not only called for limits on U.S. cruise missile production, it was predicated on Reagan's willingness to cancel U.S. INF deployments. Not surprisingly, when the INF talks fell apart in November 1983, START also collapsed.

Despite the tensions of the period—Poland, the KAL tragedy, and strident rhetoric and a continuing military build-up on both sides—the first years of the Reagan era were marked by surprising restraint on both sides. Even more surprising, within two years of their collapse, the arms control negotiations would resume and Reagan and the new Soviet leader, Mikhail Gorbachev, would hold the first of four formal summits. Détente was not dead; only sleeping. Despite the renewed tensions, the Cold War was drawing to an end.

Quotes from the Cold

If the Soviet government wants peace, then there will be peace. Together we can strengthen peace, reduce the level of arms, and know in doing so we have helped fulfill the hopes and dreams of those we represent and, indeed, of peoples everywhere. Let us begin now.

— Ronald Reagan, speech to the nation, January 1984

The Least You Need To Know

- Former movie actor Ronald Reagan became president in 1981, promising to cut taxes, reduce most government spending, and drastically increase military expenditures.
- Congress enacted much of Reagan's economic and defense proposals. The result was an improved U.S. economy and historic deficit spending.
- Initially, Reagan rejected détente with the Soviet Union, opting instead for a more confrontational approach that challenged Soviet hegemony, particularly in Latin America.
- Despite having called the Soviet Union an "evil empire," Reagan never threatened military action against the USSR. During his presidency, Reagan's rhetoric toward the Soviets was always stronger than his actions.
- After three years of fruitless negotiations, the Soviet Union abandoned arms control talks with the United States in November 1983.

Part 5 Coming Out of the Cold

The Cold War was on its last legs. Ronald Reagan was still insisting that the Soviets were "evil," but his moderate actions belied that rhetoric. By the mid-1980s, much of the bellicose rhetoric was gone, too. A new Soviet leader, Mikhail Gorbachev, not only revived détente; he dismantled the Soviet Union, helped to bring down the Berlin Wall, and put Russia on the road to democracy.

By 1990, the Cold War was a thing of the past. The United States once again counted Russia as an ally.

Chapter 23

Détente, Glasnost, and Perestroika

In This Chapter

- The Strategic Defense Initiative
- Reagan seeks improved U.S.-Soviet relations
- The rise of Mikhail Gorbachev
- The arms control breakthroughs
- Reagan goes to Moscow

Ronald Reagan's first term in the White House was characterized by his red-hot anti-Soviet rhetoric. To Reagan, the leaders in the Kremlin were evil totalitarians. But by the time his second term began in 1985, the American public had grown tired of living under the threat of nuclear annihilation. They wanted their president to tone down the rhetoric and reduce the nuclear threat. Ever the skillful politician and actor, Reagan did not miss his cue.

Sometimes, history calls upon the most improbable people to bring about historic change. The inexperienced Harry Truman, derided by his critics as soft on communism, had established the containment policy that lasted into the 1990s. Richard Nixon, the former Redbaiter, had dramatically paved the way to normalized relations with Communist China. Now, in the mid-1980s, it fell to an ultra-conservative named Ronald Reagan to preside over the beginning of the Cold War's end.

Star Wars

Realizing that the American people would not tolerate the continuing escalation of the nuclear arms race, Reagan believed he had found a solution: the Strategic Defense Initiative (SDI). Essentially a high-tech missile shield, Reagan and his national security advisors envisioned an antiballistic missile system that would use beam and particle weapons, lasers, and homing rockets to destroy incoming ballistic missiles fired at the United States by the Soviet Union. The futuristic program was soon dubbed "Star Wars" by critics who regarded the idea as the stuff of science fiction movies, not real science. Even Reagan admitted that perfecting SDI would not be easy.

High Hurdles

To be effective, the program would have to be refined so that it could intercept every one of the Soviets' 10,000 nuclear warheads. In the event of an all-out nuclear attack, even a 99 percent success rate would mean that about 100 nuclear warheads would hit American cities—and that could hardly be called an effective missile defense system.

Quotes from the Cold

I came into office with a decided prejudice against our tacit agreement with the Soviet Union regarding nuclear missiles. I'm talking about the MAD policy—"mutual assured destruction"—the idea of deterrence providing safety so long as each of us had the power to destroy the other with nuclear missiles if one of us launched a first strike. … It was like having two westerners standing in a saloon aiming their guns at each other's head—permanently. There had to be a better way.

—Ronald Reagan, *An American Life* (Simon and Schuster, 1990)

But there were other objectives behind the program than simply erecting a missile shield over American soil. The first, as one retired American general put it at the time, was to "severely tax, perhaps to the point of disruption, the already strained Soviet technological and industrial resources." The other objective was to channel enormous amounts of money—upwards of $17 billion—into research and development of new high technology systems that might provide practical applications far beyond national defense.

Despite its popular appeal (Reagan asked "Would it not be better to save lives than avenge them?") the program attracted strong opposition from the Soviets and from some American scientists and politicians.

Quotes from the Cold

What if free people could live secure in the knowledge that their security did not rest upon the threat of instant U.S. retaliation to deter a Soviet attack, that we could intercept and destroy strategic ballistic missiles before they reached our own soil or that of our allies?

—President Ronald Reagan, from his nationally televised speech, March 1983

Destabilizing?

The Soviets believed that SDI was destabilizing. They believed that it might give the United States a strategic advantage in a nuclear conflict, even if only partially successful. More specifically, they worried that it might be a ruse to gain a first-strike advantage.

The Soviet response to SDI was to accelerate the nuclear arms race by deploying their SS-20 intermediate range nuclear weapons and aim them at Western Europe. The NATO response to the Soviet response: installation of midrange Pershing missiles.

Other critics of SDI, in the United States and the Soviet Union, now worried that it would further exacerbate the arms race by forcing the Soviet Union to develop its own ABM system. And there were fears that SDI would move the arms race firmly into space—an area of conflict prohibited by the Limited Test Ban Treaty of 1963, the Outer Space Treaty of 1967, and the ABM Treaty of 1972.

It was the ABM Treaty that would prove most troublesome. In it, the United States and the Soviets had agreed to refrain from developing, testing, or deploying ABM systems that were "sea-based, air-based, space-based, or mobile land-based." If SDI were put in place, critics feared, the ABM Treaty would be dead and there would be no constraints on the development of ballistic missiles by both sides. In that event, the nuclear arms race would grow only more intense and dangerous.

Despite these and other objections, Reagan was undeterred. With congressional support, the government funded dozens of SDI research projects carried out by dozens of universities and defense contractors.

Failure

The problem with SDI was fairly simple: It didn't work. Despite all the money spent on the program during the 1980s, it never produced a reliable missile shield for the United States. Eventually, Congress drastically cut and finally eliminated funding for the program (only to be revived during the administration of President George W. Bush in 2001). Worse, as we will see, Reagan's intense devotion to the program undermined a potentially dramatic arms control agreement in 1986.

Reagan Changes Course

By 1984, Ronald Reagan was finally ready for better relations with the Soviet Union. "We've come a long way," he said in January, "since the decade of the 1970s—years when the United States seemed filled with self-doubt and neglected defenses, while the Soviet Union increased its military might and sought to expand its influence by armed force and threats."

Reagan claimed that his massive military build-up had changed the equation in favor of the United States:

> One fact stands out: America's deterrent is more credible, and it is making the world a safer place—safer because now there is less danger that Soviet leadership will underestimate our strength or question our resolve.

Cold Facts

Ronald Reagan was called, by many, "the Teflon president." Despite liking him personally and supporting him politically, many Americans disagreed with his positions on numerous issues, including his opposition to abortion and his environmental and foreign policies. Likewise, Reagan's gaffes and political mistakes didn't seem to cost him significant political support. In 1984, Democratic Congresswoman Pat Schroeder of Colorado remarked that Reagan was "perfecting the Teflon-coated Presidency … nothing sticks to him."

It wasn't just the fact that Reagan believed America was now strong enough to begin negotiating with the Soviets that prompted his new approach. He would be seeking reelection later in the year and was keenly aware that many Americans wanted a president committed to making the world safer by reducing, not increasing, the nuclear threat.

Reagan's change of heart was also prompted by a belated realization: The Soviets had rejected his earlier START proposal that called for deep cuts in Soviet land-based missiles because of their heavy reliance on those missiles. Observed Cold War historian Ronald E. Powaski in his book, *The Cold War: The United States and the Soviet Union, 1917-1991*. "The very shallowness of Reagan's knowledge of nuclear weapons issues—and indeed of the Soviet Union itself—contributed greatly to the relative ease with which he transformed himself into an arms reduction advocate late in his first term."

Now was the time, Reagan suddenly declared, for improved relations with the Soviets. And he outlined three major areas on which his administration would focus:

1. Regional conflicts in areas like the Middle East and Central America
2. Slowing down the global arms race

3. The belief that overall U.S.-Soviet relations should be "marked by greater cooperation and understanding"

Another important reason for Reagan's change of heart was the appointment of a new secretary of state, George Shultz, in June 1982. Unlike some of the more conservative members of Reagan's national security team, Shultz was conciliatory toward the Soviets. While he recognized the profound differences between the two nations, he argued they shouldn't stand in the way of improved relations. "It is obviously in our interests to maintain as constructive a relationship as possible with the Soviet Union," he said.

Shultz fought continuously with Reagan's National Security advisors. But eventually his approach prevailed. Reagan signaled his willingness to work for a closer U.S.-Soviet relationship.

At first the Soviets were wary of Reagan's new spirit of cooperation. One reason was the crisis of leadership in the Kremlin that began after the death of Leonid Brezhnev in 1982. Brezhnev was succeeded by former *KGB* head Yuri Andropov, who died in 1984. Andropov was succeeded by Konstantin Chernenko, an anti-American hard-liner, who died in 1985.

Reagan persisted. In September 1984, less than two months before the presidential election, he proposed a new round of arms-control negotiations, later called the Nuclear and Space Arms Talks (NST). Reagan's plan was to consolidate the major nuclear weapons negotiations—INF, START, and the antisatellite weapons talks (ASAT)—into one large treaty.

After Reagan's reelection victory in November 1984, the Soviets signaled their willingness to resume arms control talks with the United States. The first meetings between the two sides began in March 1985, but made little progress because of the Soviets' determined, longstanding opposition to Reagan's Strategic Defense Initiative.

Quotes from the Cold

We need to be strong, we must be ready to confront Soviet challenges, *and* we should negotiate when there are realistic prospects for success.

—Secretary of State George Shultz from October 1984 speech

Cold Words

The **KGB** was the Soviet Union's main intelligence agency, the rough equivalent of the U.S. Central Intelligence Agency.

Quotes from the Cold

How am I supposed to get anyplace with the Russians if they keep dying on me?

—Ronald Reagan to his wife Nancy after the death in 1985 of Soviet leader Chernenko, quoted in his memoirs, *An American Life* (Simon and Schuster, 1990)

Gorbachev

It was an historic time in world affairs. Reagan's new willingness to work with the Soviets on arms control and a host of other issues coincided with a dramatic change of leadership in Moscow in March 1985. When Soviet leader Chernenko died in 1985, 54-year-old Mikhail Gorbachev rose to power. Gorbachev was a new kind of Soviet leader. Well-educated and cosmopolitan in bearing and outlook, the new Soviet leader was the first Kremlin chief since Khrushchev to challenge the fundamental tenets of communism and Soviet orthodoxy.

Cold Facts

Ronald Reagan won reelection in November 1984 in a landslide over his Democratic opponent, former Vice President Walter Mondale. Reagan won 58.8 percent of the vote to Mondale's 40.6 percent. Mondale's running mate was New York Congresswoman Geraldine Ferraro, the first woman ever nominated for national office by a major political party.

Gorbachev recognized the dire straits of a Soviet economy crippled by centralized management, low productivity, and waste. In addition to working on restructuring the Soviet economy, Gorbachev quickly went to work on his nation's dire social ills, including an alarmingly high rate of alcoholism and an antiquated and inefficient health care system.

Most important to U.S.-Soviet relations was Gorbachev's acknowledgment that his country's exorbitant defense spending over several decades had seriously damaged the Soviet economy and diverted precious resources away from important social needs.

Cold Facts

During the 1970s and early 1980s, the Soviet Union devoted enormous resources to beefing up its national defenses, far more of its gross national product (GNP) than the United States or Western Europe. During this period, U.S. military spending averaged about 7 percent of its GNP. By contrast, Soviet defense expenditures during this period represented as much as 17 percent of Soviet GNP and may have approached 25 percent at one point.

Glasnost, Demokratizatsiia, and Perestroika

Gorbachev enacted a series of domestic reforms that would transform the Soviet Union and eventually cause its disintegration. In what he called *glasnost* (openness), the Soviet leader gave citizens new civil liberties, including increased freedom of speech. His *demoktratizatsiia* (democratization) program resulting in political and legal reforms. *Perestroika* (restructuring) was Gorbachev's program to revamp and revitalize the Soviet economy by moving it away from the old (and failed) Soviet centralization model. In its place were numerous free-market reforms.

New Thinking

Gorbachev's so-called "new thinking" included the U.S.-Soviet relationship. He acknowledged Soviet responsibility for much of the Cold War and put the blame on Josef Stalin, whom he criticized for his 1939 nonaggression alliance with Hitler and his occupation of the Baltic States in 1940. Later, in 1988, Gorbachev's foreign minister, Eduard Shevardnadze, would go even further when he criticized a series of Soviet foreign policy blunders, including its participation in the arms race, its pulling out of the arms control talks in 1983, and its long-running conflict with China.

Gorbachev particularly wanted to change the U.S.-Soviet relationship regarding arms control. He hoped to strike a deal with the United States and other western nations to not only end the arms race, but to completely eliminate nuclear weapons.

Quotes from the Cold

As a first step, we had to at least clear up the "snowdrifts" left over from the Cold War times and to alleviate the pressure that had borne down on us due to our involvement in conflicts all over the world and in the debilitating arms race. We had to understand that "we couldn't go on living like this", both inside our country and in world politics.

—Mikhail Gorbachev, *Memoirs* (Doubleday, 1995)

Wary of Gorby

At first, most leaders in the West, particularly Reagan, were wary of Gorbachev and his motives. Only Great Britain's conservative Prime Minster, Margaret Thatcher, seemed to trust him. After their initial meeting in December 1984, she remarked that "I like Mr. Gorbachev. We can do business together."

When Reagan and Gorbachev met for the first time in November 1985 in Geneva, they quickly established a warm rapport, but not much more. Reagan did, however, leave Switzerland believing, like Thatcher, that Gorbachev was a man with whom he could work. Nonetheless, neither side made much progress on arms control, and Reagan remained skeptical of what it called Gorbachev's "peace offensive." Some of the president's advisors believed that the Soviets were primarily working to undermine NATO.

Quotes from the Cold

As we shook hands for the first time, I had to admit … that there was something likable about Gorbachev.

—Ronald Reagan, *An American Life* (Simon and Schuster, 1990)

Reykjavik

Impatient at the slow progress of arms control talks, Gorbachev invited Reagan to join him in Reykjavik, Iceland, in October 1986. Their meeting—billed as a low-key preliminary meeting in anticipation of a subsequent conference—turned into a major summit.

Gorbachev came to Iceland with a detailed set of proposals that stunned the Americans. He suggested that both sides reduce their strategic missile arsenals by half and that they agree to abolish all their nuclear weapons within 10 years. The proposal's audacity immediately appealed to Reagan sense of drama and he expressed his willingness to discuss the plan.

But Gorbachev's idea had a caveat: Both sides must continue to abide by the ABM treaty that prohibited testing of ballistic missile defense systems, including Reagan's Strategic Defense Initiative. In the end, the two leaders could not resolve that fundamental disagreement. Reagan would not trade away SDI, even though he offered to share its technology with the Soviets.

In exchange for the total elimination of nuclear weapons by both sides, Reagan refused to forego his thus-far unworkable "Star Wars" plan. The summit ended with no agreement and its bitter failure insured that the two countries would not successfully negotiate a START treaty during Reagan's presidency.

Cold Facts

Many American conservatives were outraged that Ronald Reagan had considered giving up all American nuclear weapons at his Reykjavik, Iceland, summit with Mikhail Gorbachev in October 1986. Author Garry Wills later commented that the hawks "… resembled a crew of absent-minded Frankensteins who had fiddled at separate parts of a monster for benevolent but widely varying purposes, only to see him break the clasps and rear himself up off the table in a weird compulsion to do some monstrous Good Thing that none of them had ever believed possible."

Breakthroughs

The failure of the START treaty (at least during Reagan's term) did not mean that the two sides quit talking arms control and that the Cold War wasn't coming to an end. In short order, the two sides reached agreement on an INF treaty, and reduced the threat of war in Europe. Gorbachev also began pulling Soviet troops out of the Third World, greatly reducing U.S.-Soviet tensions in several regions of the world.

INF Treaty

The successful conclusion of the INF treaty in December 1987 (in which Gorbachev made significant concessions) was a major achievement. The treaty mandated the elimination of all short- and intermediate-range nuclear weapons by both sides. The United States would dismantle almost 1,000 nuclear warheads; the Soviets, more than 3,000.

The success of the INF treaty also encouraged both sides to continue working on the elimination of strategic weapons. Negotiators went back to their discussions on the START treaty with renewed vigor, and a treaty was eventually signed in June 1991 under the administration of President George Bush.

Soviet leader Mikhail Gorbachev and U.S. President Ronald Reagan sign the historic INF treaty in December 1987.

(Courtesy of the Ronald Reagan Library)

Eastern Europe

Like many, Ronald Reagan saw the Berlin wall "as stark a symbol as anyone could ever expect to see of the contrast between two different political systems: on one side, people held captive by a failed and corrupt totalitarian government, on the other, freedom, enterprise, prosperity."

Despite the warmer relations between the United States and the Soviets, Reagan pushed Gorbachev to relax Soviet control over Eastern Europe. And nothing symbolized that effort more than Reagan's dramatic speech on June 12, 1987 at Berlin's Brandenburg Gate. To the cheers of thousands, Reagan shouted: "Mr. Gorbachev, tear down this wall!"

In time, Gorbachev moved decisively to reduce tensions in Eastern Europe. In December 1988, during a speech at the United Nations, he announced his decision to unilaterally withdraw 50,000 troops and 10,000 tanks stationed in various Eastern European

Quotes from the Cold

Yes, across Europe, this wall will fall. For it cannot withstand faith; it cannot withstand truth. The wall cannot withstand freedom.

—Ronald Reagan, June 12, 1987, in Berlin

countries. He would also unilaterally reduce the Soviet armed forces by 500,000 men over two years.

Not only did Gorbachev's bold move reduce East-West tensions, it drastically weakened Soviet influence in those countries and, as Reagan hoped, hastened the collapse of their Soviet-style communist governments. Gorbachev's decision marked an end to the so-called "Brezhnev Doctrine," in which the former Soviet leader had pledged to prevent Soviet satellite countries from shifting their allegiance to the West.

President Ronald Reagan stands at Berlin's Brandenburg Gate in June 1987 and calls on Soviet leader Gorbachev to "tear down this wall!"

(Courtesy of the Ronald Reagan Library)

Third World

Under pressure from the United States, Gorbachev, in 1988, also began the process of ending the Cold War in the Third World. In February, he announced the withdrawal of Soviet troops from Afghanistan. The USSR would finally end its disastrous conflict in that country, a quagmire that many compared to the U.S. role in Vietnam.

American and Soviet cooperation in December 1988 also resulted in an end to the conflict in Angola and Namibia. Other world tensions were reduced when Gorbachev took the first steps toward repairing the breech between his nation and the People's Republic of China and restored the USSR's diplomatic relations with Israel.

Reagan in Moscow

At the beginning of his term in office, few could have imagined Ronald Reagan in Moscow, toasting the Soviet leaders, and counting Mikhail Gorbachev among his friends. After all, it was Reagan who had called the Soviet Union an "evil empire." Now, in June 1988, he traveled to Moscow, not as an adversary, but an ally. Were the Soviets still evil? he was asked. "I was talking," he replied, "about another time, another era."

Quotes from the Cold

We are entering an era in which progress will be based on the common interests of the whole of humankind. The realization of this fact demands that the common values of humanity must be the determining priority in international politics. … This new stage requires the freeing of international relations from ideology.

—Soviet leader Mikhail Gorbachev, from his December 1988 speech to the United Nations

That didn't mean that Reagan and other U.S. officials didn't find fault with Soviet behavior. The United States still had problems with Moscow's human-rights record. But Reagan and most other observers recognized that the Soviet Union had fundamentally altered its ways. It was moving decisively away from its communist, totalitarian past. It was moving tentatively but steadily toward democracy and free enterprise.

Reagan's Role?

What was Reagan's role in ending the Cold War? Some give him most of the credit, arguing that his massive military build-up forced the Soviets to the negotiating table and hastened the collapse of their decaying communist regime.

Quotes from the Cold

In just over five years, Mikhail Gorbachev transformed the world. He turned his own country upside down. He woke a sleeping giant, the people of the Soviet Union, and gave them freedoms they had never dreamed of. He also gave them back their own horrific history, which his predecessors had hidden and distorted for sixty years.

—Robert G. Kaiser, *Why Gorbachev Happened* (Simon and Schuster, 1990)

Reagan's policies undoubtedly contributed to the historic changes that occurred in Moscow; but he and his supporters cannot, alone, claim the credit. By the 1980s, the Soviet economy was on the rocks and sinking fast. And while Reagan's policies did prompt Soviet leaders to divert even more resources away from social concerns to military programs, the fact was that Soviet-style communism was on life supports.

Gorbachev deserves as much credit as Reagan for recognizing and addressing the economic and political failures of his nation. He knew that a status-quo policy would only deepen his country's misery, and might increase prospects for nuclear war. A bold and courageous man, the Soviet leader risked his political career with the concessions he made in the arms control talks. And he, not Reagan, instituted the social, political, and military reforms that transformed his country. The United States, led by Reagan, might have prodded and nudged the Soviets toward the dramatic reforms of the late 1980s, but it was Gorbachev who skillfully instituted them in the face of enormous domestic opposition.

In the end, it would appear that Reagan became president at a time when the Soviet Union was teetering on the brink of collapse. Another president might not have pushed as hard as Reagan did, but eventually that country's economic and political systems were bound to fail.

Ronald Reagan was the last in a long line of American presidents who struggled against the Soviets during the Cold War. And it was his good fortune to be president when the Soviet Union collapsed and the military and foreign policies pursued by Truman, Eisenhower, Kennedy, Johnson, Nixon, Ford, and Carter came to fruition. As Reagan himself once said, "We meant to change a nation [the United States], and instead, we changed a world."

The Least You Need to Know

- During his presidency, Ronald Reagan pursued a controversial missile defense program—the Strategic Defense Initiative (SDI), which its detractors called "Star Wars."
- Initially hostile to the Soviet Union in the early years of his presidency, Reagan's attitude softened as his 1984 reelection approached, and prodded by Secretary of State George Shultz, Reagan and the new Soviet leader, Mikhail Gorbachev, reinvigorated arms control negotiations.
- While negotiations with the Soviet Union over limiting long-range strategic weapons were unsuccessful during Reagan's presidency, he and Gorbachev did reach agreement on limiting and eliminating intermediate-range nuclear weapons in the 1987 INF treaty.
- Prodded by Reagan's military build-up and led by Gorbachev, the Soviet Union underwent profound political, economic, and military reforms.
- By the late 1980s, the Soviet Union had pulled its troops out of Eastern Europe and retreated from the Third World.

Chapter 24

The New World Order

In This Chapter

- George Bush's cautious reaction to the Soviet upheaval
- The liberation movements in Poland, Hungary, and the Baltics
- The Berlin Wall comes down
- Democracy on the march in China; the Tiananmen Square massacre
- The USSR begins to crumble—communism on the ropes

The late 1980s and early 1990s were a time of breathtaking change in Europe. The Soviet Union was collapsing and the winds of freedom began to sweep across the Eastern European landscape. Communism, as a power in Soviet politics, was almost dead. In Asia, meanwhile, communism also appeared to be under siege as the democratic revolution that began in Moscow began to simmer in China.

Nothing would come to symbolize the historic changes spreading throughout the world more than events in Berlin in November 1989. Thrilling images of the Berlin Wall's collapse were broadcast around the world and signaled an end to the old world order.

It was a time of closer U.S.–Soviet cooperation, as both nations struggled to find their way in what many called the "New World Order." It wasn't always easy or smooth. Sometimes U.S. and Soviet officials didn't cooperate as much as they should have. But the result was a dramatic reduction in tensions between the two countries—particularly in Europe and in the Third World.

Cautious George Presides

Vice President George Bush had an impressive resumé: former congressman from Texas, ambassador to the United Nations, chairman of the Republican National Committee, U.S. envoy to China, and director of the Central Intelligence Agency. But when he challenged Ronald Reagan for the Republican presidential nomination in 1980, few gave him much of a chance. He was a moderate Republican in an increasingly conservative party. Yet he performed better than any of Reagan's other challengers and by the time of the Republican National Convention, Bush emerged as a logical choice for vice president (that is, after former President Gerald Ford turned down the number-two spot on the ticket).

Bush served ably as Reagan's vice president and easily won his party's presidential nomination in 1988. After a bruising and sometimes nasty campaign against his Democratic opponent, Massachusetts Governor Michael Dukakis, Bush won the White House in his own right.

Caution

Despite his reputation for skill in foreign affairs, Bush reacted cautiously to the rapidly unfolding events in Moscow and throughout Eastern Europe. Like Reagan before him, Bush did not immediately embrace Soviet leader Mikhail Gorbachev, whose dramatic political and economic reforms were transforming not only the Soviet Union, but also Eastern Europe.

Quotes from the Cold

"I did not want to encourage a course of events which might turn violent and get out of hand and which we then couldn't—or wouldn't—support, leaving people stranded at the barricades. I hoped to encourage liberalization as rapid as possible without provoking an internal crackdown—as had happened in Poland in 1981—or a Soviet backlash."

—George Bush, from *A World Transformed,* written with Brent Scowcroft (Knopf, 1998)

Gorbachev's Initiatives

For most of the first year of the Bush presidency, it was Gorbachev who made all the moves. Bush sat mostly on the sidelines. It was Gorbachev, not Bush, who acted decisively to reduce East-West tensions in Europe by withdrawing 50,000 Soviet troops from Eastern Europe. It was Gorbachev, not Bush, who recommended that the United States and the Soviet Union reinvigorate the United Nations as a true peacemaking body.

In May 1989, Gorbachev announced that the Soviets would unilaterally remove 500 nuclear warheads from Europe. He also proposed deep cuts in Soviet conventional weapons. To many observers, however, it appeared that a Soviet leader was finally extending a hand of friendship and cooperation to the United States—and that a cautious American president was shrinking from the historic opportunity to decisively end the Cold War.

Bush Responds

Despite exhortations from Ronald Reagan and former Secretary of State Henry Kissinger to increase the pace of the new relationship, Bush opted to drive the car of détente slowly. Bush and some of his advisors believed that Reagan had been too quick to embrace Gorbachev (he had actually been painfully slow). Defense Secretary Richard Cheney defended Bush's reluctance to embrace the Soviet leader by explaining that he did not believe Gorbachev's reforms would succeed.

Bush finally got around to offering his own initiative for closer U.S.-Soviet relations in late May 1989. He proposed cutting NATO and Warsaw Pact forces in Europe and suggested a ceiling of 275,000 Europe-based troops for each country.

In Bush's defense, he and his aides feared that the end of the Cold War didn't necessarily mean a safer world. "For all its risks and uncertainties," explained Deputy Secretary of State Lawrence Eagleburger, "the Cold War was characterized by a remarkably stable and predictable set of relationships among the great powers." In the post-Cold War world, Eagleburger and Bush feared that "the chances for instability increase[d]."

Cold Facts

One of President George Bush's proposals for improving U.S.-Soviet relations, made in May 1989, only emphasized the cautious nature of his approach to foreign affairs. Bush reached back to the Eisenhower administration to revive a 1955 proposal to institute the "Open Skies" plan that would have permitted mutual aerial reconnaissance flights over both countries. Bush's national security advisor, Brent Scowcroft, later observed that the "proposal smacked of gimmickry" and "wrongly [gave] the impression that we did not have the brain power to think of something innovative."

The Walls Tumble

While historians might debate what impact Ronald Reagan had on hastening the Cold War's end, most would say that George Bush had little to do with the revolutions that swept through Eastern Europe beginning in 1989. Through it all, Bush was little more than an observer. He and his aides adopted a passive posture, fearing that the situation might unravel or move too quickly, resulting in a Soviet military backlash.

Bush's only real effort to take the initiative came in July 1989 when the new president traveled to Poland and Hungry, where he challenged Gorbachev to put into practice his recent call for a "common European home." Bush said: "There cannot be a common European home until all within it are free to move from room to room." However, despite urging Eastern Europe's liberation, Bush still harbored fears that the fires of revolution that Gorbachev had ignited might burn out of control.

Those fires might not have been out of control, but they were beginning to burn in ways that few would have imagined.

Hungary

In Hungary, in early 1989, the country's communist-controlled parliament instituted political reforms that allowed for freedom of speech and assembly. Next, parliament made it possible for other parties to compete for political power. By March, 80,000 citizens tested out their new freedoms when they marched peacefully through the streets of Budapest, demanding free elections and the expulsion of Soviet troops. By May, the Iron Curtain finally began to fall when Hungary removed the barbed-wire fence on its Austrian border.

The following year, in free parliamentary elections, the Hungarian Communist Party received only 9 percent of the vote. Hungarian communism was officially declared dead.

Poland

In Poland, meanwhile, the political changes were even more dramatic. In elections in June 1989, the country's main opposition party, Solidarity, captured an astounding 160 of the 161 contested seats in the lower house of parliament. In the upper house, its victory was just as complete: It controlled 99 of 100 contested seats. Soon, Solidarity—once oppressed and now allied with two small noncommunist parties to build a parliamentary majority—peacefully assumed control of the government it had long challenged.

Gorbachev's Kremlin predecessors would have probably sent Soviet troops to restore communist rule. Gorbachev, by contrast, adopted what one of his aides called the "Sinatra Doctrine." Referring to singer Frank Sinatra's popular song, "My Way," the Soviets signaled that their former Eastern European satellites were now free to determine their political destinies.

But Gorbachev did more than just sit on the sidelines. He worked aggressively to ensure that the approaching political and social upheaval did not spin out of control. If riots broke out in Eastern Europe, he knew that he might be forced to restore order with troops. To prevent this, he strongly urged Eastern European governments to begin implementing reforms to prevent civil unrest. In Poland, in particular, he urged communist leaders to relinquish power peacefully.

The Baltics

Encouraged by events in Hungary and Poland, unrest began to brew in the Baltic States—Latvia, Lithuania, and Estonia. Stalin had seized the three republics as war bounty in 1940 and now their communist-led governments began making sounds about independence. By May of 1989, the legislative bodies of Lithuania and Estonia declared their "sovereignty," just short of an independence declaration. Two months later, Latvia followed suit. The Soviet Union would not officially recognize Baltic independence until 1991, but the path to freedom from Soviet domination was clearly underway.

Berlin

One consequence of the fall of the Iron Curtain between Hungary and Austria was a massive influx of East Germans who fled their country for Austria (and ultimately West Germany) by way of Hungary. The lengths to which East Germans went to escape communist rule only highlighted the political problems mounting for East Germany's communist President Eric Hoenecker.

When Gorbachev visited East Germany in early October 1989, large crowds of East German citizens cheered the Soviet leader. Some chanted, "Freedom! Freedom!" A larger contingent shouted, "Gorby! Gorby! Help us!" Gorbachev, again concerned that events might be moving too fast, nonetheless warned Hoenecker and other East German leaders that without significant political reforms their government would not long survive.

Hoenecker did not listen. In mid-October, after he disastrously threatened repressive measures to disperse a large demonstration in Leipzig, the East German leader was forced to resign. By November 4, a groundswell of public protest began to threaten the government itself. On that day, an enormous crowd numbering upwards of a half-million gathered in East Berlin and demanded the right to travel freely into West Germany.

On November 9, word leaked out that the government would soon grant exit visas to any citizen wanting to leave the country. This was not

Cold Facts

During his visit to East Germany in October 1989, Soviet leader Mikhail Gorbachev hinted his opposition to the Berlin Wall. Asked if the wall might some day fall, he replied: "Nothing is eternal in this world." With Gorbachev's cryptic acquiescence, the wall collapsed in a matter of weeks.

entirely accurate; but news of the reported order spread so quickly and was greeted with such enthusiasm in East Berlin that the ebullient citizens began storming the Berlin Wall. Stunned East German guards watched helplessly throughout the day and night as joyous citizens began scaling and methodically destroying the world's most famous symbol of Soviet-style communism.

The Cold War was over. Now it was the Soviet Union that was crumbling.

Quotes from the Cold

"When Gorbachev did not intervene to save communism in strategically important East Germany, which hosted the best Soviet divisions, some 380,000 troops, he demonstrated that he would not act to prevent its collapse anywhere else in Europe. By the end of 1989, communism in Eastern Europe was finished."

—Ronald E. Powaski, *The Cold War: The United States and the Soviet Union, 1917–1991*

Bush Responds

When the Berlin Wall finally fell, Bush reacted, in the words of one writer, "as if he had just seen his dog run over by a truck." While he cautiously welcomed the news out of Berlin, he did not declare, boldly and eloquently, a formal end to the Cold War. Questioned about his muted response to the electrifying news, Bush replied: "The fact that I'm not bubbling over, maybe it's … maybe it's getting along toward evening." Later, he added, "We are handling it in a way where we are not trying to give anybody a hard time."

Quotes from the Cold

"Even as the walls of the modern Jericho come tumbling down, we have a president who is inadequate to the moment."

—House Majority Leader Richard Gephardt on George Bush's muted reaction to the collapse of the Berlin Wall, November 1989

In reality, Bush's muted reaction was a result of his desire not to gloat over what many viewed as a Soviet defeat. He believed that an American celebration of the Berlin Wall's collapse might offend the Soviets and make Gorbachev's job more difficult.

Romania and Czechoslovakia

The breathtaking events in Berlin were really only the beginning of the Soviet Union's rapidly declining influence in Eastern Europe. In December 1989, the hard-line communist government of Romania's Nicolae Ceausescu fell. Four days later in Czechoslovakia, Vaclav Havel, a dissent playwright and poet jailed by authorities for his political activities, was elected president of that nation's new parliamentary democracy.

Quotes from the Cold

"We are living in extraordinary times. The human face of the world is changing so rapidly that none of the familiar political speedometers are adequate."

—Czechoslovakian President Vaclav Havel, from his speech to a Joint Session of the U.S. Congress, February 1990

Revolt in China

Eastern Europe was not the only place where repressed people were yearning for freedom. In China, the world's most populous nation, a nascent democracy movement was blooming.

The pro-democracy movement was led primarily by university students, frustrated that their country's progression toward capitalism was leaving them behind. Chinese university teachers were poorly paid and under trained. The government had allowed many university facilities to deteriorate. "Our education," admitted China's education minister in 1989, "is backward, our people's attainments fall short, and our low level of education has become a major constraint on our country's modernization and reform." Chinese university students might have been under educated, but that did not mean they were entirely ignorant about the prosperity of the West and the dramatic social, political, and economic changes underway in Eastern Europe.

But the frustration with the Chinese communist system wasn't confined to the university campuses. Millions of Chinese citizens of all walks of life were increasingly angry about the corruption and indifference of their government leaders. Throughout the mid-1980s, the unrest gradually escalated. Chinese authorities discouraged the dissent, but never cracked down in a brutal fashion. Emboldened, the students and other dissidents began speaking out more loudly and forcefully.

Tiananmen Square

The arrival of Mikhail Gorbachev in May 1989 spurred the growing protest movement to greater action. Speaking in Beijing, the Soviet leader appeared to bless the students' protests when he declared: "Economic reform will not work unless supported by a radical transformation of the political system."

That was exactly what a group of Chinese students had in mind on April 18 when they first marched on Beijing's Tiananmen Square and hung a pro-democracy banner over the Monument to the Revolutionary Martyrs. They were prompted to action by the death of Hu Yaobang, a former general secretary of the Chinese Communist Party who had largely supported the pro-democracy movement in 1987.

The next day, emboldened, a crowd of almost 10,000 students marched on the residential compound of China's political leadership. The day ended peacefully. But the following day, as the crowd grew, police descended on the protesters and dispersed them.

The memorial to Hu Yaobang was quickly transformed into a massive pro-democracy movement that centered on Tiananmen Square. Trying to quell the growing protests, the government declared martial law on May 20. But the protests only grew. Eventually, as many as a million students, workers, intellectuals, civil servants, and other citizens converged on the square to demand government reforms in early June 1989.

Massacre

Finally, on June 3 and 4, China's People's Liberation Army swept into the square and brutally crushed the protests. Thousands of people died and were arrested. Thousands more were injured. Following the violence, the Chinese government enacted repressive measures, banned the foreign press, and placed onerous restrictions on the Chinese media.

Cold Facts

President George Bush was at best a passive observer of events in China in June 1989. At worst, he offered support to the brutal actions of Chinese leaders who attacked and killed thousands of pro-democracy protesters.

Bush responded to the violence at Tiananmen Square by suspending meetings between U.S. and Chinese military leaders and ending, temporarily, U.S. arms sales to China. He did not, however, make any moves to punish China by revoking its most-favored-nation trade status with the United States. In July, Bush sent two of his top advisors to Beijing to explain to Chinese leaders that his retaliatory steps were merely attempts to placate public opinion and not a genuine expression of condemnation.

The Sun Sets on the USSR

Despite the miraculous political and economic transformation he had sparked in Eastern Europe, Mikhail Gorbachev couldn't rescue the Soviet economy. In fact, his program of *perestroika* may have deepened the country's economic troubles. While Gorbachev had pushed for economic reforms at home, they had often been half measures that preserved some of the worst aspects of the old Soviet centralized economy. Despite his efforts at creating a market economy, inflation, shortages, and worker unrest were rampant.

Gorbachev had other problems at home. Angry and frustrated Communist Party leaders watched helplessly as the reforms their leader had encouraged in Eastern Europe resulted in the steady decline of Soviet influence and power. By late 1989, Gorbachev's popularity within Russia was at an all-time low.

Quotes from the Cold

"Ultimately, the facts of Soviet life—objective reality, as a Marxist might put it—were Gorbachev's greatest enemy. He could open up the Soviet Union, restore its history, initiate debate on fundamental issues, even convert a nation of sheeplike followers into a vibrant new political organism, but he could not overcome the fundamental terms of existence in his country."

—Robert G. Kaiser, *Why Gorbachev Happened,* (Simon and Schuster, 1990)

Communism Takes a Hit

Gorbachev also unwittingly set up the Soviet Communist Party for disaster in 1988 when he had engineered a new Soviet constitution. The new document featured a dramatic new democratic reform—creation of a Congress of People's Deputies, most of whom would be chosen in free elections in March 1989.

Those elections just about snuffed out the Communist Party, as dozens of opposition party leaders were elected to office. Among the political figures elevated to new prominence in the elections was Boris Yeltsin, a gregarious and charismatic independent from Moscow who won a smashing victory over his communist opponent.

Soviet communism was clearly on the way out, a fact emphasized in February 1990, when hundreds of thousands of Russians took to the streets protesting continued communist control of their government. Having seen this story played out the previous year in Hungary, Poland, and elsewhere in Eastern Europe, Gorbachev knew better than to stand in the way. He quickly proposed amending the constitution to end the Communist Party's monopoly over the country's government. To lessen his reliance on the party for his power (he was general secretary of the Soviet Communist Party), he persuaded Soviet leaders to name him president of the Soviet Union.

Falling Apart

Until 1990, the greatest threat to Soviet power had been the steady falling away of Soviet satellites like Hungary, Czechoslovakia, Poland, and Romania. Now, Gorbachev faced a different problem: the growing desire of Soviet republics for their independence. The Baltic States had already asserted their "sovereignty" and would soon demand their independence from the USSR. First, however, it was ethnic unrest in Soviet Armenia and Azjerbaijan in February 1988 that prompted Gorbachev to dispatch troops to quell the violence. (He was not entirely successful.)

In March 1990, however, a much greater problem to Soviet integrity presented itself when the Lithuanian parliament declared its independence. Gorbachev knew that the Kremlin's

Cold Facts

Mikhail Gorbachev's repressive measures in response to the Lithuanian independence movement in 1990 sparked a massive outpouring of citizen protest throughout Russia. In Moscow, marchers held aloft signs that declared: "Gorbachev Is the Saddam Hussein of the Baltics!" and "Down with the Executioner!"

leaders might tolerate his efforts to reform Soviet society. They would not, he understood, allow him to remain in office if he allowed the Soviet Union to fall apart.

In response to the Lithuanian declaration, Gorbachev dispatched Soviet troops, imposed an economic blockade of the small nation, and threatened to depose its leaders. When members of the independence movement seized the government-controlled television station Vilnius, Gorbachev sent in Soviet paratroopers to reclaim the facility. At least 14 Lithuanians were killed and dozens more injured in the fighting.

U.S.-Soviet Relations

While Gorbachev struggled with his domestic problems, he still had to worry about the Soviet Union's relations with the rest of the world—particularly the United States.

President George Bush (left) meets with Soviet leader Mikhail Gorbachev at a summit meeting in Finland in September 1990.

(Courtesy of the George Bush Presidential Library)

In Washington, George Bush viewed the unfolding events in Moscow and throughout Eastern Europe with characteristic caution. U.S. officials doubted Gorbachev could hold on to power for long. But they wanted to encourage his political and economic reforms hoping, as always, that events would not spiral out of control. If the Soviet Union was about to crumble, Bush did not view that as an entirely positive development. What was left, he feared, might be an unstable and dangerous entity that threatened world peace.

Cold Facts

In the aftermath of World War II, Harry Truman and George C. Marshall persuaded Congress to spend more than $12 billion to help rebuild Europe's war-torn economy. George Bush's response to Eastern European distress at the Cold War's end was as puny as Truman's was ambitious.

During the Soviet Union's deep economic crisis in 1990, the United States proposed to assist reform movements in Russia and Eastern Europe with a paltry $300 million. Complained Democratic Senator Bill Bradley of New Jersey: The money was "barely enough to bail out a failed savings and loan institution, much less jump-start national economies that have been dead for decades."

When it came to Lithuania in particular, Bush adopted what he considered a moderate, middle-ground approach. The American president informed Gorbachev that while the United States would not do anything to make matters worse for Gorbachev in Lithuania, any further use of force would harm U.S.-Soviet relations. In response, Gorbachev lifted the economic embargo he had placed on Lithuania.

Cold Facts

The United States held China and the Soviet Union to vastly different standards over human rights during George Bush's presidency. Because of Soviet policy against the free emigration of Soviet Jews, Bush refused to grant the USSR most-favored-nation (MFN) trade status. China, meanwhile, was a different story. Following the 1989 violence in Tiananmen Square, the United States renewed China's MFN status and only mildly criticized the brutal suppression of the country's pro-democracy movement.

Closing Out the Cold War

Despite their differences over Baltic independence, U.S. and Soviet leaders found much to agree upon in the early 1990s. The two countries led the way in negotiating the terms of German reunification in September 1990. By December of that year, East and West Germany were again one.

The year was also a good one for arms control. In November 1990, the United States and the Soviets signed the Conventional Forces in Europe (CFE) treaty which established limits on the numbers of tanks, armored combat vehicles, combat aircraft and helicopters, and artillery pieces each side could deploy in Europe. The U.S. Senate ratified the treaty in November 1991.

The CFE treaty represented another landmark in U.S.-Soviet relations. The treaty's language officially declared an end to the Cold War. The two sides affirmed they were "no longer adversaries" and stated their "steadfast commitment to democracy … for all countries."

In Afghanistan, in 1991, Gorbachev attempted to end the hostilities by proposing that both sides end their policy of supplying arms to the combatants. Bush readily accepted the proposal.

Gorbachev also reduced or ended Soviet military influence in Cambodia, Cuba, and Nicaragua. And in 1991, the United States and the Soviets began working together to bring about a peaceful end to the war in El Salvador—an effort that resulted in the signing of a peace treaty in January 1992.

From Eastern Europe to Central America, Mikhail Gorbachev had acted decisively and courageously to end the Cold War disputes that had pitted his nation against the United States for the last half of the twentieth century. In Ronald Reagan and George Bush he found two unwitting and hesitant partners who, it often seemed, did not grasp the enormity of the changes occurring around them.

Despite U.S. reticence and caution, those dramatic changes were taking place. And the Cold War was officially over. In a matter of years, the Soviet Union would dissolve and Gorbachev would be ousted from power. And despite the Soviet leader's bold initiatives, and his role in issuing the war's death knell, it was the United States—or, rather, capitalism and democracy—that emerged victorious.

One large question remained: Now that the United States was the world's only military and economic superpower, how would it use its power and influence to promote democracy and capitalism around the world? The answer to that question would be left to the next three post-Cold War presidents: Bush, Bill Clinton, and George W. Bush.

The Least You Need to Know

- As political and economic reform spread throughout Europe, President George Bush reacted cautiously to the unfolding events.
- During the Bush presidency, Soviet leader Mikhail Gorbachev played the leading role in establishing the tenor of U.S.-Soviet relations.
- In 1989, the communist governments of East Germany, Czechoslovakia, Poland, Hungary, and Romania began to crumble while the Soviet Union did nothing to try to stop the political upheaval.
- The Chinese government responded to students' pro-democracy protests at Beijing's Tiananmen Square with a brutal military offensive that resulted in the deaths of thousands of protesters.
- Despite his popularity outside the Soviet Union, Mikhail Gorbachev's popularity at home plummeted in 1990 as his country's economic woes deepened, and despite the high stakes involved in continued economic and political stability in the region, the United States responded by offering only meager economic assistance.
- By the early 1990s, the Soviet Union was on the verge of disintegration, as its various republics—particularly the Baltic States—began to demand independence.

Chapter 25

The Post-Cold War Era

In This Chapter

- Gorbachev encounters domestic opposition; his power wanes
- Civil and political upheaval in the USSR
- Boris Yeltsin becomes president of Russia
- Bush's China policy sparks domestic dissent
- Bush grapples with the post-Cold War world—Panama, North Korea, and Cuba

It was a new world. After almost seven decades marked by open hostility between the United States and the Soviet Union (excluding the years of World War II), the two nations were again allies. It was not the kind of symbiotic relationship enjoyed by the U.S. and Great Britain. But in many ways the relationship between two nuclear powers was more important in terms of world peace. Both nations still possessed enough nuclear bombs to destroy the world several times over. That they were now formally at peace caused the world to breathe easier.

But the Soviet Union was also on its last legs. And so was Mikhail Gorbachev. By the end of 1991, the USSR would dissolve, as would Gorbachev's power. Rising to take Gorbachev's place on the world stage would be the charismatic reformer and born-again anticommunist, Boris Yeltsin, president of Russia.

The end of the Soviet Union simplified the world for U.S. leaders, but not to the degree they had hoped. A host of difficult challenges still vexed President

George Bush. Relations with China were still a problem. The Middle East and Persian Gulf regions were caldrons of violence and aggression. Communist North Korea, isolated and angry, threatened the peace and stability of Asia. And, in America's back yard, Fidel Castro stubbornly ruled one of the world's last remaining communist regimes.

Simply put, the post-Cold War world was not as simple or peaceful as some might have hoped.

Gorbachev Fading

Mikhail Gorbachev was torn between competing desires. He hoped to complete the political and economic reforms he had initiated, but he also did not wish to preside over the disintegration of the Soviet Union. Increasingly, however, it was becoming apparent that those desires were mutually incompatible.

With the USSR's economy spiraling downward and the country's power eroding, the Kremlin's hard-liners quickly lost patience with Gorbachev and his leadership. His erratic behavior in the summer of 1990 certainly did little to inspire confidence.

Yeltsin's Plan

In August 1990, Gorbachev endorsed a free-market reform plan drafted by Boris Yeltsin, chairman of Russia's popularly elected parliamentary body. But the plan, which mandated a 500-day transformation of the Soviet economy, would have ended centralized Soviet control of the markets and hastened the nation's disintegration. Changing course, Gorbachev staged a sudden, rightward shift and aligned himself with the hard-liners, many of whom he appeased by giving them important governmental posts.

Cold Facts

Soviet leader Mikhail Gorbachev was awarded the 1990 Nobel Peace Prize for his bold domestic and foreign policy initiatives of the late 1980s. The honor, however, did little to enhance his popularity and standing at home.

Gorbachev's perplexing reversal—including his repressive measures against the free press and his brutal, hard-line response to the Lithuanian independence movement (see Chap-ter 24, "The New World Order")—earned him the enmity of reformers. In March 1991, after Gorbachev's allies tried to remove the popular Yeltsin from office, 100,000 Russian citizens gathered in Moscow to denounce the Soviet leader and voice support for Yeltsin and his reforms.

Gorbachev may have given rise to the reform movement sweeping the Soviet Union; but he simply could not keep up with it. His desire to reform, but not eliminate communism, as well as his dogged determination to preserve the basic structure of the Soviet Union, held him back.

Union Treaty

In 1991, Gorbachev devoted considerable effort to building public support for saving the Soviet state by persuading the Soviet republics to recast their alliance. His proposal was a looser confederation of the 15 republics under what he called a "Union Treaty" federation.

In the nationwide voting, Gorbachev's Union Treaty earned a comfortable majority and the Soviet leader again began pushing for the political and economic reforms he had once championed. But Gorbachev's return to the role of reformer would come too late. While he remained a tremendously popular and respected world leader, at home his stature and popularity were all but expended.

Cold Facts

Although they both faced daunting domestic challenges, U.S. President George Bush and Soviet leader Mikhail Gorbachev successfully completed negotiations on the Strategic Arms Reduction Talks (START) treaty in July 1991. The success of START was the result of nine years of negotiations between the two nations and required both sides to drastically reduce their arsenals of deployed strategic warheads and launchers.

The Rise of Yeltsin

Boris Yeltsin was the reformer who most captured the imagination of the Russian people in 1991. As the new leader of the Russian parliament, Yeltsin enjoyed a prominent platform to espouse his ambitious plans for transforming the Soviet economy.

A burly former construction worker, Yeltsin joined the Communist Party in 1961 and by 1985 had risen, thanks to Gorbachev's patronage, to the rank of Moscow party boss. Elected to the ruling Politburo in 1986, he soon clashed with Gorbachev over the pace of Soviet political and economic reform. His populism and blunt outspokenness also earned him a considerable following among the Russian people.

Yeltsin's 1990 proposal, that Gorbachev embraced and later rejected, would have decentralized the Soviet economy by giving broad economic authority, including the right to tax, to the individual republics. Gorbachev countered with his Union Treaty proposal; but ultimately, the gambit would be no substitute for the sweeping reforms Yeltsin demanded and that the Soviet people desired.

Gorbachev's Union Treaty was popular with Soviet citizens. But before the question was put to voters, Yeltsin persuaded the Russian parliament to simultaneously ask voters to decide whether to create the office of Russian president. When the ballots were cast, 85 percent of Russian voters expressed a desire to elect their own president. In the ensuing June 1991 election, Yeltsin won handily and became, next to Gorbachev (who remained leader of the USSR), the most prominent Soviet officials and the nation's loudest voice for political and economic reforms.

Cold Facts

Under President George Bush, the United States did little to assist Soviet leader Mikhail Gorbachev as he tried to revive his nation's shattered economy. Struggling with a U.S. recession and worried that any assistance would be misused by dishonest and inept Soviet officials, Bush offered only paltry help to Gorbachev. In 1991, U.S. aid to the Soviet Union amounted to little more than a $1.5 billion credit for agricultural purchases.

Gorbachev in Trouble

With Yeltsin as his main rival, Gorbachev's "passion" for reform now looked weak and defensive. Making matters worse, what steps Gorbachev took to enact economic and political changes only alarmed Kremlin hard-liners—many of whom, thanks to Gorbachev, were serving in powerful positions.

Particularly alarming to the hard-liners was the realization that Gorbachev's Union Treaty meant that the country would soon be governed by a coalition of leaders selected by the various republics. Reforming the nation's economy was difficult enough for these leaders to swallow; now Gorbachev proposed, via the treaty, to throw them out of their jobs.

Coup

On August 19, 1991—the day before a preliminary Union Treaty was to be initialed by representatives from several republics—Gorbachev's opponents staged a coup. With the Soviet leader vacationing in the Crimea, the State Emergency Committee removed him from power, citing "health reasons," and placed him under house arrest. The hard-liners dissolved the treaty and announced imposition of a six-month state of emergency.

He was no ally of Gorbachev, but Yeltsin recognized the danger the coup posed to Russia's democratization. Hoping to head off disaster, he rushed to Gorbachev's defense. In a dramatic scene that gained worldwide attention, Yelstin defiantly climbed atop a Soviet tank that the hard-liners had positioned in front of the Russian parliament building, known as the White House.

Quotes from the Cold

The reactionaries will not achieve their goals; the army will not go against the people.

—Russian President Boris Yeltsin, speaking atop a Soviet tank during the August 1991 Soviet coup

Led and inspired by Yeltsin's courage, ordinary Russian citizens rushed to defend the building. When KGB troops ignored orders to storm the White House, the coup collapsed.

By August 21, only three days after the revolt had begun, the Soviet troops and tanks were gone and the coup's hard-line leaders were arrested.

Yeltsin Takes Command

Yeltsin quickly filled the vacuum created by Gorbachev's incapacitation. Although Gorbachev quickly returned to Moscow to resume power, it was Yeltsin to whom most Russian citizens now looked for leadership.

Yeltsin accused the Communist Party of planning and staging the coup. And the punishment he meted out was severe: He banned further party activities in Russia and seized the party's property. The communist parties of several other Soviet republics soon met the same fate.

Within only a few days, the Soviet leadership began to bear the imprint of Yeltsin's considerable influence and popularity. The imprisoned Kremlin hard-liners were replaced, not by allies of Gorbachev, but by nominees put forth by Yeltsin.

President Bush and Russian President Boris Yeltsin at their January 1993 Moscow summit where they signed START II arms control treaty.

(Courtesy of the George Bush Presidential Library)

Gorbachev tried to recover by hastening the end of the Soviet Communist Party. Days after returning to Moscow, he resigned as the party's general secretary and disbanded its Central Committee. At his behest, the national Congress quickly suspended all party activities.

The USSR Dissolves

Soon, the Soviet Union would meet the same fate as its Communist Party. As leader of a hastily formed "transitional" government, Gorbachev gave the Baltic States (Latvia, Estonia, and Lithuania) their independence. Hoping to preserve some semblance of the Soviet Union, Gorbachev worked to persuade the Baltic States and the other Soviet republics to remain associated under his Union Treaty plan.

Cold Facts

President George Bush helped force Soviet leader Mikhail Gorbachev to grant independence to the Baltic States in 1991 by extending U.S. diplomatic recognition to the three nations. Four days later, Gorbachev formally acknowledged Baltic independence.

But the genie of independence had been released. It could not be forced back into the bottle. By October 1991, all of the Soviet republics, save Russia and Kazakhstan, had declared their independence from the Soviet Union. In December, Yeltsin and the leaders of Ukraine and Belarus sounded the death knell for the USSR when they announced formation of the Commonwealth of Independent States (CIS). Within weeks, eight more republics joined the CIS. With no nation left to govern, on December 25, Gorbachev resigned as president of the Soviet Union and transferred control of its nuclear weapons to Russia. The USSR was no more.

Quotes from the Cold

The world has changed, and so have the nature, role, and place of [U.S.-Soviet] relations in world politics. For too long they were built under the banner of confrontation, and sometimes of hostility, either open or concealed. But in the last few years, throughout the world people were able to heave a sigh of relief, thanks to the changes for the better in the substance and atmosphere of the relations between Moscow and Washington.

—Soviet leader Mikhail Gorbachev, from his resignation speech, December 1991

Confusion over China

With the Cold War over, U.S. leaders in the early 1990s were unsure about the relationship their country should enjoy with China. The reason: The 1989 Tiananmen Square massacre destroyed the favorable impression most Americans had of the vast Asian nation. Before Tiananmen Square, many Americans viewed China as an increasingly progressive nation moving toward greater economic and political freedom. Afterwards, however, most saw a politically backward country ruled by a repressive, communist regime.

Since the days of the Nixon presidency, American policymakers had usually viewed China as a counterbalance to Soviet hegemony. Presidents Nixon and Carter, particularly, had used warmer relations with China to punish or cajole the Soviet Union. But the Cold War's end, however, diminished China's geopolitical value.

Economically, however, the nation of one billion people was still an enticing and valuable market for U.S. exports, as well as a dependable, low-cost supplier for imported goods. And for George Bush, this was the quandary: how to satisfy the public and congressional desire to punish China for its deplorable human rights record while maintaining strong economic relations that helped American consumers.

Cold Facts

Throughout the 1990s, the People's Republic of China came under heavy criticism from human rights advocates around the world. China's poor human rights record was the basis for continuing congressional opposition to granting the nation most-favored-nation (MFN) trading status.

A 1996 U.S. State Department report summarized China's dismal human rights record: "Abuses included torture and mistreatment of prisoners, forced confessions, and arbitrary and lengthy incommunicado detention. Prison conditions remained harsh. The Government continued severe restrictions on freedom of speech, the press, assembly, association, religion, privacy, and worker rights. Some restrictions remained on freedom of movement. In many cases, the judicial system denies criminal defendants basic legal safeguards and due process because authorities attach higher priority to maintaining public order and suppressing political opposition than to enforcing legal norms."

Most often, Bush came down on the side of strengthening economic ties to the nation, hoping that, as in Eastern Europe, free markets and democracy would grow hand in hand. Despite the annual battles in Congress over granting most-favored-nation (MFN) trading status, the United States maintained its economic relations with China after the passions over Tiananmen Square diminished. In 1990, Bush lifted the congressional ban on Export-Import Bank loans to U.S. firms doing business in China and allowed the Chinese to buy three communications satellites from the United States.

Quotes from the Cold

There is no doubt in my mind that if we present China's leaders with an ultimatum on MFN, the result will be weakened ties to the West and further depression. The end result will not be progress on human rights, arms control, or trade. Anyone familiar with recent Chinese history can attest that the most brutal and protracted periods of repression took place precisely when China turned inward, against the world.

—President George Bush's message to Congress, March 1992, upon vetoing legislation denying most-favored-nation trading status for China

Bush did exert gentle pressure on the Chinese to improve their human-rights records. And he reversed 10 years of U.S. policy toward Taiwan in September 1992 when he approved the sale of 150 F-16 fighter jets.

Bush and the Tin-Horn Dictators

One of the more profound challenges for U.S. presidents in the post-Cold War era turned out to be the unrest fomented by the dictatorial leaders of nations like Panama, Iraq, and North Korea.

In each instance, the dangers posed by these regimes were different and resulted in unique responses by the United States. One regime threatened world peace, another jeopardized the world's economy, and another ran afoul of U.S. drug laws. Finally, there was the troublesome Cuban regime of Fidel Castro, a thorn in the side of U.S. presidents since John F. Kennedy.

The Panama Shuffle

The brutal Panamanian dictator, Manuel Antonio Noriega, increasingly became a problem for the United States in the late 1980s. After taking power in 1983, Noriega, the corrupt former head of Panama's intelligence service, ruled with an iron fist. He routinely murdered political opponents, tolerated corruption throughout the government, and allowed the nation's economy to crumble.

For years, Noriega had served the United States as a CIA informant and as a conduit for U.S. aid to anticommunist Contras in Nicaragua. In 1988, however, a federal grand jury indicted him on drug trafficking charges and his friendly relations with the U.S. government ended. In Panama, public hostility toward his brutal regime also began to blossom.

By 1989, Bush decided that it was time for Noriega to go. First, U.S. officials pressured him to resign. When that failed, Bush ordered a trade embargo and imposed other economic sanctions on Panama. In the face of U.S. opposition, Noriega grew only more hostile and defiant.

Matters finally came to a head on December 15, 1989, when Panama's legislature declared war on the United States. That same day, Panamanian military forces killed a U.S. marine.

On December 20, Bush ordered a U.S. invasion of the Central American nation, ostensibly to bring Noriega to justice, but also to restore democracy to the nation and to protect American lives and assets. In all 27,000 American troops took part in the invasion. Within days, "Operation Just Cause" was over. Noriega was deposed and arrested by U.S. forces and later convicted and imprisoned for drug trafficking. By 1994, the nation conducted free elections and voters choose as president, Ernesto Pérez Balladares, an economic reformer dedicated to ending drug trafficking.

Cold Facts

The December 1989 invasion of Panama was the largest U.S. military operation since the Vietnam War.

America Discovers Kuwait

A long-simmering border dispute between Kuwait and Iraq erupted in August 1990 when 150,000 Iraqi troops invaded neighboring Kuwait, installed a puppet government, and formally annexed the nation. President Bush and other world leaders reacted quickly, condemning the invasion and denouncing the Iraqi leader Saddam Hussein as a ruthless dictator. Within a week after the invasion, the United States began mobilizing more than 400,000 troops for duty in the Persian Gulf region, mostly in Saudi Arabia, which Iraq had also threatened. Other nations in the hastily assembled international coalition supplied another 200,000 troops.

Cold Facts

The international coalition of nations arrayed against Iraq in the 1990 and 1991 Persian Gulf War was impressive. Those countries supplying troops and equipment included: Saudi Arabia, the United Kingdom, France, Kuwait, Egypt, Syria, Senegal, Niger, Morocco, Bangladesh, Pakistan, the United Arab Emirates, Qatar, Oman, Bahrain, Canada, Italy, Argentina, Belgium, Denmark, Greece, Norway, Portugal, Spain, Czechoslovakia, New Zealand, the Netherlands, Poland, and South Korea.

At first, the United Nations imposed severe economic sanctions on Iraq. But on November 29, 1990, after the sanctions failed to force Iraqi troops from Kuwait, the United Nations Security Council gave its permission for member states to "use all necessary force" to expel Iraq from Kuwait.

In the United States, a fierce congressional dispute erupted over using military force. Many Democrats argued that the sanctions should be given more time to work. Others opposed military action because they believed the conflict was more about economics (the free flow of oil) than about human rights or democracy. After several days of debate, however, the U.S. Congress narrowly approved legislation authorizing Bush to employ the U.S. military in the Persian Gulf region.

On January 17, 1991, UN coalition forces launched a massive air attack. After more than five weeks of intense bombing, they commanded the skies over Iraq and Kuwait, and had drastically weakened Iraqi defenses.

The ground attack began on February 24, 1991, in southwestern Iraq. Within two days, Iraqi troops were routed and Iraq announced its plans to leave Kuwait. On February 28, after 100 hours of ground fighting, the international coalition of nations declared a cease-fire.

President George Bush, accompanied by Army General Norman Schwarzkopf, visits U.S. troops in Saudi Arabia in November 1990. That summer, Bush ordered 400,000 American troops to the region in response to the Iraqi invasion of Kuwait.

(Courtesy of the George Bush Presidential Library)

Cold Facts

Despite the rhetoric of American political leaders in 1990 and 1991, the Persian Gulf War was not fought to restore democracy to Kuwait. The nation was and is a nominal democracy, at best. For example, women are not allowed to vote. To participate in elections, a male citizen must be at least 21 years of age and have lived in Kuwait for no less than 20 years. Law enforcement officers and military personnel cannot vote.

The war was over, but its consequences would be felt for more than a decade. Saddam Hussein remained in power, a perpetual threat to world peace and economic stability. By the late 1990s, the UN sanctions were still in place, UN weapons inspectors were ousted, and Iraq was suspected of manufacturing weapons of mass destruction. At least two more American presidents would find the Iraqi regime one of their most vexing international problems.

Should We Still Hate Castro?

Cuba was another nettlesome problem for the United States, and had been for 30 years. How to deal with one of the world's last hard-line communist regimes—and one just 90 miles from the United States—was a difficult question.

Were there not so many virulently anticommunist Cuban exiles living in vote-rich southern Florida, the question might have been more easily solved. Indeed, had George Bush been consistent, he would have approached relations with Cuba as he did those with

China. But instead of encouraging democracy by encouraging free enterprise and increased trade (the China policy), Bush and the two presidents that followed him, adhered to the politically safe, decades-old policy of complete political and economic isolation.

With the collapse of the Soviet Union in late 1991, the USSR's annual $3.5 billion in economic assistance and trade subsidies, and an additional $1 billion in military assistance, came to an abrupt end. To some, Castro's days seemed numbered.

In 1992, congressional leaders acted in hopes that they could hasten the Cuban leader's political demise and passed the 1992 Cuban Democracy Act, the first major change in U.S. policy toward Cuba since the Kennedy administration. The law dramatically tightened economic restrictions on Cuba and was aimed at further isolating Castro by prohibiting any foreign-based subsidiaries of U.S. companies from trading with Cuba. U.S. citizens were banned from travelling to the island. Despite predictions by its sponsors that the law's provisions would quickly topple Castro, he remained firmly in control of Cuba into the twenty-first century.

Cold Facts

Despite its widespread poverty and its status as one of the world's last remaining Soviet-style communist regimes, Cuba has almost no illiteracy. It is also the only Latin American country to offer all its citizens free health care.

North Korea and the Bomb

Perhaps the most erratic and potentially dangerous communist regime in the world was—and still is—North Korea. Ruled since 1946–1998 by Kim Il sung and since 1998 by his son, Kim Jong Il, the nation became one of the world's most politically isolated and unpredictable regimes during the Cold War years.

During the late 1960s, particularly, the United States found itself in conflict with the North Korean government. In 1968, the country's navy captured a U.S. intelligence ship, the *Pueblo*, and held its crew hostage for 11 months. The following year, North Korea shot down a U.S. reconnaissance plane. These incidents, however, were minor compared to the concerns about North Korea's nuclear weapons program that arose in the late 1980s and early 1990s.

Beginning in the late 1980s, the United States began working hard to end North Korea's isolation by encouraging cultural, scholarly, journalistic, athletic, and other exchanges with communist regime. Hoping to further reduce North Korea's estrangement, in 1991 the United States supported UN membership of both North and South Korea. The next year brought another encouraging sign when both governments signed a nuclear safeguard agreement that permitted the International Atomic Energy Agency (IAEA) to inspect their nuclear facilities.

By 1993, however, North Korea raised fears that it was producing nuclear weapons in violation of its 1992 agreement when it denied IAEA inspectors access to sites suspected of nuclear weapons production. By December 1993, the CIA reported that North Korea had probably assembled at least one nuclear weapon.

Quotes from the Cold

Communism died this year. Even as president, with the most fascinating possible vantage point, there were times when I was so busy helping to manage progress and lead change that I didn't always show the joy that was in my heart. But the biggest thing that has happened in the world in my life, in our lives, is this: By the grace of God, America won the Cold War.

—President George Bush, from his 1992 State of the Union Address

In January 1994, after U.S. officials threatened economic sanctions against North Korea, President Kim Il-sung ominously warned that such threats might lead to "catastrophe."

By mid-1994, after the intervention of former President Jimmy Carter, the potential crisis was defused when the North Korea agreed to IAEA inspections and closed all facilities capable of making weapons-grade nuclear material. In return, the United States promised oil shipments and replacement of two aging nuclear power reactors with more modern light-water reactors.

Defeat for Bush

George Bush believed that he had skillfully managed U.S. foreign policy through some of the more challenging years in U.S. history. He had presided over the end of the Cold War and had led the UN coalition to victory in the Persian Gulf, the most successful large-scale U.S. military operation since World War II.

But despite his considerable skills, Bush lacked the vision to articulate or implement a coherent post-Cold War foreign policy around which Americans and their allies could rally. He had vacillated over China, reacted passively to the collapse of the Berlin Wall, reluctantly supported economic aid for Russia, and did little to address the growing civil war in the Balkans. His inherent caution and lack of what he jokingly called "the vision thing," caused many Americans to view him as weak and indecisive.

In spite of his anemic foreign policy, Bush achieved astounding popularity with the American public in the months following the Gulf War (his job approval rating soared above 80 percent). His military successes suggested that a second term was his for the asking.

But then recession hit and Bush's indecisiveness reappeared. He was slow to respond to the nation's economic woes and reluctant to begin his reelection campaign. As a result, his high poll numbers slowly disappeared.

As the recession deepened, memories of the Cold War and the success in the Gulf War faded from the minds of Americans who became more concerned with their day-to-day economic struggles. Challenged by Democratic Governor Bill Clinton of Arkansas and Reform Party candidate H. Ross Perot, Bush found himself battling for his political survival less than two years after his triumphant Gulf War victory.

To most voters in 1992, foreign policy concerns were secondary. On Election Day, Bill Clinton won. And while he gladly assumed responsibility for the nation's domestic affairs, he would also find himself accountable for managing the nation's foreign policy in the uncertain, uncharted waters of the post-Cold War era.

Quotes from the Cold

Bill Clinton's foreign policy experience is pretty much confined to having had breakfast once at the International House of Pancakes.

—Republican presidential candidate Patrick Buchanan, 1992

The Least You Need to Know

- Ironically, the very political and economic reforms that Soviet leader Mikhail Gorbachev initiated to keep his nation together threatened to tear apart the USSR.
- Disgust with Gorbachev among the Kremlin's leaders culminated in the summer of 1991 when they staged a coup, deposing Gorbachev from power and placing him under house arrest.
- The 1991 coup quickly crumbled in the face of public outrage, skillfully stoked by the reform president of Russia, Boris Yeltsin.
- Yeltsin used the failed coup not only to discredit the communist hard-line Soviet leaders and destroy the Soviet Communist Party, but to exploit the resulting power vacuum and emerge as the preeminent Soviet politician.
- Despite his relative success in managing the nation's foreign policy in the immediate post-Cold War era—including the spectacular military victory in the Persian Gulf War—President George Bush lost his reelection bid in 1992.
- Bush was widely criticized for his failure to articulate a clear vision for U.S. foreign policy in the post-Cold War period.

Chapter 26

Cold War Legacies

In This Chapter

- Bill Clinton, "New Globalism," and the post-Cold War world
- Clinton tackles the Balkans, the Middle East, Iraq, and Northern Ireland
- The United States supports Yeltsin and his reforms
- George W. Bush and the war on terrorism

The new president, Bill Clinton, was the first Baby Boomer elected president and the first to come of age during the Cold War. During one of the major conflicts of that period—the Vietnam War—Clinton was a protestor, not a participant. In fact, Clinton would be the first president since Franklin Roosevelt who entered the White House without an active-duty military record.

As George Bush had learned, the Cold War's end didn't necessarily bring about a safer world. During his presidency, Clinton would face numerous foreign policy and military challenges. But his emphasis would be on what some called "economic globalism," a belief that U.S. economic security depended upon the ability of the country to trade freely with other nations. That free trade philosophy often brought him into direct conflict with leaders of his own Democratic Party.

Unlike presidents Reagan and Bush who preceded him, Clinton would face no momentous foreign policy challenges before he left office in 2000 under a legal and ethical cloud. Enormous challenges, however, would await Clinton's successor, George W. Bush.

Until the terrorist attacks of September 11, 2001, many feared that Bush was about to revive the Cold War with his bellicose and unilateral foreign policy. But instead of reviving the Cold War, Bush inherited a different kind of conflict. The deadly attacks on New York's World Trade Center and the Pentagon ushered America into what many called a "New War"—a deadly and dangerous struggle with international terrorism, the end of which no one can be certain.

Bill Clinton and the New Globalism

Bill Clinton entered the White House in January 1993 with little foreign policy experience, but a strong belief that the nation's continued security depended on its economic relationships with other countries. "There is no longer a division between what is foreign and what is domestic," Clinton said in his 1993 inaugural address. "The world economy, the world environment, the world AIDS crisis, the world arms race—they affect us all."

Quotes from the Cold

Today, a generation raised in the shadows of the Cold War assumes new responsibilities in a world warmed by the sunshine of freedom but threatened still by ancient hatreds and new plagues.

—President Bill Clinton from his first inaugural address, January 1993

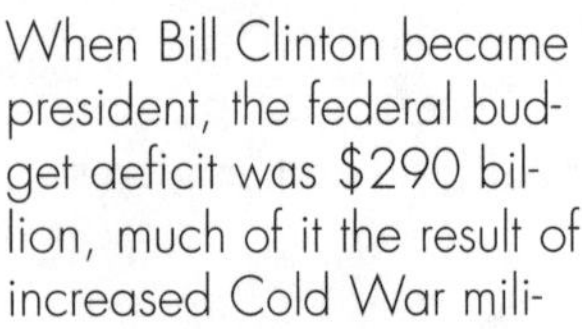

Cold Facts

When Bill Clinton became president, the federal budget deficit was $290 billion, much of it the result of increased Cold War military spending. By 2000, the federal government boasted a $160 billion surplus.

NAFTA and GATT

Clinton preached what was called "economic globalism" and pushed through Congress two major trade accords during his first term: the North American Free Trade Agreement (NAFTA) in 1993, and the General Agreement on Tariffs and Trade (GATT) that created the World Trade Organization. Both agreements generated strong domestic opposition, particularly among Democrats and organized labor, who argued that lowering import tariffs would cost American jobs. But Clinton argued forcefully that free trade would actually increase jobs by allowing the nation to export more goods. After a fierce debate, the U.S. Senate ratified both agreements.

The record thus far suggests that Clinton was correct. Throughout the 1990s, increased trade kept inflation low and—combined with the elimination of the federal budget deficit—fueled the longest economic expansion in the nation's history.

China

Quotes from the Cold

America should not trust the Chinese government to make progress on its own and unilaterally surrender our nation's ability to influence Chinese policy through trade.

—House Democratic leader Richard Gephardt, April 2000

Before his election, Clinton had attacked George Bush for his policy of accommodation with China. Once in the White House, however, Clinton changed his mind and signed a landmark trade agreement with the Chinese that promised to lower or eliminate many trade barriers between the two nations. Over the concerns of many that China did not deserve permanent "normal trade relations," the House and Senate approved the deal in 2000.

Other than attempts by congressional Republicans to remove Clinton from office, no issue characterized Clinton's presidency more than his effort to encourage greater international trade. With the Cold War over, Americans generally agreed with their president when he argued: "We can build a global economy and a global society that leaves no one behind, that carries all countries into a new century that we hope will be marked by greater peace and greater prosperity for all people." By the time Clinton left office, his administration had negotiated almost 300 trade agreements with other countries.

A World of Problems

When he ran for president in 1992, Clinton had criticized George Bush for failing to articulate a "new American purpose" in the post-Cold War era. Throughout his presidency, Clinton would endure the same criticism. Clinton, however, did have a vision; but with the Soviet Union dissolved, his policy of "globalism" was judged by many an uninspiring theme around which to build a foreign policy.

"From the beginning of his presidency," observed the editors of *Foreign Policy* magazine in 2000, "Clinton recognized that the dominant factors of international relations were shifting from nuclear throw weights to flows of foreign direct investment and trade." Clinton, they argued, had correctly viewed "the global economy not only as a vehicle for increasing U.S. prosperity, but as a medium for enhancing international stability."

But some Americans and many of Clinton's Republican critics, long accustomed to a Cold War foreign policy directed by military and national security concerns, demanded more. They wanted to know: Where did the world's only remaining military superpower fit into the world? How did America and its president propose to lead the community of free nations? To what larger purpose would America's wealth and military might be applied?

Cold Words

Nation building is the process by which a nation or a group of nations endeavor to establish or reestablish the political, economic, and social structures of another nation.

Other critics argued that with the Cold War over, the United States military should be used sparingly around the world and they argued for a minimalist U.S. foreign policy. They especially decried Clinton's willingness to use U.S. forces for humanitarian purposes and for *nation building*.

President Bill Clinton, elected after the Cold War's end, promoted what became known as "economic globalism." Despite his success in winning approval for several historic free trade agreements, Clinton endured harsh criticism for what some considered a muddled and unfocused foreign policy.

(Courtesy of the Library of Congress)

Clinton's answer to his critics was that America, as the world's only remaining superpower, must use its might in concert with other nations to protect and defend basic human and civil rights—as long as doing so did not endanger the nation's security or deplete resources for important domestic needs. His application of that policy, however, met with inconsistent results.

Quotes from the Cold

The successor to a doctrine of containment must be a strategy of enlargement—enlargement of the world's free market democracies.

—Anthony Lake, national security advisor to President Bill Clinton, 1993

Peacekeeping

Clinton had mixed success when it came to defending human rights around the world. An unpopular military humanitarian mission to Somalia, initiated by President Bush to address widespread famine, went sour in 1993 when 18 American soldiers were killed by hostile troops. At first, Clinton doubled the troop commitment, but withdrew the forces in 1994.

The failed mission to Somalia prompted Clinton to hesitate in the face of a more serious crisis in 1994 in Rwanda, where a brutal civil war resulted in the murders of up to one million innocent citizens. Clinton sent 200 troops to the African nation, but called them home within a few months and later acknowledged that the international community did almost nothing to stop the genocide.

Clinton achieved greater success in Haiti, where in 1994 he sent a larger military force to the Caribbean nation to restore to power the country's democratically elected president, Jean-Bertrand Aristide, who was overthrown by military leaders in 1991. Just before the U.S. troops were to land on the island, former President Jimmy Carter persuaded the country's military leader to surrender the presidency to Aristide.

Cold Facts

In 1999, the U.S. Senate rejected the Comprehensive Test Ban Treaty, signed by President Bill Clinton in 1996. The treaty would have prohibited nuclear weapons testing by all signatory nations. Despite the embarrassing rejection by the Senate, Clinton pledged that the United States would not test nuclear weapons.

The Balkans

The ethnic fighting in Bosnia and Herzegovina also consumed much of Clinton's energy during the early years of his presidency. Beginning in 1992, Bosnian Serbs who wanted their nation to remain part of the Yugoslav federation battled Bosnian Muslims and Croats who favored independence. In 1995, Clinton brokered a peace agreement between the warring factions that resulted in an independent Bosnia composed of two separate entities managed by a single government.

War broke out again in the spring of 1998, this time in Federal Republic of Yugoslavia (made up of Serbia and Montenegro) when Serb forces invaded the southern province of Kosovo. Serb atrocities against ethnic Albanians prompted NATO to act militarily for the first time against a European country.

In March 1999, NATO forces, led by the United States, began bombing Serb military sites in Kosovo and Serbia. By June, the Serbs withdrew from Kosovo and agreed to a peace plan for the region.

Cold Facts

NATO responded to the 1998 crisis in the Balkans partly out of concern that the conflict might spread. Those concerns were well grounded in history. The First World War grew from the Balkan Wars of 1912–13, and was sparked in 1914 when the Austrian Archduke Francis Ferdinand was assassinated in the Bosnian capitol of Sarajevo.

The Middle East

Clinton never sent troops to the Middle East, but throughout his presidency he engaged in intensive diplomatic efforts to achieve a lasting peace in the region. He believed that with enough American influence, the seemingly intractable Middle East problems could be resolved. History, unfortunately, would prove him wrong.

Less than a year after taking office, Clinton helped broker a peace deal between Israel and the Palestine Liberation Organization (PLO). Signed at the White House in September 1993, the agreement permitted limited Palestinian self-rule in the Israeli-occupied West Bank and Gaza Strip. The following year, Clinton scored another Middle East victory when he facilitated a peace agreement between Israel and Jordan.

Cold Facts

President Bill Clinton achieved his greatest successes in the domestic arena. Under his leadership, the enormous deficits of the 1980s and early 1990s were eliminated. Clinton also presided over the longest and most robust economic expansion in the nation's history.

Despite Clinton's efforts, including a second treaty between Israel and the PLO in 1995, the agreements did not end the Middle East conflict. Violence continued to plague the region.

In October 1998, Clinton brought Israeli Prime Minister Benjamin Netanyahu and Palestinian leader Yasir Arafat together for intense negotiations at a resort in rural Maryland. Terms of the resulting accord committed Israel to transferring more of its territory to the Palestinian National Authority in return for Palestinian pledges to curb terrorism. Within months, however, the deal collapsed.

Some critics accused Clinton of exacerbating the violence by affording so much credibility to Arafat, who many regarded as a terrorist.

Cold Facts

In December 1998, President Bill Clinton became only the second U.S. president to be impeached by the U.S. House of Representatives. Charged by the House with perjury and obstruction of justice relating to his acknowledged affair with a White House intern, Clinton was eventually acquitted by the U.S. Senate and, ironically, left office with the highest job approval ratings of any president in the modern era.

Until almost the last day of his presidency, Clinton worked unsuccessfully to bring about an end to the Israeli-PLO conflict.

Iraq

The Iraqi regime headed by Saddam Hussein was a persistent problem during Clinton's presidency. The Iraqi leader constantly violated the 1991 cease-fire agreement that ended the Persian Gulf War, including denying inspection of sites where UN officials suspected the government was manufacturing weapons of mass destruction. Hussein relented in December 1998 after Clinton ordered air strikes against Iraqi military targets. Ultimately, however, the inspection process failed when Iraq expelled UN weapons inspectors.

Cold Facts

Throughout the 1990s, the United States refused to pay its United Nations dues. Among the congressional Republicans opposed to paying the $1 billion the United States owed was Senator Jesse Helms of North Carolina, chairman of the Senate Foreign Relations Committee. Helms and others were angry that some UN organizations advocated abortion rights. In 1999, threatened with the loss of its vote in the UN General Assembly, the United States finally agreed to pay $800 million of its back dues.

Northern Ireland

Clinton's greatest foreign policy achievement was undoubtedly his success in helping end the war between Catholic and Protestant factions in Northern Ireland. In 1998, Clinton's representative, former U.S. Senate majority leader George Mitchell, brokered a peace agreement between the two sides and the British government that permitted creation of a new Northern Ireland assembly governed by Protestants and Catholics. On several occasions, the deal threatened to collapse. Clinton, however, worked successfully to persuade both sides to uphold the agreement.

Boris and Bill

As president, Bill Clinton encouraged continued political and economic reforms in Russia. After his January 1994 summit with Russian President Boris Yeltsin, the two leaders affirmed their commitment to "a dynamic and effective U.S.–Russian partnership that strengthens international stability." Demonstrating his support for Russia's reforms, Clinton persuaded Congress to approve $2.8 billion in economic assistance for Yeltsin's government.

However, critics would later allege that Clinton lost interest in the Russian reforms. They furthermore charged that he relinquished stewardship of the Russian aid program to the International Monetary Fund and that a Russian organized crime syndicate stole much of the money.

NATO Expands

Clinton counted among his foreign policy accomplishments the expansion of NATO, over Russian objections, to include the former communist states of Poland, Hungary, and the Czech Republic. Yeltsin feared that expanding NATO to include former Soviet satellites would fuel the Russian citizenry's fears about Western expansionism and might spark nationalist sentiments.

To many Russians, NATO was simply a bitter reminder that the West had won the Cold War. Clinton tried to assure the Russians that NATO had no aims to dominate Russia and, in fact, he said that Russia itself might one day be invited to join the alliance.

Bill Backs Boris

The Russian forces arrayed against economic and political reform were still powerful, as Yeltsin learned in the fall of 1993. On September 21, the Russian congress, known as the Duma, barricaded itself in the "White House" parliament building, impeached Yeltsin, and installed Alexander Rutskoi as the nation's new president.

From the beginning of the crisis, Clinton offered Yeltsin his unwavering support. But the crisis was one that only the Russians could resolve. That they did in early October, when thousands of Russian citizens protested by attacking the state-owned television station. The next day, Yeltsin and his defense minister directed an armed assault on the Duma and forcefully reclaimed the government. It was, some commentators observed, communism's "last gasp" in Russia.

Later that month, in a visit to Moscow, Secretary of State Warren Christopher offered Yeltsin the United State's unqualified support: "History is on your side—the side of democracy—and so are we."

> **Quotes from the Cold**
>
> The public wanted American leadership, and Clinton gave it to them—but too sporadically and often too hesitantly. … Clinton stumbled from crisis to crisis, trying to figure out what was popular, what would be effective, and what choices would pose the lowest risk to his presidency, and, especially, to his reputation.
>
> —William G. Hyland, *Clinton's World: Remaking American Foreign Policy*

George W. and the New War

After the closest presidential race in American history, George W. Bush, the son of the forty-first president, entered the White House in January 2001.

Bush came into office insisting that the United States would not shrink from its international leadership role. In his inaugural address he declared: "The enemies of liberty and our country should make no mistake: America remains engaged in the world by history and choice, shaping a balance of power that favors freedom."

For the first eight months of his presidency, however, it appeared that Bush's focus would be on domestic concerns. When he did delve into foreign and military affairs, he led some to believe that he favored a unilateralist approach. That is, some suspected that he wanted to impose U.S. policies upon other nations without consultation or negotiation. Other critics worried that Bush's actions might lead to a revival of the Cold War.

U.S. allies, especially in Europe, were disconcerted by Bush's unilateral rejection of the Kyoto Protocol, a treaty addressing global warming, and his insistence on abrogating the ABM Treaty in order to pursue a missile defense plan reminiscent of Ronald Reagan's Strategic Defense Initiative.

> **Cold Facts**
>
> George W. Bush (forty-third president), son of President George H.W. Bush (forty-first president), was the second son to follow his father's footsteps into the White House. The other father-son presidential team was John Adams (second president) and John Quincy Adams (sixth president).

The devastating September 11, 2001, terrorist attacks on New York's World Trade Center towers and the Pentagon in Washington fundamentally altered Bush's presidency. Most questions about his legitimacy vanished. Reflecting the historic American impulse in times of national crisis, Bush's popularity soared, especially after he ordered air strikes on terrorist training sites in Afghanistan in early October.

President George W. Bush (right) and Defense Secretary Donald Rumsfeld inspect damage to the Pentagon following the September 11, 2001, terrorist attacks on Washington and New York.

(Courtesy of the U.S. Department of Defense)

While Bush persisted with his antiballistic missile system plans, the terrorist attacks necessitated greater U.S. cooperation and consultation with its allies. As did his father during the Persian Gulf War, Bush and his aides skillfully assembled a broad coalition of world nations in support of what many called "America's war on terrorism."

Bush entered office as a two-term Texas governor with limited foreign policy experience. The terrorist attacks, however, moved foreign policy to the top of his agenda and transformed the way Americans and much of the world viewed him.

Ten years after the Cold War had ended the United States found itself enmeshed in an another conflict that threatened to consume its attention and resources. Within months, Bush proposed large budget increases for national defense and homeland security. Combined with an economic recession and Bush's $1.35 trillion tax cut, the military and national security increases returned the nation to a new period of deficit spending.

While some feared the war on terrorism might rival the Cold War in its length and cost, America's newest conflict would be fundamentally different in several ways. In this war, the adversary would not always be a nation, but rather a dangerous array of shadowy terrorist organizations. And Russia—as well as most of the former Soviet republics and satellites—would support the United States. Indeed, except for a smattering of nations—Iraq and North Korea most prominently—this war did not promise to divide the world as did the Cold War.

Yet as the United States began the twenty-first century facing the uncertainty of a new war that had already brought death and destruction to American soil, it was clear that the Cold War's end had not simplified the world, especially for the United States. Rogue nations and terrorist groups now threatened the free world with weapons of mass destruction, including, it was feared, nuclear weapons.

Quotes from the Cold

Great harm has been done to us. We have suffered great loss. And in our grief and anger we have found our mission and our moment. Freedom and fear are at war. The advance of human freedom, the great achievement of our time and the great hope of every time, now depends on us. … We will not tire, we will not falter and we will not fail.

—President George W. Bush, speech to Congress, September 20, 2001

In language reminiscent of the Cold War, Bush characterized the struggle as one between "good and evil." In his 2002 State of the Union address, the new president identified three nations—Iran, Iraq, and North Korea—as an "axis of evil" that threatened the world's peace and security.

To many, it was evident that America—because of its military might, its economic strength, its pervasive culture, and its open society—would always have mortal enemies. If anything, the post-Cold War world appeared as dangerous and foreboding as ever.

The Least You Need to Know

- Entering the White House after the Cold War's end, President Bill Clinton promoted what became known as "economic globalism," the belief that robust trade among nations was an effective means of fostering capitalism and encouraging international stability.
- Critics sometimes faulted President Clinton for pursuing a muddled and reactive foreign policy and for the way he sometimes used the U.S. military in humanitarian relief missions.
- President Clinton's foreign and military policies experienced mixed success.
- Clinton's attempts to secure a lasting peace in the Middle East were largely unsuccessful; however, his efforts to end the decades-old violence in Northern Ireland resulted in a more permanent peace accord.
- Clinton and Russian leader Boris Yeltsin forged a close working relationship; however, the suspected misuse and theft of U.S. economic assistance ultimately discredited Clinton's Russian policy.
- The September 11, 2001, terrorist attacks on the United States drew the country into a worldwide war against terrorism and transformed and legitimized the presidency of George W. Bush.

Appendix

Glossary

antiballistic missile (ABM) system An array of detectors and weapons designed to intercept and destroy incoming long-range ballistic missiles. The Strategic Defense Initiative (SDI), if successful, would have been an ABM system.

Baby Boomer A member of the generation of American children born from 1946 to 1965. The "Baby Boom" following World War II was marked by a significant increase in the rate of childbirths.

ballistic missile A missile that is first propelled to its target by a rocket and is then in free flight along a high arcing trajectory.

Bolshevism The Russian word for "greater" or "majority." It was the radical, communist ideology that inspired the Russian (or Bolshevik) Revolution of 1917. An adherent of Bolshevism was a Bolshevik.

brinksmanship A diplomatic art advocated in the 1950s by Secretary of State John Foster Dulles in which representatives of a nation push a confrontation to the brink of war in order to achieve a desired result.

capitalism An economic system that encourages free enterprise; that is, the private or corporate ownership of business property. In such an environment, markets generally devise their own rules and are free of direct control by the government.

Cold War The period of hostility between the United States and the Soviet Union that began after World War II and ended in the late 1990s.

collective security A group of nations acting in concert to guarantee the defense of its individual members.

communism A political and economic ideology that advocates elimination of most or all private property. Communist governments, like the Soviet Union, are usually totalitarian systems ruled by a single party. Under communist rule, all property is owned communally; that is, by the state.

containment A U.S. foreign policy and military strategy that heavily influenced U.S. relations with the Soviet Union during the Cold War. During most of this period, U.S. leaders sought to halt, by various means, the spread of Soviet influence in Europe and in the Third World.

cruise missile A guided, unmanned, self-propelled missile, which can fly at low altitude and thus elude detection by many radar systems.

democracy A form of government in which absolute power is invested in the people.

détente A relaxation of tension. In this case, the warming of relations between the United States and the Soviet Union that began in the 1960s and accelerated in the 1970s and late 1980s.

dissident A person who speaks out against the policies of his or her country.

domino theory The belief applied to U.S. policy in Southeast Asia in the 1950s and 1960s that the fall of one nation to communism would eventually result in the fall of neighboring states. During the Cold War, the theory was sometimes used to justify U.S. containment policy.

dove A term that became popular in the 1960s to describe opponents of the Vietnam War. Generally, however, it can be used to describe any advocate of peace. (See also, hawk.)

Eastern Bloc Nations such as East Germany, Poland, Romania, and Czechoslovakia that were aligned with and whose governments were controlled or heavily influenced by the Soviet Union during the Cold War.

espionage The practice of spying or obtaining sensitive information about one country for another country or organization.

fascism A totalitarian political philosophy that exalts the nation above the individual. Fascist regimes usually impose stringent forms of economic and social discipline and wage sometimes brutal retribution against political opponents.

foreign aid Economic assistance provided to one nation from another. One example of U.S. foreign aid is the Marshall Plan, which helped rebuild Western Europe after World War II.

glasnost Russian word for "openness" and one of the reform policies pursued in the 1980s by Soviet leader Mikhail Gorbachev. Under glasnost, Soviet officials allowed freer public debate of political and social issues and relaxed media restraints.

hawk One who advocates a military solution as a way to resolve a particular conflict between nations. During the Vietnam War, those who supported the war or advocated stronger military measures were commonly referred to as "hawks." See also, dove.

hegemony The dominance that a nation exerts over others.

hot line Not connected to a specific phone, but rather to a system of instant communications between Washington and Moscow established by both countries in 1963.

ICBM Intercontinental ballistic missile. ICBMs have a range of more than 5,500 kilometers. They are land based and are generally delivered by a rocket booster, at least one reentry vehicle, and penetration aids.

INF Treaty The Intermediate-Range Nuclear Forces (INF) Treaty was signed by the United States and the Soviet Union in 1987 and required the elimination of all ground-launched ballistic and cruise missiles with ranges between 500 and 5,500 kilometers.

internationalism The opposite of isolationism. A belief in the need for cooperation among nations.

Iron Curtain A metaphor for the dividing line between Eastern and Western Europe during the Cold War. Coined in a 1946 speech by Sir Winston Churchill, the phrase symbolized the Soviet-imposed barriers to open communication and free travel.

isolationism A philosophy opposed to political, military, or economic cooperation among nations. An isolationist, however, might oppose a military or political alliance with another nation, but support economic cooperation with the same.

linkage A diplomatic negotiating strategy that demands progress toward an objective be linked to the success of resolving otherwise unrelated issues.

MIRV Multiple independently targetable reentry vehicle. MIRV missiles can deliver two or more nuclear warheads to separate targets.

mutual assured destruction (MAD) The belief that neither side in the Cold War would launch a nuclear first strike for fear of overwhelming retaliation by the other. MAD was the governing principle of the defense policies of the United States and the Soviet Union during the Cold War and was used to justify the nuclear arms race.

NATO The North Atlantic Treaty Organization. NATO was established in 1949 by a collective self-defense treaty, primarily for the defense of North America and Western Europe.

neutral nation A nation not aligned with either the Soviet Union or the United States during the Cold War.

nuclear proliferation The spread of nuclear weapons or nuclear weapons components or technology.

perestroika The Soviet word for "restructuring." The term was used to describe the economic and social reforms initiated in the 1980s by Soviet leader Mikhail Gorbachev.

proletariat The laboring or industrial class, usually among the poorest and least powerful workers in a society.

protectorate A country that has subordinated itself to another, especially in its foreign and defense policies.

proxy war A war in which the conflict of one or more combatants is largely waged by the army of another country. During the Cold War, two examples are the Korean War (the North Koreans were seen as proxies of the Soviet Union) and the Vietnam War (in the beginning, the South Vietnamese were proxies of the United States).

realpolitik Politics or foreign policy based solely on pragmatic or realistic concerns, and not ideology.

red or **reds** A derogatory, slang term for communist.

reparations Compensation for damages which are demanded of a nation defeated in war.

SALT Strategic Arms Limitations Talks. Bilateral negotiations between the United States and the Soviet Union from 1969 to 1979 over limiting strategic nuclear offensive systems and antiballistic missile (ABM) systems. The talks resulted in the 1972 SALT I Treaty and the 1979 SALT II Treaty (never ratified).

satellites A nation dominated or controlled by another. During the Cold War, East Germany, Hungary, and Poland were among the Soviet Union's satellites.

SEATO Created in 1954 and disbanded in 1974, the Southeast Asia Treaty Organization was a loose association of nations—Australia, France, Great Britain, New Zealand, Pakistan, the Philippines, Thailand, and the United States—whose purpose was to protect the region from communist aggression. During the Vietnam War, SEATO members did not act in a unified way and SEATO was generally regarded an ineffectual association.

Soviet An elected governmental entity in a communist state.

START Strategic Arms Reductions Talks. Bilateral negotiations between the United States and the Soviet Union from 1982 to 1993 over limiting and reducing the arsenals of strategic offensive nuclear weapons. The talks resulted in the 1991 START I Treaty and the 1993 START II Treaty.

Strategic Defense Initiative (SDI) The unsuccessful, high-tech antiballistic missile system initiated by President Ronald Reagan in the 1980s. The program was called "Star Wars" by its critics.

summit meeting A gathering of governmental leaders or heads of state. During the Cold War, summits between U.S. and Soviet leaders were sometimes held to discuss or sign arms control and other treaties.

Third World A term used widely during the Cold War to characterize underdeveloped nations (mostly in Asia, Africa, and Latin America), or nations that lacked many of the basic elements of an advanced society. During the 1980s and 1990s, the term was increasingly replaced by "developing nation" or "emerging nation." The term Third World was also used during the Cold War to describe the unaligned nations of Africa and Asia.

totalitarianism A repressive system of government in which the lives of citizens are controlled, in near absolute terms, by the state.

Vietnamization A term coined by President Richard Nixon during the Vietnam War to describe his policy of transferring the fighting in Vietnam to the South Vietnamese military.

Warsaw Pact The Soviet Union's answer to NATO. A mutual defense alliance, signed in Warsaw in 1955, the pact included Albania, Bulgaria, Czechoslovakia, East Germany, Hungary, Poland, Romania, and the Soviet Union. It disbanded in 1991.

Zionism A political movement whose original goal was to establish a Jewish national state in Palestine and which now supports the nation of Israel. Adherents are commonly called Zionists.

Appendix B

U.S. Defense Spending During the Cold War

Year	In Billions	Percent of Gross Domestic Product (GDP)
1945	82.9	37.5
1946	42.6	19.1
1947	12.8	5.5
1948	9.1	3.5
1949	13.1	4.8
1950	13.7	5.0
1951	23.5	7.3
1952	46.0	13.2
1953	52.8	14.2
1954	49.2	13.0
1955	42.7	10.8
1956	42.5	9.9
1957	45.4	10.1
1958	46.8	10.2
1959	49.0	10.0
1960	48.1	9.3
1961	49.6	9.3

Year	In Billions	Percent of Gross Domestic Product (GDP)
1962	52.3	9.2
1963	53.4	8.9
1964	54.7	8.5
1965	50.6	7.4
1966	58.1	7.7
1967	71.4	8.8
1968	81.9	9.4
1969	82.4	8.7
1970	81.6	8.1
1971	78.8	7.3
1972	79.1	6.7
1973	76.6	5.8
1974	79.3	5.5
1975	86.5	5.5
1976	89.6	5.2
1977	97.2	4.9
1978	104.4	4.7
1979	116.3	4.6
1980	133.9	4.9
1981	157.5	5.1
1982	185.3	5.7
1983	209.9	6.1
1984	227.4	5.9
1985	252.7	6.1
1986	273.3	6.2
1987	281.9	6.1
1988	290.3	5.8
1989	303.5	5.6
1990	299.3	5.2

Source: U.S. Office of Management and Budget

Appendix C

Further Readings

Ambrose, Stephen E. *Nixon: The Triumph of a Politician, 1962–1972.* New York: Simon and Schuster, 1989.

Asinof, Eliot. *1919: America's Loss of Innocence.* New York: Donald I. Fine, 1990.

Barson, Michael, and Steven Heller. *Red Scared! The Commie Menace in Propaganda and Popular Culture.* San Francisco: Chronicle Books, 2001.

Bourne, Peter G. *Jimmy Carter: A Comprehensive Biography from Plains to Post-Presidency.* New York: Scribner, 1997.

Brands, H.W. *The Devil We Knew: Americans and the Cold War.* New York: Oxford, 1993.

Cannon, James. *Time and Chance: Gerald Ford's Appointment with History.* New York: HarperCollins, 1994.

Cole, Wayne S. *Roosevelt and the Isolationists, 1932–1945.* Lincoln: University of Nebraska, 1983.

Conquest, Robert. *Stalin: Breaker of Nations.* New York: Viking, 1991.

Divine, Robert A. *The Reluctant Belligerent: American Entry into World War II.* New York: John Wiley, 1965.

Evans, Harold. *The American Century.* New York: Alfred A. Knopf, 1998.

FitzGerald, Frances. *Way Out There in the Blue: Reagan and Star Wars and the End of the Cold War.* New York: Simon and Schuster, 2000.

Freidel, Frank. *Franklin D. Roosevelt: A Rendezvous with Destiny.* Boston: Little, Brown, 1990.

Gaddis, John Lewis. *The United States and the Origins of the Cold War, 1941–1947.* New York: Columbia University, 1972.

———. *We Now Know: Rethinking Cold War History.* Oxford: Oxford University Press, 1997.

Gorbachev, Mikhail. *Gorbachev: On My Country and the World.* New York: Columbia University, 2000.

Guinsburg, Thomas N. *The Pursuit of Isolationism in the United States Senate from Versailles to Pearl Harbor.* New York: Garland, 1982.

Halberstam, David. *War in a Time of Peace: Bush, Clinton, and the Generals.* New York: Scribner, 2001.

Herring, George C. *America's Longest War: The United States and Vietnam, 1950–1975.* New York: John Wiley, 1979.

Hoopes, Townsend. *The Devil and John Foster Dulles.* Boston: Atlantic Monthly Press, 1973.

Hyland, William G. *The Cold War: Fifty Years of Conflict.* New York: Times Books, 1991.

Keegan, John. *The First World War.* New York: Knopf, 1999.

———. *The Second World War.* New York: Penguin, 1990.

Kennedy, David M. *Freedom from Fear: The American People in Depression and War, 1929–1945.* New York: Oxford, 1999.

Kissinger, Henry. *Diplomacy.* New York: Simon and Schuster, 1994.

Isaacson, Walter, and Evan Thomas. *The Wise Men: Six Friends and the World They Made.* New York: Simon and Schuster, 1986.

Johnson, Haynes. *The Best of Times: America in the Clinton Years.* New York: Harcourt Brace, 2001.

Mann, Robert. *A Grand Delusion: America's Descent into Vietnam.* New York: Basic Books, 2001.

McCormick, Thomas J. *America's Half-Century: United States Foreign Policy in the Cold War and After.* Baltimore: Johns Hopkins, 1995.

McCullough, David. *Truman.* New York: Simon and Schuster, 1992.

McElvaine, Robert. *The Great Depression: America, 1929–1941.* New York: Times Books, 1994.

O'Neill, William L. *American High: The Years of Confidence, 1945–1960.* New York: Free Press, 1986.

Painter, David S. *The Cold War: An International History.* London: Routledge, 1999.

Parment, Herbert S. *George Bush: Life of a Lone Star Yankee.* New York: Scribner, 1997.

Patterson, James T. *Grand Expectations: The United States, 1945–1974.* New York: Oxford, 1996.

Perret, Geoffrey. *Eisenhower.* New York: Random House, 1999.

Powaski, Ronald E. *The Cold War: The United States and the Soviet Union, 1917–1991.* New York: Oxford, 1998.

Powers, Richard Gid. *Not Without Honor: The History of American Anticommunism.* New York: Free Press, 1995.

Reeves, Richard. *President Kennedy: Profile of Power.* New York: Touchstone, 1993.

Reeves, Thomas C. *The Life and Times of Joe McCarthy: A Biography.* New York: Stein and Day, 1982.

Remnick, David. *Lenin's Tomb: The Last Days of the Soviet Empire.* New York: Random House, 1993.

Riasanovsky, Nicholas Valentine. *A History of Russia.* New York: Oxford, 1999.

Service, Robert. *Lenin: A Biography.* Cambridge: Harvard University, 2000.

Stokesbury, James L. *A Short History of the Korean War.* New York: William Morrow, 1988.

Volkogonov, Dmitri. *Stalin: Triumph and Tragedy.* New York: Grove Weidenfeld, 1988.

Whitfield, Stephen J. *The Culture of the Cold War.* Baltimore: Johns Hopkins, 1991.

Index

Numbers

A

B

C

D

E

F

G

H

I

J

K

L

M

N

O

P

Q–R

S

T

U

V

W

Y-Z